MEDIA PRESSURE ON FOREIGN POLICY

Palgrave Macmillan Series in International Political Communication

Series editor: Philip Seib, University of Southern California (USA)

From democratization to terrorism, economic development to conflict resolution, global political dynamics are affected by the increasing pervasiveness and influence of communication media. This series examines the participants and their tools, their strategies and their impact. It offers a mix of comparative and tightly focused analyses that bridge the various elements of communication and political science included in the field of international studies. Particular emphasis is placed on topics related to the rapidly changing communication environment that is being shaped by new technologies and new political realities. This is the evolving world of international political communication.

Editorial Board Members:

Hussein Amin, American University in Cairo (Egypt)
Robin Brown, University of Leeds (UK)
Eytan Gilboa, Bar-Ilan University (Israel)
Steven Livingston, George Washington University (USA)
Robin Mansell, London School of Economics and Political Science (UK)
Holli Semetko. Emory University (USA)
Ingrid Volkmer, University of Melbourne (Australia)

Books Appearing in this Series

> *Media and the Politics of Failure: Great Powers, Communication Strategies, and Military Defeats*
> By Laura Roselle

> *The CNN Effect in Action: How the News Media Pushed the West toward War in Kosovo*
> By Babak Bahador

> *Media Pressure on Foreign Policy: The Evolving Theoretical Framework*
> By Derek B. Miller

MEDIA PRESSURE ON FOREIGN POLICY

The Evolving Theoretical Framework

By

Derek B. Miller

MEDIA PRESSURE ON FOREIGN POLICY
© Derek B. Miller, 2007.

First published in 2007 by
PALGRAVE MACMILLAN™
175 Fifth Avenue, New York, N.Y. 10010 and
Houndmills, Basingstoke, Hampshire, England RG21 6XS
Companies and representatives throughout the world.

PALGRAVE MACMILLAN is the global academic imprint of the Palgrave Macmillan division of St. Martin's Press, LLC and of Palgrave Macmillan Ltd. Macmillan® is a registered trademark in the United States, United Kingdom and other countries. Palgrave is a registered trademark in the European Union and other countries.

ISBN-13: 978-1-4039-7970-4

Library of Congress Cataloging-in-Publication Data is available from the Library of Congress.

A catalogue record for this book is available from the British Library.

Design by Newgen Imaging Systems (P) Ltd., Chennai, India.

First edition: July 2007

10 9 8 7 6 5 4 3 2 1

Printed in the United States of America.

Transferred to Digital Printing in 2008

The Stability and very Being of any Government consists in its Credit and Reputation; in the high Esteem and Veneration it retains in the Breast of its Subjects, and the proportionable Respect paid to it by Foreigners.

Francis Squire, 1740, Uxbridge, England,
in *A Faithful Report of a Genuine Debate
Concerning the Liberty of the Press Addressed
to a Candidate at the Ensuing Election*

Contents

List of Figures

ACKNOWLEDGMENTS

Many people who helped me research and produce this book have my thanks. Keith Krause was my dissertation advisor in Geneva and provided highly valued advice in structuring this project and ensuring its completion. David Sylvan directed me toward the rigorous study of social phenomena. Steven Livingston served as a member of the review committee and made extremely detailed comments on every page and every footnote of an early draft of the manuscript. It was inspiring and intimidating and I owe him a tremendous debt. Rom Harré agreed to correspond with me about positioning theory and suggested I come to Linacre College at Oxford to work with him, probably having realized I needed as much help as I could get. The Europeaeum Consortium provided the scholarship and the Bodleian library provided the inspiration and the material. Phil Seib saw value in this work when it was a mere presentation at an academic conference and helped its maturity into a manuscript and now a book.

My family and friends say that now it's in print they may actually read it. My wife, Camilla Waszink, is a constant source of encouragement when I need it, guidance when I lack it, and eye-rolling when I deserve it. I require a great deal of her attention.

My grandparents, Esther and Lester Shapiro, passed away before this book was completed and would have been proud to see it in print. I can hear their voices even now (you wrote all this?). I dedicate all these weighty words to them.

Introduction

This is a study of political communication in the Liberal democratic state and how media pressure on the executive may affect state conduct in international relations. It examines this vast subject through the narrow theme of media pressure on the decision making of executives vis-à-vis security concerns. In beginning this inquiry into possible media influence, it soon became evident that to understand the significance of one voice, like that of the media, in the cacophony of Liberal democratic discussion it was necessary to ask how any voice, at all, could actually matter. From outside the war room, how can one elicit a response from inside it? To answer this question is to shed light on the decision-making processes of Liberal democratic governments and, even further, how that process might affect the conduct of these societies in the international theater as a whole.

The term "pressure" is often used as an answer to the question of how individuals or groups from outside the decision-making group can affect its performance. But what is pressure, and from that definition, how does it work? To label something pressure implies that there is a criterion that helps us distinguish *this* kind of statement from *that* kind of statement; *this* is pressure, *that* is not. It further implies that this kind of statement could, under the right circumstances, actually force the hand of the executive in a certain kind of situation.

The literatures on media influence, public opinion, and international relations were studied for clues about what pressure is. It was found that the term was used regularly, and the manner of its use appeared reasonably consistent—the meanings associated with it all seemed to cluster around a set of actions or qualities that people "naturally" associated with pressure. Though it was seldom defined, its use was in a sense understandable and therefore axiomatic, making its further definition and characterization apparently unnecessary. In short, there appeared to be a generally accepted understanding of when the executive was under pressure, and when pressure was being exerted.

Though attention was focused on media pressure, per se, different literatures reviewed all spoke about pressure as a real phenomenon—so real, and so obvious, in a way, that it didn't seem to warrant further examination. There are domestic pressures and international pressures, public pressures and group pressures, alliance pressures and old fashioned "political pressures." Leaving aside whether these are all really different actors, was *pressure* something that could be understood and studied on its own terms as a serious force in international relations, as exercised through influence on foreign policy decision making? This book argues that it is, and that comparative political communication and its capacity to create and sustain pressures on the executive should be given a good deal more attention in the study of international affairs. In short, embedded in the term pressure is a theory of state-craft itself, applicable, as it were, far beyond the confines of a study on media–government relations.

In developing a theory of media pressure in political communication in Liberal states, this study has its eye on the more distant horizon of better understanding not only the democratic system, but also what sets it apart. Conclusions of Liberal democratic uniqueness cannot be drawn without equally detailed comparative studies of non-Liberal states and how pressure is practiced and understood there. The detailing of this cultural phenomenon in the two countries studied here goes some distance in making one side of the comparison clear, explicable, and—equally important—falsifiable so that further efforts might be made on better understanding the role of political communication within, and across cultural systems. My hope is that the arguments here are sufficiently compelling to attract other researchers to pick up this question in other societies, or during other times.

*   *   *

Interest in the dynamic and complicated relationship between media and governmental decision making in foreign policy and national security has experienced renewed interest since the increased involve-ment of peacekeeping forces in complex emergencies during the early to mid-1990s. The reason for this growing interest is attributable to the coincidental end of the Cold War and the subsequent change in the overarching strategic environment, and changes and develop-ments in communication and transportation technologies. It is sheer coincidence that in the early 1990s, technological achievements made global, real-time voice and video communication a reality at just the moment the Cold War ended. Nevertheless, this coincidence led to creative applications of technology by the media industry making the fall of the Berlin Wall, for example, one of the most watched spectacles in history. Scholars soon caught on to the idea that something serious, powerful, and fundamental was changing in international affairs. The watchword was "globalization" and the media was part of it.

Editorials soon bemoaned the coming of a "CNN Effect"—named after the international television news network—whereby the media were suspected of setting the agenda of the government in foreign policy. Attentive observers of foreign policy and international relations speculated that if the press historically had a positive impact on democratic governance by educating the sovereign population in Liberal states, then America may have just crossed a sort of technological Rubicon whereby media's omniscient eye and endless storytelling now threatened to undermine the deliberative decision-making processes of democratically elected officials.

By the mid-1990s, it had become conventional wisdom, and hence axiomatic, to speak of media-inspired foreign policy initiatives. It was not suggested that all policy was driven by the media; few, however, question that it could be. It was equally common to read that the problem of media influence on government was both new and revolutionary. The ability of the media to report live and in "real time" fundamentally changed the rules of the game.

Whereas the real-time news phenomena is indeed a new reality, and technology has unquestionably improved—as measured by affordability, speed, reduced weight, and accuracy in transmission, for example—I hope to explain that a probe into the intellectual history of press and policy lays barren any claim to the discussion of media influence being either new or revolutionary. As we will see, the question of whether and how the media may influence the government has been a living concern for at least 300 years in the West, rising to heights of profound concern, as during the birth of the Liberal state in Europe and the New World from the mid-1700s to the mid-1800s, and dropping to nadirs of indifference as during the early twentieth century until the early 1990s.[1] Rather, the social power of the media and its means of pressuring the government remains exactly the same. What is different is the pace at which the conversation between the media and government takes place. In understanding the perennial and underlying social forces that explain media pressure it becomes easier to make sense of what we are witnessing, to know what is truly different and what remains the same, and, to some extent, what needs to be done about it for the benefit of good governance and social liberties alike.

Although a few writers (mostly journalists) kept the question of press–government relations from slipping into complete oblivion during the early part of the century, disciplinary constraints and traditions in academe forced the study of this relationship into the uncomfortable company of public opinion research, which, it will be argued, was not the most advantageous forum for this inquiry.[2]

These earliest twentieth-century scholars were concerned with exogenous influences on policymaking and the functioning of the democratic state. Seeing that it was the media, or press, that informed the population, it took little effort to shift the focus away from the public per se and to the supposed-progenitor of the public's opinion. In 1922, Walter Lippmann published his seminal book *Public Opinion*, which was concerned with these very matters. Though not termed as such until 1972, agenda-setting has since become a burgeoning research agenda on media influence on the public. It also benefited from a ready wealth of material to draw upon, and therefore found a comfortable intellectual home in the prior work on public opinion. One question that has fallen from the agenda, however, is whether this tradition has helped or obscured progress in the specific matter of *media influence on government*. As will be explained, public opinion researchers have still not explained in a convincing manner the *means* by which the public's opinion might actuate or affect policymaking. Without knowing how the public's opinion can influence governmental policymaking, it is difficult to know where to look to find out whether it has happened. Correlation studies of public opinion and decision making or media coverage and decision making are of little benefit unless we can make some claim about who is following whom, and why we believe that might be the case. Good theories (or even explicit ones) still remain wanting.

By taking a suspecting glance at the public opinion literature, and supposing that, perhaps, media influence is not generated by public opinion per se but rather by some as-yet-to-be-identified mechanism, we provide ourselves an opportunity to approach the question of media influence from a fresh perspective and to create a new formulation of the problem.

When retreating to this ground, we can ask two consecutive, structuring questions:

1. By what means might the media influence national security decision making?
2. Can we find evidence that the media have influenced national security decision making in the manner suspected?

Chapter 1 is an investigation into the contemporary literature. We start by examining the work of writers who are unified by a specific interest in media–government relations in the context of international affairs. The review shows how certain ideas about media influence have evolved, reached impasses, devised new solutions, and arrived today at an epistemological problem about what we mean by "pressure" and how influence is "caused."

These problems are very similar to those found in public opinion research, which is also interested in influence, only this time from the public rather than the media. As the public opinion literature is more developed—owning to a longer tradition and a wider base of scholars—we can see how they've reached the same types of problems and why a new type of argument is needed to get beyond this barrier. If we can take lessons from that field, perhaps we can avoid following their diversions and jump right to—and possibly over—the same problems they now face.

Chapter 2, "Beyond the Contemporary Debate," expands the universe of relevant voices to solve some of the theoretical mysteries uncovered in chapter 1. After noting that much work on media–government relations is now trapped by a reliance on both public opinion research and agenda-setting theory, and also that the dominant epistemological approaches complicate rather than simplify concerns over measurement and "causality," we take a radical departure and move not to another contemporary field in an untapped discipline, but farther back in time. In doing so, a world opens up to the best arguments ever produced about media influence on foreign policy decision making. This antiquarian approach revisits the towering ideas of freedom of speech and its social functions that formed the bedrock of modern political life in the West. This brief, but focused exploration leads back to the early 1700s and the mid-1800s, when Europe and the New World underwent a series of Liberal revolutions.

We see how arguments are spun on the question of free speech, liberty of the press, and freedom of expression with the full knowledge of the writers that riding on their arguments was the manner in which democracy would be forged in European statecraft. We find embedded in their arguments—ignored or long forgotten—a wealth of bold and explicit theorizing about media–government relations and the power of the press to affect the conduct of statecraft.[3] By explaining how pressure works, these arguments seem to pick up just where the modern literature stops. Recovering some of these ideas (there is much more work to do here, and this chapter is only a start) lets us recover some of our intellectual heritage and use it in a new way, hopefully with some exciting implications.

Chapter 3, "Toward a Theory of Media Pressure," forms the heart of the meta-theoretical work in this book. It fashions an explicit hypothesis about the means by which the media might be able to affect the decision making of foreign policy decision makers in Liberal states.

The chapter aims to explicate the mechanics of this hypothesis by showing how communication, in the form of rhetoric and political positioning by coalition partners, can create political imperatives for policymakers. The grounding for the coding techniques is provided here, and the details of the coding process are provided in chapters 5 and 6.

Chapter 4, "The Iraqi Civil War and the Aftermath, 1991," provides a history of the Iraqi Civil War in 1991 and the decision of the United States and British to remain "uninvolved" in the fighting until early April, when both countries launched one of the largest and most logistically complex humanitarian relief operations in history. Due to the dearth of attention placed on this important event for the entire Middle East, efforts have been made to reconstruct the events from primary source material, journalistic accounts, and the few sections of books dedicated to remembering these events.

Chapter 5, "Measuring Coverage," gets down to the nitty-gritty of measuring coverage during the crises for all sources in both countries. In examining the case study period between 1 March and 2 June 1991, every story containing the word "Iraq" in the *New York Times*, the *Washington Post*, the *Guardian*, and the *Independent* was read and every paragraph was coded. A similar process on a minute-by-minute basis was also conducted for ABC News, NBC News, and CBS News. In total, 16,607 paragraphs, 991 stories, 134 opinion pieces, and 55 editorials or lead stories were manually counted, as were 720.62 minutes of total television coverage. The latter measures were aided by the records of the Vanderbilt Archives; however, special methods were developed to solve some of the differences in the needs of this study from the data sets as they were available. This was done by a thorough review of the transcripts of ABC and CBS. Unfortunately, the BBC has yet to establish a public depository for the transcripts of their news broadcasts making such a similar measure untenable.

Chapter 6, "Measuring Pressure, Testing for Influence," analyzes media pressure as disaggregated from media coverage based on the theories of the Positioning Hypothesis. To find proof of "uptake," or direct conversational evidence of the U.S. executive taking media statements as pressure, every question posed by American journalists to the White House from 1 March through 2 June 1991—totaling 2,719 questions—was examined three times: the first time to count the total number of questions asked (2,719), the second to determine relevance to the main policy story (636), and the third to separate "pressure questions" from "non-pressure questions" (218 were pressure).

As Britain does not have an analogous institution to the White House Press Conference, the entire House of Commons HANSARD record was also examined for pressure from the Opposition (in this case Labour) during the same time period as the American study. By the end of May, the total number of words spoken on the matter (accepting a margin of error of about two percent) would be roughly 51,000.

To distinguish the independent measure of pressure from coverage, all 16,607 paragraphs were reexamined individually to check against the criteria established, and evidence gleaned from the press conferences in the United States. In Britain a rather different method was used, as is explained.

The number of stories, the number of stories on the front page, the number of paragraphs, editorials, and opinion pieces were all individually coded. As a result, chapter 7 is the first effort yet undertaken to independently measure media pressure as distinct from media coverage, and further benefits from a cross-national comparison, as well as a cross-media comparison (newspapers versus television). The results are then checked against the diplomatic records, and in the case of Britain, the records of the House of Commons.

A series of conclusions are presented about actual media influence in the United States and Britain respectively during the case study period. It draws empirical, methodological, and case study conclusions that should prove helpful to researchers aiming to better understand the relationship between media coverage and executive decision making as well as those people concerned with learning about the decision making in the case studies themselves.

Chapter 7, "Summing Up and Pressing On," recounts the primary arguments and conclusions from the study as a whole and then builds a case for how these conclusions fit into the larger literature on both media–government relations and international relations theory respectively. A special effort is made to bridge the study of political communication with the orthodox study of international relations. The section suggests ways forward for better understanding media impact on decision making in Liberal states, and for comparative studies of media–government relations in the non-Liberal world.

CHAPTER 1

The Contemporary Debate

INTRODUCTION

The purpose of this chapter is to review some of the literature that has informed the current (i.e., the last half-century) debate over media effects on foreign policy decision making in Liberal societies. In describing and assessing the state of the art we can consolidate the arguments that have produced the most notable results and organize them so that consistencies and contradictions can be revealed. This lays the framework for developing an explicit hypothesis about media pressure in chapter 3, which is then tested in the next chapters.

The central theme of this chapter is that the prevailing theoretical framework suffers from two epistemological problems that can be rectified by the same solution. The first is about the mechanism of influence between the media and the government. In the great majority of cases, scholars treat media–government relations as a study of cause-and-effect without ever explaining how exactly the media can affect the government beyond metaphors such as "pressure."

In the absense of an explicit theory we are left with a more detailed—if unresolved—discussion about "directionality" in the media–government dynamic. For some, the media pressures the government, for others, it is the government's manipulation of the media that is central, and to still others, there is some form of "bi-directional" or "mutually influential" process at play.

I argue that in identifying an appropriate theory of pressure we can render the second question irrelevant. We can do this by treating media–government relations as an on-going conversation made up of empirically demonstrable and morally significant episodes that have direct consequences on policymakers' abilities to form and maintain coalitions of support for their ideas and actions. In this model, "causality" in a mechanical sense is sidestepped entirely and is replaced with deliberate actions by the government. Directionality is moot because we're interested instead in turn-taking in a conversation.

A REVIEW OF MODERN LITERATURE

The most direct studies on the question of media effects on foreign policy are very recent, specifically the 1990s. In 1995, Steven Livingston and Todd Eachus questioned what has come to be known as the "CNN Effect," which they describe as the theory of the loss of policy control by elite decision makers to the news media. Though technology was not an explicit factor of their study, its significance was strongly implied.

In citing earlier work on the CNN Effect, Livingston and Eachus list nine predecessors who had written on the topic. On inspection, none of these references predate the 1990/91 Gulf War in part because CNN itself—and by extension all real-time news coverage—did not exist either. This underscored the technological focus of the research.[1]

Their work was an in-depth case study of one of the progenitors of the CNN Effect debate, namely the Somalia operation by the United States, and for this reason it is a good starting point for the present review. In 1992, the United States intervened in Somalia with military personnel in Operation Restore Hope to help feed starving people after the government collapsed and anarchy befell the state. In September, 1993, coincidentally just a day before the October deaths of the U.S. forces killed in fire-fights with Somali rebels lead by General Aidid, the venerable George Kennan published an editorial in the *New York Times* called, "Somalia, through a Glass Darkly."[2] In it, he argued that American foreign policy was being led by the media, and, more specifically, television. Andrew Natsios (who is highly suspicious of this argument) argued that this so-called CNN Effect "suggests that policy-makers only respond when there are scenes of mass starvation on the evening news. It also suggests that policy-makers obtain most of their information about ongoing disasters from media reports."[3]

Kennan's article was soon followed by a wealth of editorials, journalistic books, and edited volumes arguing for or against the existence of the so-called CNN Effect, especially with regard to humanitarian relief operations, or what the military then called "OOTW" or operations other than war.[4]

Livingston and Eachus wanted to know whether pressure from television and print media really had led to the initial decisions concerning U.S. intervention in Somalia. They concluded that the answer was an emphatic "no." "News coverage trends do not support the claim that news attention to Somalia led to the Bush Administration's decision to intervene."[5] They conclude instead that "the decision to intervene was the result of diplomatic and bureaucratic operations, with news coverage coming in response to those decisions." Their method was two-fold. They conducted a content analysis of news accounts of Somalia in a variety of media between late 1991 and December 1992. Second, they interviewed officials and journalists connected with the events.

Livingston and Eachus helped to dispel the particular myth that the initial decision to intervene in Somalia was caused by the media, as Kennan had suggested—a conclusion echoed by Piers Robinson in his 2002 book on the CNN Effect. What they demonstrate is that media coverage of Somalia complied with W.L. Bennett's theory of "news indexing," which states that news reports tend to follow or peg their stories to official actions and statements by policy elites.[6]

The indexing hypothesis, as it has come to be called, is at present the backbone theory of the small standing literature on media effects on government. It has received little empirical testing, and thus far no meta-theoretical challenges. W.L. Bennett was the first to name the phenomenon and provide a useful and refutably explicit hypothesis. However, the observation was made earlier. One example comes from Daniel Hallin who wrote in 1986 about Vietnam War coverage that, "day-to-day coverage was closely tied to official information and dominant assumptions about the war, and critical coverage didn't become widespread until consensus broke down among political elites and the wider society."[7] It was Bennett, however, who took such case-specific observations and proposed a general theory, which is why research on the subject is generally associated with his efforts.[8]

Jonathan Mermin presents a different argument from Livingston and Eachus about Somalia. He writes,

> [t]he argument that television contributed to U.S. intervention [in Somalia] is supported by the chronology of events and news stories presented in this study; there is no reason to doubt that the appearance of Somalia on American television just before major changes in U.S. policy in August and November of 1992 influenced the decision of the Bush administration to act. What is not clear, however, is why Somalia appeared on television in the first place, a question of central importance in understanding the scope and character of television's influence on foreign policy formation.[9]

The Livingston and Eachus study, as just discussed, provides a succinct and clear argument (two years earlier) that does give a reason to doubt this assumption of media influence. Nevertheless, his central conclusion is that "the lesson of Somalia is not just about the influence of television on Washington, but is equally about the influence of Washington on television."[10] This presumably proves that the media do not "drive" foreign policy, but contributes to its decision-making process. We are still left to wonder how.

Another study, published a year later, was written by John Zaller and Dennis Chui and was called "Government's Little Helper: US Press Coverage of Foreign Policy Crises, 1945–1991"; it strongly supported the Bennett theory of indexing, which is supported by the Livingston and Eachus and Mermin pieces as well. Being slightly more specific than Livingston and Eachus about indexing, Zaller and Chui described Bennett's 1990 argument as holding that "reporters 'index' the slant of their coverage to reflect the range of opinion that exists within the government."[11] Zaller critiques Bennett (1990) by observing that "one concern is that [the study] failed to develop a measure of congressional opinion that was independent of what the [New York Times] claimed it was."[12] This independent measurement would have been important because it would have made explicit the distance between official opinions and how they were reported. As Zaller writes, "journalists might, for example, have used officials as sources but either done so selectively or distorted their views so as to produce the results that journalists rather than sources wanted."[13] Zaller and Chui sought to correct this failing by retesting Bennett's hypothesis. Their results supported the indexing hypothesis very strongly, and their method was quite interesting.

Zaller and Chui focused on "variations in the hawkishness or dovishness of coverage of foreign affairs crises." They hypothesized that the degree of press hawkishness would depend on the degree of hawkishness in the government. The definition of hawkish and dovish was relative to the crisis. For an unbiased list of foreign policy crises from 1945 to 1991 (or at least one that was non-partisan to their investigation), they turned to John Spanier's *American Foreign Policy since World War II* (1992) and produced a subsequent list of thirty-nine crises, four of which were omitted: three because Congress was not in session, which would affect their results, and the one other because they deemed it similar enough to another to combine it with a second.[14]

They found a strong correlation. So the question is: what did they actually measure? Importantly, Zaller and Chui were forthright in observing that their correlation study of government and media, though quite rigorous, does not determine necessarily who is leading whom in the public discourse. Their interpretation that the media were indexing their stories and editorials to government opinion comes from "outside the data—from prior studies that stress, on the basis of qualitative observation, the dependence of reports on sources."[15] They conclude that this aspect of their argument is not conclusive, but does contribute to the indexing hypothesis and therefore to a greater understanding of government–media relations.

Zaller and Chui were not testing the CNN Effect, per se. Except for the last five years or so of their study, there was no CNN, and before the mid-1950s, there was no television worth considering in such a study.[16] The world was then composed of newspapers and radio, and unfortunately—though perhaps understandably—radio was not reviewed.[17] Technology, therefore, was not a variable that Zaller and Chui considered. In a stricter sense, their theory was an examination of whether media discourse and governmental discourse—during times of foreign policy crises—were similar or dissimilar and to what extent. They concluded that they were notably similar, which is a helpful finding because it sets us up to ask why.

If the indexing hypothesis seems to hold up, then what must be distinguished, and which generally appears overlooked, is whether indexing *precludes the possibility of influence.* This question takes us beyond studies that seek to find out "who is leading whom" and forces us to ask how the relationship actually works, and whether indexing makes any difference to that dynamic.

Piers Robinson wrote a review article intending to "[assess] what is meant by the term 'CNN Effect' in relation to western intervention in humanitarian crises."[18] He begins by reviewing what Herman and Chomsky call a "propaganda model" whereby, through coercive and often furtive means, the government sets the media agenda and demonstrates that it is incompatible with the CNN Effect model. After noting this incompatibility based on each theory positing a different direction of causality, Robinson wants to introduce a "media-policy interaction model."[19] Robinson argues convincingly that the research on the CNN Effect "fails to clarify whether or not the news media have (or have not) triggered recent 'humanitarian' interventions."[20]

Robinson's use of the term "triggered" is important. Like Livingston and Eachus, Robinson is primarily concerned with the initial decision to undertake an action. All three authors dismiss this as a possibility, quite rightly, in the case studies conducted in the former instance, and in the supporting literature in the latter (which is not to say it is theoretically impossible). But what about media pressure throughout the life of a policy, like in Vietnam? Isn't this a core question to understanding media–government relations? Why only questions about "triggers"?

Robinson successfully demonstrates that the literature is presently contradictory about directions of influence. But a further categorization would have been helpful, one that is as yet unaddressed: the benefit of dividing and explaining the differences between theories of political communication and theories of political economy. Zaller and Chui are primarily interested in the question of communication, that is, how, if at all, the media's words, sounds, and images might affect the outputs of the foreign policy decision-making process. Herman and Chomsky are concerned instead with the playing field on which the acts of communication are taking place. For them, structural constraints such as centralized power and ownership of media firms determines what can be addressed and what cannot. Because of this, they are dismissive of what the media does. It is already "tainted" somehow, and hence unworthy of real attention.

We need to differentiate a political communication study from a political economy study and explain their relationship. Herman and Chomsky are taking a political economy approach, that is, they are identifying and analyzing those forces that determine the structural constraints in which communication takes place, and are alleged to influence communication. These structures, of course, change through time and in each locality. Earlier in American history, for example, the press was owned and operated by the political parties. Today, they are generally owned by multinational conglomerates operating in a free-market system and political parties manage little more than their own websites in terms of publishing. Likewise, the political economy of Britain, with its combination of state and privately owned media outlets operating within a Liberal state with legal protection of free speech is different from, say, the Soviet Union under Stalin, with state-owned and -controlled media outlets and the common penalty of jail or death for the dissemination of subversive ideas or messages. All communication takes place within a structure that may be called the "political economy" and it can and should be studied.

A study in political communication itself, however, is one that seeks to identify and analyze how communication functions within a given society. It is—or should be—taken for granted that some political economy of communication exists within the community studied. But the assumption remains that *what is communicated can be studied on its own merits*, given that what is communicated can only exist as a function of the structure that supports it. It would be incorrect to argue, for example, that because there are structural constraints on communication, it is impossible to elicit an effect from that which is communicated. What must be asked instead is whether communication by or through the media is still capable of influencing policy outcomes *given* a set of structuring factors in economy, law, or political coercion, for example. Part of the trouble in unpacking the present literature on media–government relations is that the distinction between communication and economy is not being made. We're chasing different rabbits but have yet to recognize it. Eventually, when we get a better handle on each subject area we'll need to work together to better understand the social system, but at the moment our maturation is being stymied by arguments comparing apples to oranges.

This brings us to the final point about Robinson's analysis namely the issue of media pressure itself. In reviewing the work of Nik Gowing, Warren Strobel, and others, Robinson quite rightly illustrates that they tend to have difficulty in "measuring exactly the precise impact which the media have on policy, specifically whether or not the media can cause humanitarian intervention; and the significance each attaches to policy certainty (or uncertainty) in determining media influence" that there is "little evidence of a push [i.e., cause intervention] effect . . . nor is there evidence of a pull [i.e., cause withdraw] effect.[21] Robinson writes that many arguments elsewhere are essentially loose speculation about "'complex systems,' 'fluid interplay' and a 'rich and diverse relationship' between media coverage and policy outcomes—all of which sounds reasonable enough but does little to clarify things or prove a direct casual relationship between media coverage and policy outcomes."[22]

Unfortunately, when Robinson discusses the need to differentiate between immediate and underlying causes of media effects on policymaking—referring to the case of the Kurds in 1991—he writes, "Media pressure would then be understandable as the immediate factor in causing intervention" but he does not tell us what pressure actually is, how it might work, or how we might recognize it. The need to answer these questions lies in the proposed "media-policy interaction model" as a solution. The 2002 book, in which he carefully tests his theories, still does not address this problem. He writes, "this study focuses on analyzing the amount and form (via framing analysis) of media coverage with the focus upon how a particular humanitarian crisis is represented and the tone of coverage towards official policy."[23] This is indeed done with great detail and care. But it remains uncertain why the framing of the media coverage *matters at all* seeing as we remain without a theory to explain how framing affects policymakers, and second, *how we can know empirically whether media coverage mattered to the policymakers?*

The causality problem is a serious roadblock for progress in this field. Robinson's struggle with this problem is quite instructive. He writes:[24]

Post-modernism and social constructivism have taught us to be cautious of explaining the world through reference to dependent variables, independent variables and causal links. Inevitably, however, if we are to discuss the impact of media coverage on policy we become involved in making assessments as to whether a particular decision would have been made if media coverage had been different. To my mind this type of question is a reasonable one to ask although I acknowledge that some would argue the question is either unanswerable or else ill-conceived . . . In this study I occasionally use the term cause (without assuming the phenomenon is overly deterministic), and, more often, influence. When I argue that "A" influenced/caused "B" to occur I am saying no more and no less than if "A" had not been present. "B" would have been unlikely to occur . . . [t]o say that the media influenced or caused intervention is not to claim that it was the only factor, only a necessary one. As noted before this study does not pretend to offer a multi-factor explanation of intervention.

Robinson is quite right in saying that overly deterministic (or, perhaps, mechanical) explanations of causality should be cautioned against. He is also quite right in noting that for media influence to be addressed in a meaningful way one eventually wants to understand how the actions of one actor (media) can change or alter the actions of another (government). Without some argument about this, one isn't really answering anything. We might even be so bold as to say that the *point* of looking at a social phenomenon is to explain it not just describe it around the edges.

The trouble is that Robinson is forced to reject a mechanistic notion of causality but doesn't really offer anything to replace it. As he writes, "Unfortunately, influence cannot be observed in any obvious or straightforward fashion. We cannot see inside the minds of policymakers and directly observe media influence at work."[25] This is a key epistemological problem in our field and Robinson identifies it perfectly. However, I will now argue that in fact we can observe pressure in a straightforward and empirical fashion without having to read minds and that a theory of influence can be built around it.

In fact, we can even go further. Not only can we see pressure, we can also measure it on the basis of observed actions by the executive. To do so, however, requires that we build an assumptive base, offer a theory about media pressure, and then devise a coding system to make that theory testable. We can do all this by listening in a very particular way to what people say, and how it evidently affects others. This is the message and lesson of chapter 3.

The idea of a media–government interaction model, though of different character, has been suggested elsewhere. Following on Martin Linsky's work of 1986, Patrick O'Heffernan, in 1991, published the results of a three-year study supported by MIT, which built on Linsky's arguments and even reviewed all his interview data; Linsky is notably thanked for providing it. O'Heffernan examined the direct, bilateral relationship between the media and government and writes,

> Little empirical work has been published that examines direct media influence on U.S. foreign policy outputs or direct government use of media to further its foreign policy agenda, although any journalist or policy maker can tell stories exemplifying both. As a result, there are many anecdotes but no models of the U.S. foreign policy-media relationship as it exists in today's world of international mass media and worldwide television.[26]

O'Heffernan's main argument is that what once was a symbiotic relationship between media and government (by which he means mutually beneficial propinquity) has changed into one of *interdependent mutual exploitation.*[27] O'Heffernan's distinction between symbiosis and mutual exploitation is synonymous with the distinction he draws between Cohen's[28] worldview and the world of today. In Cohen's time—we are told—the government and media needed each other, and relations were generally friendly. What was once a "fraternal symbiotic relationship" has been replaced by

> two distinct global institutions—the worldwide U.S. foreign policy and diplomatic community, and the global mass media . . . . From the policymaker's perspective, a significant element of policy making involves using and influencing the media; policy making cannot be done without the media, nor can the media cover international affairs without government cooperation.[29]

The result is mutual exploitation.

This study, however, does not help us out of the problem Robinson observed. He notes that the media play an active role in U.S. policy development and execution; the media are sometimes used by government as a diplomatic proxy; at other times the media pressure the government, which prompts statements by the government. He also writes that the media have influence over the policymakers: "This influence stems from policy maker's perception of the media's importance and utility, especially of the importance of the broadcast media, and from the media's injection of certain biases into the policymaking process. The combination of these two media forces results in a new foreign policy that is media-influenced."[30] But *why?* Where does this perception come from?

He does give us a hint. Under the heading "Sources of Media Power," buried on page 88, and traversing no more than three paragraphs, O'Heffernan writes,

> [the media's] power results from their ability to locate and reveal positive and negative information which, under certain circumstances, can severely damage policies and careers or increase the likelihood of success. Insiders perceive that both positive and negative information could increase the visibility—and thus the vulnerability—of policy officials, but that negative media coverage had the strongest effect.[31]

This is interesting. It implies that the mechanism of influence is the actual media reports—that is, the communication itself—and that the "dependent variable" is the careers or policies of individual policymakers. Additionally, negative statements or information about the careers or policies of policymakers seem to have greater influence than positive ones. This is interesting too and provides a clear argument he could have taken further.

In no article—the Linsky conclusion and the O'Heffernan reformulation notwithstanding—nor in Robinson's insightful review of the work done thus far is there an actual hypothesis of the mechanics of media pressure or influence. To witness the need for such a theory consider a few examples from other authors on the subject of media and foreign policy: David Gergen writes, "It is a serious mistake for executive branch officials to make policy hastily in order to meet news broadcast deadlines."[32] According to Gergen, who has worked in two presidential administrations, they do. But why? As Robinson would have it, they feel pressured. But this simply applies a name to the problem. Marvin Kalb, who wrote the Foreword to *The Media and Foreign Policy*, one of the few volumes that directly discusses this subject, writes, "The correspondent, as well as the diplomat, is denied the opportunity for reflection. Both are part of the new, global loop of information, their fortunes intertwined. They are pressured to react quickly, in some cases, 'live.'"[33]

* * *

The time has come to abandon the mechanistic view of causality implied in this chicken-and-egg research approach and shift gears entirely to a new approach. As with most new approaches, this one is already decades old but has not bridged this particular problem of media–government relations; primarily because *communication* and how it works has not been taken very seriously. We begin with the concept of "meaning" to build that bridge.

In *Acts of Meaning*, Jerome Bruner explains that the cognitive revolution in the 1950s (of which he was a part) was "an all-out effort to establish meaning as the central concept of psychology— not stimuli and responses, not overtly observable behavior, not biological drives and their transformation, but meaning . . . It's aim was to discover and to describe formally the meanings that human beings created out of their encounters with the world, and then to propose hypotheses about what meaning-making processes were implicated."[34] Along the way, however, something happened, he explains. "[E]mphasis began shifting away from 'meaning' to 'information,' from *construction* of meaning to *processing* of information. These are profoundly different matters. The key factor in the shift was the introduction of computation as the ruling metaphor and of computability as the necessary criterion of a good theoretical model."[35]

The moment that meaning slipped into processing was the crucial moment when metaphors of computational action became reified and treated as real mechanisms of human thought. Note again how Robinson was drawn to a mechanistic model in terms of dependent and independent variables, but in rejecting this model was unable to replace it with anything new and satisfactory.

As Bruner explains, "If one falls into the habit of thinking of those complex [computer] programs as 'virtual minds' (to borrow Daniel Dennett's phrase), then it takes only a small but crucial step to go the whole way to believing that 'real minds' and their processes, like 'virtual' ones and theirs, could be 'explained' in the same way."[36]

An apt example of this comes from "The Representation of Knowledge in Minds and Machines" by Walter Kintsch. Kintsch argued in his abstract that "human knowledge can be represented as a propositional network in which the meaning of a node is defined by its position in a network. That is, the relationship between a node and its neighbors determines how this node is used in language understanding and production, i.e., its meaning."[37]

For Bruner, the "small but crucial step" here is the faith that an ability to map linguistic systems, and understanding how terms are "located" as vectors in propositional networks consisting of predicate-argument structures is the same as accounting for the creation of meaning, hence Kintsch's casual use of "i.e." above.

One consequence of this computational metaphor is that old, understandable terms associated with "mind" have lost their theoretical foothold and respect as useful terms for building arguments. As Bruner writes, "With mind equated to program, what should the status of mental states be—old-fashioned mental states identifiable not by their programmatic characteristics in a computational system but by their subjective marking? There could no place for 'mind' in such a system—'mind' in the sense of intentional states like believing, desiring, intending, grasping a meaning."[38]

In shifting from processing to meaning, from causality to conversation, and from directionality to communicative episodes, we will now enter a fascinating world: the world of reputation and moral positioning. And to do this, we need to take a step back to the time when the power of language and the power of the printed word were changing the face of Western civilization at the dawn of Liberalism.

CHAPTER 2

Beyond the Contemporary Debate

Contemporary scholarship and casual discussion on media–government relations and security decision making, as discussed in chapter 1, has a demonstrably strong tendency to emphasize the power of the press to shape the agenda of the government through the indirect, and still opaque, mechanism of public opinion. Likewise, the main avenue of inquiry has been through the lens of technology, driven by the fear that the deliberative organs of government are being subverted by contemporary media organizations with powerful communication technologies, few legal restraints, and no mechanisms of democratic accountability.

From this staging ground, those scholars and writers interested in either empirical investigations or theory building on the question of media influence on decision making often start with the premise that it is technology and technological advances in communication and transportation that have made questions about media power so salient today. As a result, there is a decidedly "modern" focus to our current work, thereby forcing the voices of writers and thinkers from the pre-electronic era into a category of obsolescence or irrelevance because of the allegedly revolutionary nature of the present era. More often still, these thinkers and writers of the past are not even considered at all.

This absence of historical inquiry is unfortunate; lost in the current framing of the issue is a surprising wealth of material that is directly related to modern concerns, most of which is found not in social theory but in law—a discipline that long predates modern social science and exists with it in parallel today. Beginning with the first laws in England against gossiping, some 700 years ago, Western scholars and lawyers (often the same individuals) have continually engaged in argument, theorizing, and legal exegesis on the subject of public speech and writing and its effects on the state, with the greatest concentration coming during the 1700s and the early 1800s, at the birth of Liberalism in Western civilization. This vast material makes clear that with each law passed against slander, libel, seditious libel, and defamation came an accompanying *explanation*—either by the arguing lawyers or by the jurists in the record of their decisions—of the social ills that resulted from the spread of what Shakespeare once called "foul whisperings."[1] Implicit in each argument is a theory of influence—that is, what speech *does* to people and societies.

From the earliest periods through the present, these laws demonstrate a remarkable consistency across time. The main consistencies lie in two areas. The first is in the observations made by these societies about what public statements do to those who are the subject of them; and the second is on what grounds those aggrieved by such statements (be they verbal or written) are to be compensated or remedied.

What has changed is how societies in the United States, France, and Great Britain, for example, view the social value of these spoken or written words and therefore whether they should be suppressed—by arguments against freedom of speech—or supported—in arguments in favor of freedom of speech.

These explanations for or against public speech and publishing remain the richest and most clearly untapped vein of what today we would call social theorizing about political communication and its affects on governance. From the perspective of methodology, the uncovering or rejoining of this work also opens an intellectual gold mine of empirical material in the form of countless legal cases brought against those who alleged that a slander or libel had taken place. These arguments about whether or not damage has been inflicted (or earlier, whether a crime has been committed) provide modern social scientists with positive, documented evidence about the values of a given society during an examined era.[2] Of even greater interest to the task at hand is the sophistication the court cases and exegesis on the rulings reveal in their understanding and analysis of press–government relations.

It is strongly suggested here that the study of the legal exegesis of slander, libel, and especially seditious libel represents the greatest depository of Western writing and thinking about the power of the spoken or the written word. And the greatest density of this material, the most thoughtful argumentation, and the most passionately presented appeals come from the eighteenth century and early-to-mid nineteenth century, when the very question of Liberalism was born: a philosophy of people and state that would later overturn the entire social and political order of Western civilization.

This "classical" work, therefore, is not simply a historical remnant. Instead, the ideas and arguments of writers from the eighteenth and nineteenth centuries are worthy of serious consultation in the same manner as those writers reviewed in the pervious chapter. One of the first lessons we learn from these early writers on freedom of the press is that the "essence" of how communication functions to challenge governmental or executive authority appears to be *the same* today as it was as far back as the thirteenth century, when the first laws against sedition were penned in Britain. In the world of medieval Europe, power was centralized in the Church and the feudal lords; books were owned and read by the select, educated few who could gain access and read Latin, Greek, Arabic, and Hebrew; and public opinion, as we use the term today, was utterly meaningless except for concerns about revolution. If in this bygone world, writers expressed the same, consistent worry about the power of the spoken or written word to undermine their power or ability to act—across this expanse of political, social, cultural, and technological time and change—then it stands to reason that modern concerns over technology having "changed every-thing" about how the press affects governmental decision making would seem to be rather overstated.

The arguments put forward about the benefits or harm that free speech and publishing might do to government and therefore all of social life in the West were quite explicit about how freedom of speech affected the government. The common thread through all these arguments, the laws against and later for freedom of speech, and the compensation provided to those "harmed" by it was that all considered words a force that could change a person's moral stand-ing in society. All were equally clear that by changing a person's moral standing detrimentally, it also denigrated that person's power to persuade others of the rightness of action. As one American Law report from 1986 explained, "While such basic rights as freedom of speech and of the press appear to mandate unfettered freedom of expression, an action for compensatory damages for libel or slander is based on the countervailing consideration that individuals should be free to maintain their reputations unimpaired by false and defamatory statements and attacks."[3]

That denigrated power was of greatest concern when the figures harmed were the men and women who ruled nations. The two greatest forms of moral damage that could be caused were calling people either un-Christian or untrustworthy. As the earlier insult has fallen from favor as a slander of choice, our attention shifts to the second still-poignant threat to one's reputation.

The centrality of being "untrustworthy" and its connection to both law and governance can be explored through the essential and perennial role of law in forming the vocabulary, language, and methods of political thought in the West. Adda B. Bozeman explains:[4]

> It is a noteworthy aspect of our civilization that all basic orientations to life have traditionally been encased and communicated in the language of secular law, nowhere more so than in the fields of internal and external politics. Classical Roman jurists in the pre-Christian era thus defined the state as a partnership to a bond in law, while the common law in England accepted Burke's definition of the state as a compact between successive generations meant to endure through time.
>
> Contract, as illustrated by these two instances, as well as by the medieval Gruetli Oath—an accord that bound a few liberty-loving Swiss cantons in a common political destiny and has since been the rock on which Switzerland's model democracy rests—thus emerges from the West's long history as the core concept of the state. Also, and in tune with the same sentiment and logic, contract is the core of constitutional democratic government, and therewith the condition precedent for legally enforceable civil liberties.

Contract itself emerges as a legal possibility with the treatment of and belief that each human being is somehow alone in the universe, and that the individual mind is the central authority for making choices and entering into relationships. In the Judeo-Christian world—underscored magnificently by Martin Luther's rejection of interlocutors in the Church—this meant relations with God. In Roman Civil law, it meant relations among men. Through the conjoining and maturity of these ideas, contract emerged as a unique social bond in the West. "The individual mind," writes Bozeman, "[is] recognized as the exclusive source of the human imagination" in Western society. This is relevant to artistic development, moral accountability, and all matters of human rights. Being free in such manner, the individual is able to "commit himself voluntarily and rationally in associations with others."

This ability to commit an act, in word or deed, in good faith implies a confidence in "the other" as *equally* capable of entering into contractual obligations. What this implies is that the contractual relations between free minds, able to act morally on a promissory basis, create a unique confidence in what she calls "notions of the future." "It would be difficult," she writes, "not to conclude from the records that law [and hence contract] has been consistently trusted in the West as the main carrier of shared values, the most efficient agent of social control, and the only reliable principle capable of moderating and reducing the reign of passion, arbitrariness and caprice in human life."[5]

The parameters of Liberal democratic statecraft now takes shape. Liberalism, capitalized, may not have a universal definition, but invariably it has something to do with recognizing the individual person as the autonomous moral actor on life's stage, with the Liberal state being a form of government consistent with that recognition.

Liberalism is the foundation of all Western governance, and the related—but distinct—term democracy is helpfully differentiated as the *process* by which Liberalism now manifests itself as a means of governance. The two terms Liberalism and democracy, however, are often incorrectly treated as interchangeable, and worse, people speak of democracy without considering the Liberal foundations that form its philosophical substratum. This, incidentally, is why democracy in its Western variety is so hard to export. Because exporting a process is not the same as exporting a philosophy.

Liberalism emerged gradually from the early eighteenth century as an awakening to the notion that some individuals are not inherently superior to others in the context of commoners and aristocrats. By 1776, the notion was a foundation to the political philosophy of the Americans during their revolution against feudal Britain (which was unique in that it threw off British control but did not rebel against an indigenous feudal system). This supported and encouraged the French Revolution, ripened during the Napoleonic Wars, and finally in the mid-nineteenth century all of the New World and much of Western Europe was finally swept by a wave of Liberal revolution in 1848, or else saw the peaceful overthrow of the *ancien régime* by this period. This is to say that Liberalism as a political philosophy and form of statecraft is young, fragile, and has only existed for less than 200 years in a very small number of countries; even fewer have experienced it continually, having been occupied by anti-Liberal powers such as Fascist Germany, or the Communist Soviet Union.[6]

If these characterizations of Liberalism and democracy are well founded—and they were certainly evident in the eighteenth and nineteenth centuries—then it stands to reason that to be "untrustworthy" in a democratic system is to be a threat to the future. The nature of that threat comes from the individual's capacity to undermine the confidence of others in the future. Those who are a threat to the future should naturally not be in charge of it, and so in the final analysis, those who break their contracts should not rule over the lives of others. If the public can demonstrate a ruler to be a liar, and the public has any say in the matter, that ruler's days are numbered.

The only way for the public to communicate this notion of being "untrustworthy" to others is through the printed word and through free assembly (though the Internet and other electronic media allow for text to be transmitted in novel forms these days). These two topics, more than any other, became the most heated topics of the Revolutionary Age. Does the populous have the moral right, in lands ruled by a feudal system, to challenge the moral worth of God's anointed? Should not the printing presses be controlled to ensure that governance remains possible, and that the vulgar, uneducated masses not spread falsehoods—or indeed, even truths!—that might threaten the standing of kings not only at home but on foreign shores? Should there be freedom of speech, knowing what harm it can do?

THE SEDITIOUS LIBEL TEST
AND THE LIBERAL DIVIDE

On behalf of a certain J. Roberts, at the Oxford Arms in Warwick Lane, a pamphlet was published in 1740 by a local attorney of Exford who was also vicar of Cutcombe and Luxborow. The writer's name was Francis Squire and the name of his long-since forgotten piece was *A Faithful Report of a Genuine Debate Concerning the Liberty of the Press Addressed to a Candidate at the Ensuing Election.*[7] Squire, twenty-two years earlier, had written a sermon entitled "Wickedness, high-treason: or, All vicious subjects enemies of their governors," and by the time of this particular local election, his views on loyalty to the crown had changed rather little. In the later pamphlet, Squire explains why he would most certainly not be voting for the candidate in question, and, in doing so, offers us an invaluable portrait of pre-Revolutionary European philosophy on the liberty of the press and why this liberty was considered such a threat to Britain. Though neither the first nor only example of its kind, Squire's piece provides a rare, clear, and accessible first argument about media influence on foreign policy decision making in non-Liberal societies. That he is not a particularly unique or original thinker, but rather a more common if colorful pamphleteer, is helpful as it recounts how the ideas he expresses were common currency at his time of writing.

Francis Squire was decidedly discontent with the manner in which anonymous publications were then speaking with "unexampled Rudeness and Indecency" about "every Thing and person most honourable, or most sacred" in Britain in the early 1700s:

> Is it possible for an Englishman of any Spirit, to behold his Sovereign, his Protector, his political Father talk'd of in a Style that no Gentleman

of Virtue or Breeding would use towards his Enemies? Can you read with a Smile, a Smile of Approbation, the detestable Ribaldry of a Gang of Vagrants, escaped, or driven out of the Bogs of Ireland, or the High-Lands of Scotland; Vagrants without Lot, Stake, or Portion of the Common-wealth, without any Inheritance other than a Two-penny Standish? Who yet start up, and take upon them to be censors and Judges, to criticize in quotidian Libels on the Measures of Government, to deride their Counsels and condemn their Proceedings, together with the most sausy affronts and Insults to their Authority, and Person?[8]

To turn his outrage into a polemic, Squire adopts a literary device that introduces three characters as surrogate voices for his opinions. Each character has a distinct political orientation and personality, but all—we are told—are "unanimous in their Fidelity to their King and Country; but it sometimes happened," he explains, "that they were divided in Opinion about the *Means* of promoting the Publick Good."[9] From his title, we are to understand this portion of his pamphlet as a "faithful report of a genuine debate."

These gentlemen, with Squire in quiet attendance as the fourth party, gathered at a local tavern to have a few drinks and discuss politics just prior to Squire putting pen to paper on the subject. All shared the conviction that the liberty of the press had enabled the scourge of the kingdom to express the most abominable views about men who were most assuredly their betters.

One of these tavern patrons would offer:

For tho' Men in the *highest Stations* are but Men, and subject to the *Failings*, and *Corruptions* of Morality; yet it ought not be permitted to *Fellows of no Rank, Commission or Authority*, publickly to censure them. It is impossible for Men, whose Circle of Knowledge is within a Garret or Coffee-house, to be acquainted with the *Grounds* of the Governors Counsels, or the *Motives* of their Actions: And if such may be allowed to set up for *Demagogues*, at their Pleasure, to harangue the giddy Vulgar into Sedition, to *father* all the Accidents, or Misfortunes of the Age on their Sovereign or his Councils to persuade the People that every Evil they feel or fear; is only the Effect of *Male-Administration*; who can wonder at the Numbers they gain over in this prodigal, dis-solute, untoward Generation . . . in short, every *Creature of evil Principles* or no Principles at all, are ready for Impression?[10]

This character insists that a prime minister would be derelict of his duties were he not to "vigorously . . . repress" these "professed enemies to peace and piety," concerned as he was with the reputation and state of both the monarchy and religion in Britain. He calls these supposedly cunning individuals "old foxes," who adroitly escape prosecution by making use of claims to colors of irony, anagram, or double entendre.[11]

The free press, in Squire's age, indeed took liberty with satire and defamation of those in positions of authority. The crux of the problem with these pamphleteers—for those who wanted to suppress their voices, that is—was that the government officials in question had their positions at the pleasure of the sovereign, and the crown was always to be above the ridicule of the masses. To insult an official of the king's parliament was therefore to insult the sovereign indirectly because it was the crown who maintained this person in power. Sedition, which is a subversive attack on the state, and libel, which is a written defamation of the character of an individual, were for centuries conjoined under the legal term "seditious libel." Seditious libel was understood as a libelous attack on a government official that in turn must be treated as an attack on the state itself. To commit libel against a member of the government—even if the accusations were true—was sedition because of its effect on the reputation of the government. Importantly too, *veracity of the accusations was no defense.*

Squire is not unaware of the possible difficulty this legal arrangement might cause if a government were in fact corrupt. He does admit to concern over tyranny, but his answer is unsatisfying to the modern ear. "We are apt [says a second character] to deplore the Want of Liberty in the Subjects of arbitrary and despotick Governments. But is there a Monarch in the World more insupportable than thousands of *private Tyrants* would be found, if they were suffer'd at Random to execute the malicious Purposes of their hearts . . . ?"[12] It is, we are told, the final purpose of these writers in the free press to "vilify Dignities, and disgrace the Administration; to discredit, depreciate, and expose the Commonwealth . . . and to extirpate the *Principles* of all *Religion* . . ."[13]

The idea of the tyranny of a monarch being a better alternative to "thousands of *private Tyrants*" was logic common to royalists throughout the pre-Liberal years. It finds thorough expression in a poem written by J. Delapp and dedicated to the Prince of Wales about fifty years later in 1792, when Britain was under Liberal attack by ideas from America and Revolutionary France. In the mocking tone of the new Liberals of Britain (the Levellers in particular, especially Thomas Paine), Delapp writes in the third and fourth stanzas of his poem *Ode to Sedition*:

> III.
> Down with distinction! level all!
> Creation's voice th' avouch declares.

No high, no low, no great, so small!
Cobler and King, are Adam's heirs.
Yon neighb'ring ARCHETYPE behold;
There stands the PATRIOT firm and bold;
Who speaks what nature hides from none,
That equal heaven ne'er meant for mortal man a THRONE!
Thus, ancient titles, reverend names,
And achives of nobility,
In heaps are hurl'd into the flames,
With haughty, democratic cry.
The lowering eyeball marks the man;
The surely, proud republican;
Forward with daring hand to bring
Mockery's insulting cap—*depose*, or *kill* a KING.

IV.
Yet, were this Liberty's loud son,
Who down *subordination* trod,
Himself a Sov'reign, every one
Must crouch beneath his iron rod.
Drop but the visor; all within,
Is jealousy, pride, malice, spleen.
With not one genuine patriot part,
Each LEVELLER'S an envious tyrant at the heart.

And so, having had their fill of drink and talk, Squire's local philosophers adjourn, and elect to meet again the next day. Nestor, the mediator of the group, returns in the morning and brings with him a proposed bill for the "regulation of the press," which he drafted the previous evening as something of a working document for their succeeding conversation. This short document forms the basis for their discussions that session, and Squire concludes his story *cum* argument with the character's complete agreement on the bill's basic tenets, after some further discussion and modification. The proposed bill—which Squire then presents to the candidate for office in his pamphlet—makes it a punishable offense for any writer to publish material of wicked or malicious intent against the government, or against religion, or to blaspheme. And thus, it is argued, the liberty of the greatest number of people is assured.

Francis Squire is no simple supporter of nobility, however, and though his views are "conservative," he shows an awareness of some of the Liberal concerns emerging in the American colonies and in the British Isles themselves. One of his three characters takes the position of expressly supporting the ideas of liberty, which was a Promethean form of freedom from tyranny. Assuming Squire recorded his words faithfully as promised, we find this speaker demonstrating that these ideas are worthy of serious consideration, and in recording them, so too does Squire. This individual, against the common law of the period, supports and convinces the others to support the notion that truth in the accusations of a writer or publisher should be grounds for the dismissal of a case. This was a radical idea, and such a notion would not in fact enter into common law until the passage of Fox's *Libel Act* of 1792.[14]

Squire concludes his bill provisos by suggesting that in cases of violence, bribery, misapplication of the public treasure, or any other crime of a national or political concern, the truth may be published just so long as the writer can actually prove it. And he also goes so far as to say that "no man should incur the least Penalty, or Censure for printing and publishing true Copies of the Speeches made by our Representatives in Parliament," which was also not allowed at the time. In suggesting these modifications to standing law, Squire would allow the actions of government to be held to the scrutiny of the people—a Liberal idea—but not to such an extent that even gross wrongs might challenge the authority of the crown—a classical non-Liberal idea. Squire's world was grounded in law as the foundation for legitimate political action in the state—as so wonderfully illustrated by Squire's letter to a candidate, of all things, and his choice of drafting mock legislation as the preferred mechanism for social change—but it did not conform to the Liberal criterion of the sovereignty of the state residing in the will of the citizenry.

For Squire, because the sovereign and the state were one, indulging in criticism of the king undermined the integrity and strength of the state *itself*. The result of a weakened sovereign would be a threat to what liberties the British did possess, which had by then made the nation such a formidable cultural and world power. Seeing as these freedoms were far-reaching and impressive in their day, press freedom was a threat to national security *and* liberty because liberty was only granted at the discretion of the crown, which was the state.[15]

But Squire did not stop with explaining the power of speech on policymaking, and instead pushed on regarding the foundations of his claims, which is worth discussing. He presented the idea that "The Stability and very Being of any Government consists in its Credit and Reputation; in the high Esteem and Veneration it retains in the Breast of its Subjects, and the proportionable Respect paid to it by Foreigners." To libel the sovereign, in Squire's model (so to speak), was to weaken the integrity and strength of the state through the mechanism of undermining the reputation, esteem, and veneration that foreigners and subjects alike accorded the British crown. What emerges from Squire's argument is that the power of the British press was manifest in its ability to defame the character of individuals or the state, thereby rendering them effectively impotent to act in their given community.

Laws on libel, therefore, conjoined topics of national security, as we would term it today, insofar as the press became a means of undermining the ability of the executive to govern domestically or conduct its affairs internationally—either by sowing discontentment at home and thereby threatening revolution, or else positioning the state in a manner that gave leverage to others. This recognition of the power of political communication to subvert the will of the state made possible and necessary the creation of laws that would restrict political communication in order to protect the security of the state both domestically and internationally. Such a law, which is uniquely sustainable through legal argumentation in the non-Liberal world, is called the law of seditious libel.

It would be mistaken to conclude that the existence or absence of seditious libel laws (or practices) creates or dismantles the foundations of the Liberal state. Instead, its existence or absence is only a type of proof about whether or not a legal concept is sustainable in a given polity. If it is, it must be verbally defended. If it can be defended on the basis of protection of the state from the will of the population, then the manner in which the argument is presented will reveal the essential incompatibility of seditious libel with Liberal ideals. For this reason of incommensurability, the existence or absence of seditious libel as a criminal offense in a state is proof positive of whether a state has crossed the Liberal divide. As one legal commentator argued quite rightly:[16]

> The concept of seditious libel strikes at the very heart of democracy. Political freedom ends when government can use its powers and its courts to silence its critics. My point is not the tepid one that there should be leeway for criticism of the government. It is rather that defamation of the government is an impossible notion for a democracy. In brief, I suggest, that the presence or absence in the law of the concept of seditious libel defines the society. A society may or may not treat obscenity or contempt by publication as legal offenses without altering its basic nature. If, however, it makes seditious libel an offense, it is not a free society no matter what its other characteristics.

If Squire presents us with a sound argument about how the press can influence the state in a non-Liberal model, we can usefully contrast it to the arguments of Jeremy Bentham, about a hundred years later, to better understand the contours of the Liberal model. But first we might take a moment to summarize Squire's claims so they can be easily compared:[17]

1. The sovereignty of the state rested in the crown, and the liberty of the people was granted at the pleasure of the crown.
2. Press freedom threatened the reputation, and hence the authority of the sovereign to govern domestically (i.e., esteem in the breast of its subjects) *and* conduct international affairs (i.e., respect paid to it by foreigners).
3. Reputation was the most important asset of a government in its ability to conduct its self-styled affairs.
4. This reputation could be enhanced, threatened, or undermined by communicative acts of the press in the public theater.
5. The press (broadly understood) was the most powerful actor in the dissemination of libelous or slanderous words that could in effect undermine the reputation—and hence governing power— of the sovereign.

ACROSS THE LIBERAL DIVIDE

In the contrasting Liberal worldview that would emerge in Western civilization during the century after—if admittedly not because of— Squire's pamphlet, seditious libel came to be fashioned as logically and philosophically incompatible with the freedom of the press, because any ruling that supported seditious libel would impede the free expression of ideas that is essential to meaningful and successful self-governance by the newly sovereign people of the state.

According to the American Bar Association, the notion of seditious libel, or criminal libel against the government, was a crime used, "if not created, by the court of the Star Chamber as a means to protect the elite. De Scandalum Magnatum, a 1275 law, jailed 'gossipers' who disparaged the kings and his lords in order to induce them to lead the court to 'the first author of the tale.' "[18]

In the American colonies, prior to the Revolution, laws against seditious libel remained common law, and charges such as those brought against John Peter Zenger in 1735 were common. However, after the American Revolution, publishers generally ignored criminal libel considerations until the short-lived and generally despised *Seditious Libel Act* was passed in 1798.[19]

But the American and French Revolutions that established the first Liberal republics changed the underlying social contract of the state on which seditious libel legally rested. In 1790, less than a year after the French Revolution, an English expatriate living in France named Robert Pigot wrote a letter addressed to the National Assembly of France effectively pleading with them not to restrict in any way the newfound liberty of the press in France, lest the country backslide into being like Britain. Discussing at the outset the condition of press restrictions in the land of his birth, Pigot's first caustic comments were directed at the libel laws. Note how his language adopts the new philosophy that the "nation" is the *people* and not the *crown*:

> Little do you think, Gentlemen, how England is at this time governed; how many are the ways of Ministers and Judges, to impose on the Nation, and oppress it; how many hireling writers are employed for that wicked purpose, and by the Law of responsibility, which judges have attached to authors and printers; all liberty of the press is nearly at an end . . . Amongst the very many that are tried, all are found guilty, in so much that our Ministers are seen to be almost perfect masters of the news-papers and other writings, where they calumniate your glorious revolution, and endeavor to render French-men most odious, on that account, in order to deceive the Nation, as in the war of America; fearful also that it should be tempted to follow your example.[20]

Shortly after Pigot wrote his piece to the French National Assembly, the laws in Britain that he railed against would be ameliorated, but would still remain highly oppressive to dissenting literature in practice. The 1792 parliamentary change to the sedition process came in the form of Fox's *Libel Act*, which transferred the power to determine criminality for sedition from the judge to a jury. The significance of this move should not be downplayed, but as Zechariah Chafee Jr. explains, "[s]editious prosecutions went on with shameful severity in England" even after the passage of the new law.[21] So while the process towards a freer press became manifest in the jury process, the practical restraint on publishing continued, in large part—Chafee suggests—because of the public sentiment during the Napoleonic wars and a general desire to protect the state from France.

Even after the wars ended, Jeremy Bentham would make a very similar argument in 1820 about the continued restrictions on press freedom and its effects on the conduct of a free society. By the time Bentham addressed the subject, however, the Liberal ideas from the Continent and the New World were weighing on Britain. Unlike in Squire's time, when they could be presented as from a minor character in a tavern conversation, now it was a social force that threatened revolution in one of Europe's great powers. On seeking a proper understanding of just what seditious libel was, Bentham answered rhetorically:

> The principle is . . . [that] no discussion shall have place, either in spoken speech, or in writing—neither evidence nor argument, shall be employed—on any other than one side, and that side is theirs: in a word it may be styled the principle of despotism, as applied to political discourse.

In a fascinating and rather upsetting piece of logic, the foundations for guilt in cases of libel were proved by the act of the injured party simply taking action against the supposed libeler. Bentham quotes Lord Ellenborough in 1804 as saying, "If in so doing individual feelings are violated, there the line of interdiction begins, and the offence becomes the subject of penal visitation." Bentham mocks him to the point:

> "If Individual feelings are violated"—i.e. in plain English, if, on the part of any one of the persons so situated, any uneasiness is in this way produced,—as often as any written discourse, productive of this effect, is published, every person, instrumental in the publication, is to be punished for it. Now, if there be any sort of proof by which, more than by any other, a man's having experienced uneasiness, for the cause in question, is effectually demonstrated and put out of doubt, it is surely the fact of his having imposed upon himself the expense, and trouble, and odium, of prosecuting it. Admit but this, and the consequence is as satisfactory as it is simple. It is—that, in every case of libel, "on the members of government," the very act of prosecution is conclusive evidence of the guiltiness of the part prosecuted, and the verdict of guilty ought to follow, of course.

Bentham explains that in order to be able to publish anything within these guidelines, one needs to know at what point a reader's feelings will be hurt, so that the writer might freely express himself below that threshold. He suggested facetiously the sale of a "pathological thermometer: an instrument, by which shall be indicated the degrees of mental caloric allowed to have place, as being favourable to the health of the body politic, as, in an ordinary thermometer, in a line with the work of temperate, the degree of physical caloric regarded as most favourable to the health of the body natural is indicated."[22]

He asks on behalf of the skeptical reader, "Oh, but what is this you would have us do? Would you have us destroy the Government? Would you leave the Government of this country without protection? Its reputation, upon which its power is so perfectly dependent,— would you leave that most valuable of its treasures without protection?"

Recalling that Squire identified "reputation" as the soft underbelly of the body politic that must be protected from the press, it might seem remarkable to find that eighty years later, and on the other side of the Liberal divide, Jeremy Bentham did the same; identifying reputation as the one aspect of governance the state needed most to protect.

But the seeming coincidence between Squire's use of the term "reputation" in 1740 and Bentham's in 1821 is not a coincidence at all nor an academic sleight of hand. The reason is that during the interim period, *the term had never fallen from favor* as an explanation for what damage the liberty of the press was able to inflict on government as either a threat to the state in the non-Liberal model, or else as a check on governmental tyranny in the Liberal. The reason for this, in turn, was that the very concept of libel—which, as we have seen, stretches back in various forms some 700 years from the present day—relies on the identification of "reputation" as being that which libel law protects. Why then does this idea of reputation of the government not appear as central to the media–government literature detailed in chapter 1? Why has "public opinion" and its often nebulous connotations and definitions replaced it? I think there are two reasons. The first is that the study of reputation in political science became profoundly narrowed to notions of "credibility" apropos deterrence theory. A state, in other words, could have a reputation for resolve or lack of resolve and this has consequences for relations with allies and adversaries. Jonathan Mercer's *Reputation and International Relations* (1996) was a good example of this. However, as Christopher Brewin aptly noted, Mercer's approach to reputation, "[l]ike other deterrence theorists . . . does not consider that reputation might ever be about justice and tolerance."[23]

I would push Brewin's point even further and say that though the notion of social standing or reputation may be universal, what remains unknown in all cases is what *constitutes* reputation in a distinct social community. To learn this requires cultural research that takes communication as a central domain of study. To foreshadow discussion in chapter 7 about comparative communication studies in international relations, it would be extremely helpful to empirically derive from the historical record the constitutive elements of reputation in different places at different times. Though the effort was beyond the scope of this project, a highly fecund avenue for research would be to review, and then compare, the rulings by courts against individuals charged with seditious libel in the period 1300–1850 (or any time therein), in order to illuminate the very characteristics that comprised the term. This work would provide a very refined examination of the essential reputational characteristics of Western statecraft as understood by Western states. The logic is that any *successful* claim that the words of a citizen (or member of the public) were seditious libel will allow a researcher to clearly code certain words, ideas, concepts, or phrases as being threatening to a reputation, thereby allowing the constitutive elements of reputation to appear. If we know where the edges are, we know the form. The same logic should presumably hold in other cultural settings, even if law cases are not the proper domain or site for archival research.

The other reason for reputation falling off the scanner, so to speak, was that seditious libel itself faded into obscurity in the West. Once these laws were overturned, legal protection for the government against defamatory statements was all but relegated to history. Public officials now had *less* protection than ordinary citizens. Consequently, the subject was simply not given a great deal of attention in legal circles as there was no reason to. By the time social science (and political science in particular) became a distinct subject of study in the twentieth century, the concept was long dead and there had been no scholarly attention to the matter for a good fifty years or more. What *was* receiving attention was democratic theory as a bridge between political philosophy and the upstart political sciences. Wanting to understand how democracy functioned placed attention squarely on the electorate, and hence the opinions on which the electorate made their judgments. Somehow, the voting mechanism was given center stage in this relationship and matters of reputation were considered, perhaps, too "soft" to deserve serious attention. We recall here Bruner's discussion of how intentional states of mind, like "belief," became outmoded and denigrated in the new computational metaphors of social science and psychology in the 1950s onward—just when matters of democratic theory and public opinion research were really taking off. Reputation, as the term is used in daily speech, was severely limited in political science and international relations when it was rediscovered in the context of deterrence theory. The time has come to free it entirely and even let the term roam around the world to find its own distinct and stable cultural meanings.

As the American Bar Association explained implicitly, some of the earliest laws on seditious libel, before the printing press was even invented in Europe, treat reputation as a primary component of political power—hence the laws against gossiping—and it was with the uttered or printed word that reputation could be damaged and political control undermined. Worth noting as well is the fact that in all Western states (and in many non-Western states as well), the concept of libel is today alive and well, and remains grounded on precisely the same concept of injury, which is on the reputation of an individual in his or her community. Since the expulsion of seditious libel as a law in the West, however, no connections have remained in our literature on media influence between libelous or defamatory communication and threats to executive governance.

The implication for modern questions of media influence should now begin to coalesce. The nebulous and undefined term "pressure" that was so omnipresent in chapter 1 now is revealed to be threats to the reputation of the executive and is the primary means by which the power of the press is realized. Looking back over the work of all writers who used the term "pressure" to explain how the media had an impact on government, as given in chapter 1, we find that by replacing it with the idea of a threat to reputation, their arguments become more explicit and—equally important—maintain their logic.

A quick inversion of this premise helps to illustrate the point and three examples come to mind. The first is censorship during times of national crisis in Liberal states. During the World Wars, for example, all Liberal states censored—to one degree or another—the words and writing of the populous. Some, of course, was strictly to maintain military secrets. More interesting, however, was the uniformity of these censoring techniques in covering or silencing domestic opposition to executive policies, and all statements, images, or rumors about the immorality of executive action, or the lack of capability of the leaders.[24] That Roosevelt, who was confined to a wheelchair, was (almost) never photographed in one; that Kennedy's back troubles were virtually unknown to the American public—along with his philandering—and that all differences between the Congress and executive would "stop at American shores" all help illustrate that the thing which censorship attempts to protect is the reputation—both moral and agentive—of the executive.

The second example is what Mueller calls the "rally around the flag effect" during times of national crisis. America and Britain are equally subject to this dynamic, which by all accounts appears to be quite real. What happens during this period? When the World Trade Center was destroyed by terrorists and thousands were brutally murdered, national support for George W. Bush rose from 51 percent the weekend before the attack to 86 percent just after. George W. Bush did not become a better, more loved, or more capable leader in seven days—whatever his skills were prior. Instead, the country rallied around its symbols, its institutions, and its decisions, and by doing so strengthened them (in their capacity to act in the latter cases) against the foreign aggressor.[25]

The third example is what the press calls the "honeymoon period" of a new president, wherein the press and media in general give the new president breathing room as he settles into office. This takes the form of *less criticism* of the capacity, decisions, and moral "character" of the person at the helm.

What nations do—and do not do—during periods of national rally tells us what they consider damaging to or supportive of their executives generally. It is suggested that these three phenomena—wartime censorship, the rally-around-the-flag effect, and the honeymoon period—all support the theory of reputation suggested by Squire, Bentham, and others in the pre–social science era, when words such as morality were well integrated into the study of statecraft.

Even if a name has now been put to the mysterious pressure of the media uncovered in chapter 1, perhaps the objection stands that the relevant community for this threat to reputation and governing authority is actually the public. Perhaps the written or spoken words of the media do in fact damage the character of the executive thereby creating imperatives for action, just as the law on libel describes. But is it not likely that the audience in question is still the public itself? And if this is the case, do we not return immediately to the Public Opinion Hypothesis as an explanation for the power of the press, only now with more of an understanding of how this works?

One way to challenge this idea is to look at a second great source of consistency in the legal tradition of libel law, as practiced in British and U.S. common law: assessing damages caused by slanderous or libelous words.

The purpose of legal remedies is to provide compensation, in one form or another, to the subject of an injurious act. Having established that defamatory communication is well established as an injurious act based on damage to one's reputation in a community, the question becomes: How does one determine how badly one's reputation has been damaged? As proportionality in compensation is a tenet of legal remedies, it would seem that the court would have to do some sort of public opinion poll to ask the members of the injured party's community (however determined) to what extent they now thought less of that person, based on what they had heard, and to award damages accordingly.

According to Zitter, "the measure of compensatory damages [to a plaintiff in tort law] may be affected by such factors as the circumstances and nature of the imputation made, the extent of the publication of the defamatory material, the plaintiff's reputation, and the relative positions of the parties." Though the executive is not able to claim damages against the media for pressure brought to bear against it during press conferences, for example, it certainly can suffer those damages in a measurable way. Do these measures align themselves to the logic of media–government relations? They certainly appear to. The circumstances and nature of an imputation can easily be seen as relevant. An attack on a prime minister's morality at a press conference at a summit meeting televised globally would logically be more damaging than an imputation of bad taste made during a closed session. The extent of the publication of the defamatory material goes to the same point, namely the extent to which the imputation was televised, printed, or otherwise disseminated—which is not to say with certainty that it was *heard or read*, only that the likely chance of having the imputation heard or read was higher. The next point is less clearly connected, as the reputation of the individual holding the office of the presidency or prime ministership may be hard to untangle with the reputation of the office itself and its necessity to maintain a certain level of authority. However, the final point is again salient because the relative position of the accuser and the executive can each be understood as grounded on the standing reputation each has for veracity. An imputation made by the *New York Times* or the *Guardian* will likely cause more damage due to relative standing than accusations made by Internet blogs or small-time papers.

Proof of damage to reputation in turn being the primary cause for something disadvantageous—like not getting a job, being turn down for a loan, or other such matters—is regularly considered and admitted in assessing damages in libel or slander cases. Social science and law differ, however, on two extremely important matters: what constitutes evidence of "causality" and by what mechanism that proof is attained.

In court, the amount of damage is considered a matter of fact, as opposed to a matter of law. Paraphrasing Daniel Dobbs, the damages are determined by the "finders of fact," which is usually a jury, except in a bench trial (i.e., a trial without a jury), where the judge is him or herself the "finder of fact." The factors mentioned earlier would usually be given to the jury by the judge to consider in its deliberations, but the jury can use any relevant evidence that it cares to credit (as long as its deliberations are themselves considered proper). On appeal, the findings by the "finders of fact" can only be overturned on a showing of "clear error."[26]

Tolerance in the social sciences is of course much narrower. The finders of fact, so to speak, are the social scientists themselves, and avoiding clear error is hardly the criteria for publishing original research. Nevertheless, the grounds on which the jury or judge were to find fact need not be any different from that of the social scientist, only the extent to which evidence in this field will be considered admissible. It is precisely this threshold that chapter 3 aims to establish and the following chapters aim to provide.

Damage, then, is determined first and foremost by the *act of publication*, and only secondarily by the known *effects of that publication*. The first is usually a matter of clear proof, especially in libel cases as the offending document can be produced. The second, though treated as seriously as possible by the finders of fact, need only avoid "clear error" for their findings to have legal force. As explained by the American Bar Association:

> At common law, in contrast to traditional tort principles, damages in a defamation action were "presumed" to result from the act of publication and were thus recoverable without a showing of pecuniary loss, reputational damage, or any other form of injury. Although the rationale was the difficulty of proving injury despite the likelihood that a serious injury had occurred, presumed damages were also an invitation to juries to punish unpopular opinions.[27]

In short, damage to one's reputation happens immediately. It is the immediacy of this damage, and the centrality of reputation to effective governance in Liberal states, that makes the media–government dialogue of such incredible interest and concern to the executive.

Consider the applicability of this logic to the problem of media influence. It would imply that the pressure on the executive comes not through the public's actual opinion after having heard and responded to media reports, but rather the damage to the executive happens *at the moment of publication*. The implications of this observation are very significant. Some of the first implications are as follows:

1. The executive can be affected, or "pressured," through the communicative acts of the media themselves, independent of whether or not the public at large has had time to develop an actual opinion. The communication by the media has force in itself.
2. Technology may indeed provide new means by which the media can gather information and disseminate it (we'll return to this later) but this does not determine how pressure "works," because it does not explain how that information affects the ability of the executive to govern. Instead, it may influence whether pressure is capable of being generated. This would address the

concern of people such as Linsky and Livingston, who both wrote about the decision-making process being speeded up due to media coverage. Our historical insight into matters of reputation begin to tell us why this may take place, but more work needs to be done to explain this process (see chapter 3).

3. If the media have the power to damage the reputation of the executive through communicative acts alone, then the subject of our attention—in creating empirical measures of media pressure—are not on the *effects* of media reports, but in the qualitative *statements* of the media themselves to see how they position the executive. This is an important shift in approach and becomes a direct challenge to the agenda-setting literature (insofar as that literature remains focused on how the media affect the public alone), as we must now open up the field to examining direct relations between the media and government through the mechanisms of political communication and threats to governing ability, without going through the middleman of public opinion.

CHAPTER 3

Toward a Theory of Media Pressure

The time has come to reconcile the concerns of chapter 1 with the arguments unearthed and dusted off in chapter 2 by providing an argument about media pressure and how it can be understood conceptually from a communication standpoint.

PRESENTATION OF THE POSITIONING HYPOTHESIS

The Positioning Hypothesis that follows uses technical language that will be helpful to only a small group and utterly useless to a broader readership. I've opted to present it first in the more technical form, reiterate it in more reader-friendly language, and then use this chapter to unpack the ideas that ground it.

The Hypothesis is as follows:

(Part A) Media pressure is the perlocutionary impact of the media's communicative acts that demonstrably defame the reputation of the executive, or the executive's policy, as defined by the local moral order. The political significance of defamation is that it functions as an instrument of faction, consequently leading to difficulties in forging or maintaining coalitions needed to govern or lead. Media pressure can, in turn, be observed in the executive acts of rhetorical redescription or repositioning in response to the media's communicative acts as they regard the reputation of the executive or the executive's policy. These positioning acts can be measured (as a first pass) as a rate of occurrence.[1]

(Part B) Influence itself is discernible by deliberate changes in executive policy intended to function as verbal or nonverbal forms of rhetorical redescription and/or repositioning that defend or recover the executive's authority so that superordinate strategic objectives can be maintained or advanced. These policy shifts aim to end rhetorical challenges by or through the media, thus potentially bringing threats to the executive's authority to a resolution. Because these are almost never admitted, they are very hard to prove. Rather, false claims can be disproved using this logic, and a basis for reasonable suspicion can be advanced in others.

In less verbose language, the media can say or publish things that damage the reputation of the executive among the people it needs to get things done. The type of damage done by various speech acts is determined, and determinable, by the moral or ethical values of the community engaged in the discussion about the executive or its policies. This presumes that not all moral worlds are the same and societies value certain actions and motivations more than others and often quite differently. The reason reputational damage matters is that executives need partners to keep them in power or to support their policies. We can see that the reputation of the executive is under threat, not by looking at the comments of the media—outrageous though they might be sometimes—but by the *responses* of the executive to those comments. Only in the responses can we be sure that the executive itself felt under threat. Otherwise, we are making assumptions that are not empirically grounded, logical though they may seem. Influence is when the executive acts to alleviate the pressure it is under. Statements or actions that *specifically* respond to the pressure being applied may be indicative of media influence in the absence of other compelling explanations.

All this requires explanation as well as theoretical defense, which is the next step. We need to see how communication can function as pressure; why the media and government can be said to be engaging in a conversation; and how one can actually code communication to create falsifiable arguments—like proving that the media *was* pressuring the government, or that the government was not influenced by that pressure.

POSITIONING THEORY

Positioning theory was defined by Rom Harré as being *the study of local moral orders as ever-shifting patterns of mutual and contestable rights and obligations of speaking and acting.*[2] He continues, writing:

> [I]n recent years [positioning theory] has come to take on a quite specific meaning for developing work in the analysis of fine-grained symbolically mediated interactions between people, both from their

own individual standpoints and as representatives or even exemplars for grounds. In this technical sense a position is a cluster of generic personal attributes, structured in various ways, which impinges on the possibilities of interpersonal, intergroup, and even intra-personal action through some assignment of such rights, duties and obligations to an individual as are sustained by the cluster. For example, if someone is positioned as incompetent in a certain field of endeavor they will not be accorded the right to contribute to discussions in that field.

Positioning theory is rooted in the work of social constructionism in that "social constructionism stresses that social phenomena are to be considered to be generated in and through conversation and conversation-like activities."[3] What is particularly important about social constructivism for our purposes is the centrality of social inter-action, and *conversation*, as the location in which things "happen." Concerns over market forces and news production, tax breaks and information access, though all worthy of study, are shelved. We are dealing, fundamentally, with the act of talking in a given social world and trying to understand how that talk is socially significant.

We are left with three main concerns. The first is establishing that a conversation is actually happening. This is not nearly as straightfor-ward as it sounds and requires a bit of background if we are to treat conversations as real events that can be studied and even measured. The second is setting out a theory for how a conversation (any con-versation) can affect the participants in it. The third step, of course, is empirical. Can we actually find evidence that our theory has played out as expected?

Can we really make the leap to understanding media and govern-ment interaction as a conversation? Consider again the arguments of policy practitioners such as David Gergen or George Kennan. These are insiders *extraordinaire*. They are referring to "television democracy" and CNN Effects based on a worried conclusion that the government is reacting to the media based on the media's prior *reports* and that the nature of the reaction from government has brought democracy and foreign policy to a crisis. They are motivated by an insider's knowledge that there is an action–reaction phenomenon taking place.

All of Linsky's and O'Heffernan's interviewers draw the same con-clusions, and both explain how the reports themselves speed up the decision-making process and push matters up the bureaucracy, and how most people interviewed were certain the media can impact govern-ment, even though they could not quite explain how. Marlin Fitzwater, the former White House press secretary, mentioned casually in response to a question he was having trouble answering that, "I asked for response [*sic*] to the story, and that's what they told me . . . ," showing us that preparation for White House press conferences takes seriously the media–government dialogue.[4]

In chapter 1 it was shown how Livingston tried to find out who said what first, and proved quite well that the government actually had policies in the pipeline before the media began their coverage, specifically in the case of Somalia. He and Eachus were trying to figure out, in a sense, where the causal power might have resided, on the assumption that whoever "spoke" first was responsible for the actions to follow, or at least for the "initial decision." But how could that be? He proved that U.S. policy toward Somalia preceded media interest, disproving Kennan's claim that the Somalia intervention was caused by the media. His theory was very simply argued on the law of intertemporality, that is, what comes later cannot cause things that come earlier. But is it possible that in the subsequent conversation between media and government, the policymakers might still have adapted actions based on media coverage, even though it was indexed?

Here, the waters get very cloudy, and the foundations for further arguments about causality are too obscured in a "media–government interaction model." A fine description of this murkiness is Warren Strobel's introduction to *Late Breaking Foreign Policy*. He begins with an anecdote, dateline "Kislovodsk, USSR, April 25, 1991." In the story, James Baker, the U.S. secretary of state at the time, traveled to the USSR to speak with the Soviet Foreign Minister Aleksandr Bessmertnykh about the Arab–Israeli peace negotiations. Baker was there to try and put some pressure on the process. He wanted the foreign minister's endorsement of the process as ammunition before his trip to the Middle East. Bessmertnykh was noncommittal and the reporters were about to file their stories saying Baker didn't get his endorsement. But Baker's spokeswoman, Margaret Tutwiler, "caught wind of what the press corps was about to report." The reporters were called back, and Bessmertnykh then uttered the magic words in a "Take Two" press conference, where a Soviet journalist—after being prompted by Bessmertnykh's aide—asked the magic question.[5]

The problem Strobel observed and the paradigm of causality he used made his task impossible:

> I open with this anecdote because it offers a view of the relationship between the news media and foreign policy officials that differs from the popular image of distance and confrontation. It is a view that undergirds this study. The relationship, examined up close, is so intertwined that at times it is all but impossible to determine who is affecting whom—who

is setting the agenda and who is following it. Was it the news media that set the course of events that day in Kislovodsk? . . . Did the news media force a change in Soviet policy—or merely in rhetoric? Or were the officials using the media?

These questions, and others addressed below, are not simple ones. But attempting to answer them is vital in an age when information and images move around the world instantaneously, seemingly affecting the lives of millions, the outcomes of wars, the foundations of states.

Strobel is quite right about the stakes involved, but he makes little headway in solving the problem. This was Robinson's critique; That Strobel insisted there was an effect, but he could not prove "push" or "pull." If we recognize, however, that the media are incapable of "causing" U.S. deployment of troops (or their withdrawal) because only those authorized to order the deployment can "cause" it, then we can start to look at how the media can affect those who *can* cause such deployments. What the media can do is create an imperative that ensures the agents feel compelled to act. The question now is to understand how conversation creates that imperative, or in our common vocabulary, pressure.

Let us ask a series of questions that will lead us away from Strobel's paradox and towards an understanding of conversations. First, if the media and the policymakers are engaged in conversation, what are the characteristics of this conversation? Second, what might be the motivation for the policymakers to engage in this conversation, seeing that they are under no exogenous requirement to do so? Third, how are these stakes operationalized into a clear formulation and workable theory of media pressure?

Characteristics of Conversation

Although the positioning approach operates under different assumptions about cause and effect than do the studies reviewed thus far, the difference principally rests on issues of explanatory power, not necessarily as regards observations. This means that we do not have to reject the findings presented thus far in chapter 1 as being of value. Indeed, they form the foundations for the core literature of the field. However, the analysis of the observations needs to be approached rather differently.

Let us begin with Bennett's indexing hypothesis, Strobel's observation about the difficulty in untangling the cause and effect of the media–government relationship and the arguments of numerous writers who claim that the media and government affect one another, rather than one simply affecting the other (Mermin, Robinson, Bennett, Zaller and Chui, O'Heffernan, Orren).

One feature that these observations have in common is the assumption that the government and media are involved in a conversation that is characterized by *purposeful interaction*. By interactive we mean that the act of one actor serves as a stimulus for a *deliberate* (i.e., not automatic or necessitated) response by the second actor. By purposeful, in commonsense terms, we mean that words are not spoken idly. The speaker intends for those words to have an effect. Here, we may tentatively accept Carolyn Smith's proposition that the president's general purpose in the press conference is persuasion, and that the general purpose of the media is to seek accountability.[6] While we cannot predict what will actually be said or done by either conversant, we can nevertheless make two structuring observations about the conversation that ensues. First, because each actor is engaged in the discourse, we can be certain that their objectives in the discourse will be to further whatever aim is motivating them to remain engaged (again "persuasion" and "accountability" being two reasonable possibilities at a broad level). We are saying only that there must be a continued *value* for the actor in remaining a participant in the conversation, otherwise that actor would extricate him- or herself from the conversation.

A second structuring observation is that the conversation is patterned on the basis of rules of interaction. This is a controversial statement for many social psychologists, and does not flow naturally from the conclusions of the authors reviewed thus far. It therefore needs a brief explanation.

Billig makes a convincing pitch for the importance of understanding argument as an integral and inextricable part of thinking—particularly the importance of deliberative rhetoric as first explicated by the likes of Aristotle and in particular Protagoras.[7] In his book, he draws attention to, and takes some issue with, Harré's own work on what Billig calls the "rule theory approach." He explains Harré's work as constituting an argument that "coordinated social behavior would be impossible, if there were no rules of conduct for the various situations in which people find themselves. One way to uncover these rules is to treat episodes of everyday life as if they were formal rituals or games, for we are accustomed to the idea that rituals and games have rules."[8] Billig quotes Harré and Secord as saying, "It can hardly be denied that we are rule-following, self-monitoring agents."[9]

Billig's counter-argument is that "the problem with using the game metaphor to understand social rules is that the metaphor only deals with one aspect of rules: their acceptance. It does not deal with the creation of rules."[10] This issue of rule-following is important, as is Billig's critique, because if rules are followed in the media–government conversation on questions of foreign affairs, then we can reasonably say that both actors understand (or act as though they understand) that their relations must follow a prescribed pattern that is mutually intelligible. Rule following, in a sense, makes communication possible. Otherwise, two actors would be "sending signals" but none would be received. This prevents interaction as defined above, and makes the word "purposeful" meaningless.

Whether supporting Harré or Billig's point on rules, let us only conclude at this point that the conversation is *interactive* and that there is a grammar of give-and-take in the conversational pattern, and that whether or not there are rules per se, there are mutually agreed upon patterns of interaction that serve as normative standards by which each side can be expected to act, and furthermore, that these norms are *evolving* and being rewritten with each encounter that derives from a previous pattern.

Motivations for Conversational Engagement

Policymakers have both a stake *in* a conversation, and a stake in being *outside of* the conversation. There is something at risk that makes the continued involvement in the conversation an imperative to which the policymakers "must" respond. If a motivation for the engagement of policymakers in a conversation with the media is that there is something to be lost by not participating, or alternately, to be gained by doing so, what is that "something"? This takes us to the core of our argument. The answer may not be exciting, but I hope to argue

How politicians want to position themselves as determined by their role	Agentive	Non-agentive
Moral	Desired position	Alternative desired position
Non-moral	Undesirable	Undesirable

Figure 3.1   Positionings in reputational authority

convincingly that it is powerful and important: *reputational authority* (see figure 3.1).

Reputational Authority and Media Pressure

Reputational authority is the socially negotiated and maintained quality of having the right to speak or act in particular ways that affect other members of a group through those acts. Whereas one's role—such as prime minister—guarantees by law that certain formal powers will reside with the individual in that particular role, it does not guarantee that this individual will retain individual authority to influence the political machinery of a state through non-legal powers. As Richard Neustadt said famously about the U.S. presidency, the power of the president is the power to persuade. I offer that this persuasion is communicative and is made possible by reputation.

This problem of loss of authority is extremely important in those circumstances where coalitions—or political partnerships—are necessary to advancing a policy. Almost all national security decisions—especially those that involve the use of military personnel, and then again for extended periods of time—require the creation of and the maintenance of coalitions (whether opposition parties, voters, other nations, or whomever). Reputational authority becomes the glue that holds these coalitions together, not the law.

According to Carolyn Smith, U.S. President Jimmy Carter

> claimed early on that he would hold press sessions twice a month. He did so through July 1978 and then reduced the number to one a month. He held only six in 1980, during the Iran hostage crisis. When reporters asked Press Secretary Jody Powell why Mr. Carter stopped press conferences, since they were one thing he did fairly well, Powell replied, "We just didn't think they were good for us."[11]

Smith identifies the primary purposes of presidential rhetoric to be persuasion, which is aligned with Richard Neustadt's arguments, but this anecdote she provides reveals something more. Why would press conferences dwindle during periods of national crisis?[12] As Powell suggested, it was not good for the president. This might have meant that press conferences were not the best mechanism for the White House to communicate with the public and they preferred another technique. But it probably meant that press conferences themselves can *hurt* the president. This is implied through her argument about the purpose of the media as being to seek accountability. If the danger is deemed significant enough, the best policy by an executive is to change the rules of the threatening game by simply having fewer encounters. The "hurt" identified here is the potential or actual loss of reputational authority.

* * *

A president or prime minister maintains authority through different functions. In that person's line of work, one might need to prove they are decisive in crisis situations, or perhaps can heal the wounds of a nation during times of civil unrest. Newspapers would not be deemed more "authoritative" if they were to participate in either of these activities, and may even be less so. The point here is that while authority can be concisely defined, the nature of those rights to speak and act are locally derived—which means that they come from the group in which they are seeking authority.

Now consider Harré's definition of position theory, on which we rested a definition of reputational authority: it is the study of local moral orders as ever-shifting patterns of mutual and contestable rights and obligations of speaking and acting. Relying on this definition of positioning theory, we can now view actors as authoritative or nonauthoritative, based on his or her (or its) position in a conversation. This is not an abstract constructivist metaphor, but an actual chit-chat between people—in this case, speaking on behalf of institutions.

Reputational authority can be subdivided into *moral authority* and *agentive authority*. For each situation—for presidents and prime ministers—we need a means of understanding how communicative acts by the media can position policymakers as authoritative or nonauthoritative. Three assumptions are made:

1. Policymakers, at all times, need to have reputational authority in order to successfully accomplish their tasks as defined by their social roles (minister of foreign affairs, ambassador to the United Nations (UN), chairman of the Joint Chief of Staff, etc.).
2. This authority is based on two characteristics: a moral quality—that is, one has a right to lead or act.
3. An agentive quality—that is, one has an ability to lead to act.

At certain points in a conversation, a conversant may be positioned as authoritative or nonauthoritative along these two axes. Like justice, authority is never achieved, but must be fought for every day. For Harré and van Langenhove the fight for authority is actually sentence by sentence.

If authority requires the cooperated appreciation of one's moral and agentive characteristics, then one must ensure that one's public persona is managed so as to maintain authoritative characteristics. Acts by an institution that purposefully manage its public image serve as evidence of the need, if those acts function to ensure the perpetuation of that institution's (or individual's) moral and agentive authority. The proliferation of public relations firms in both Washington and London and their indebtedness to elected politicians for their livelihoods may illustrate the point. While not all managed acts will necessarily or successfully function toward this end, it would be consistent to observe that no acts—whatever their purpose—would try and go *against* this objective. In circumstances where reputation suffers, it would be consistent to find some indication of the act in question being labeled "wrong"—either as a mistake or failure of some kind by the institution or individual, or else some form of "damage control" to readjust the public understanding of the act.

How can positioning theory be used to generate coding techniques in inter-institutional conversations, in order to identify threats to executive reputational authority? How can we take this rather abstract theory and create real proof of media pressure? The next section provides some of the tools necessary to perform a positioning analysis, but also contributes some thoughts on how to make the move to analyzing inter-institutional conversations rather than interpersonal ones.

INTER-INSTITUTIONAL CONVERSATIONS
AT THE INTERPERSONAL NEXUS

"What I have to say here is neither difficult nor contentious"; began J.L. Austin at a lecture in 1955, "the only merit I should like to claim for it is that of being true, at least in parts. The phenomenon to be discussed is very widespread and obvious, and it cannot fail to have been already noticed, at least here and there, by others. Yet I have found no attention paid to it specifically."

Austin was introducing the idea of "performative utterances" to a wider audience, and by doing so explained how certain statements were not mere descriptions or statements of fact (or nonsense), but rather deeds in themselves. Performative utterances indicate an action by the speaker. The action is constituted in *illocutionary force*, or what is achieved in saying something. The response provided, in turn, demonstrates *perlocutionary force*, or what is achieved by saying something. In recognizing the difference, we make it possible to appreciate that one's intention in speaking or acting does not always elicit an anticipated (or preferred, or expected) result in the listener. The perlocutionary force of one's statement may in fact be shockingly unexpected to a speaker. And therein lies the impossibility of coding media pressure based merely on what the media do. Proof of pressure will depend on showing perlocutionary force in discrete conversational episodes.

It is a noteworthy aside that deriving meaning from social episodes (that is, the statement *and* response) was also explored by Murray Edleman who wrote in 1967 that "[o]f the possible meanings of a language style inherent in its structure, the researcher identifies its actual meaning for a particular public by observing their response to it. This procedure accords with [Margaret] Mead's behavioral definition of meaning in terms of response."[13]

Where philosophers such as Austin opened doors to understanding the function of certain utterances as deeds in interpersonal communication, they have yet to sufficiently turn their attention to the words spoken on behalf of groups, such as institutions, tribes, nations, or states. When a single individual is empowered to speak for a group, does that not often widen the criteria by which we must view certain utterances as "performative"? Likewise, is the authority to speak for others simply an extension of formal powers or is it perhaps more tenuous as well, based on local definitions of moral authority? While the answers to such questions may not be universally applicable—a matter raised at a later point—it appears very much the case in a study of American and British political communication that a broader conception of "performative" than that supplied by Austin needs to be applied to public statements by individuals empowered to speak on behalf of collectives.

The idea of performative utterance by collectives—or plural performatives as they might be called—will also be seen to be dependent on some of the observations we made about contract societies, and hence liberal statecraft, in chapter 2. If one is expected to "keep one's word" (i.e., *pactus sunt servanda*) as a means of maintaining one's reputation, and if utterances are taken as plural performatives (or promises of implicit action) in more cases at the institutional level than the interpersonal one, then it means that a listening audience in, for example, the United States or Great Britain, will take even *descriptions of events by the executive as being implicit moral arguments that, in turn, are identifiable as actions taken by the state vis-à-vis that which is being described*. One listening audience that certainly does this is the media.

An illustrative example of this sensitivity to descriptions of events, and how that is understood by the executive itself as placing an onus of responsibility on subsequent events, can be seen clearly in an exchange between a reporter (unnamed) and U.S. President George

Bush at a press conference on 7 April 1991.[14] At the time, Iraqi Shiites and Kurds were engaged in a failing insurrection in Iraq in which they were being slaughtered by Iraqi forces.[15] Two days earlier, the president had announced the beginning of a significant humanitarian relief effort (later to be called Operation Provide Comfort) for the refugees from the embattled areas. Bush was being blamed on several fronts for allegedly saying he would aid the uprisings to topple Saddam Hussein, and then failing to take such action, which in turn resulted in the deaths of thousands.

> Q: *Mr. President, you've repeatedly said that you have not encouraged the Kurds and the Shiites to rise up with the expectation that the U.S. would be in there fighting with them. And yet the Kurdish representatives this morning on one of the talk shows are saying that that's clearly the impression they got from listening to the Voice of Free Iraq, which they understood to be supported by the U.S. Would you clarify just what the role the U.S. played in running that radio station?*[16]
>
> President Bush: No, I don't have the details on it. But I will reassert, I never in any way implied that the United States was going to use force beyond the mandate of the United Nations.
> Thank you all very—
>
> Q: *Well, is that because that station could be an embarrassment to you, sir?*
> President Bush: No, I just don't know the details of it. I just don't know the details of it.
> And if it had anything—
>
> Q: *Were they naive?*
> President Bush: Well, I mean, you call it whatever you want. They were not misled by the United States of America. And that is now I think very, very clear. I went back and reviewed every statement I made about this, every single one. And there was never any implication that the United States would use force to go beyond the objectives which we so beautifully have achieved. None. And I hope that helps clarify it. Thank you all very much.

The press itself was well aware of the significance of the statement. ABC News that evening ran the following parts of a story, incorporating part of Bush's statement:

> **Ann Compton**: On This Week with David Brinkley a voice for those Kurdish refugees complained today the Kurds were certainly led to believe the United States would help them when President Bush called on the Iraqi people to overthrow Saddam Hussein.
> **Barham Salih**: [TWWDB] Without that I'm sure the Iraqi people as a whole would not have risen to be left alone and to be abandoned and to be butchered and massacred by Saddam's forces.

Ann Compton: President Bush has been stung by such criticism.

President Bush: They were not misled by the United States of America, I went back and reviewed every statement I made about this. There was never any implication that the United States would use force to go beyond the objectives which we so beautifully have achieved. None.

George Bush "went back and reviewed every statement . . . made about this," looking for "any implication," because he knew, as do all executives in America and Britain, that what the executives say on behalf of their countries is taken as performative by all listening audiences. What Bush and his advisors seemed to fail to understand—or successfully manage, at any rate—is that the criteria by which something can be taken as an "implication that the United States would use force" is in fact far broader than he and his staff realized as they "went back and reviewed every statement." Chapters 5 (coverage) and 6 (pressure) will go over the same material that the president and his staff examined, and see what it is they might have missed that led to the political and moral backlash that he faced in late March though mid-April 1991.

★   ★   ★

Some believe that seeing media pressure is obvious. Such complicated ideas as "plural performatives" and the like are unnecessary for rigorous analysis. As discussed earlier, that venerable statesman George Kennan was convinced he had seen it when the United States sent troops to Somalia in 1993. A few days after publishing his article on the subject in the *New York Times*, American troops were killed in action, forcing a solemn introspection on media and foreign policy. With the gravity of what had happened, it seemed Kennan might have been right.

Former U.S. undersecretary of state Lawrence Eagleburger once said, "I will tell you quite frankly television had a great deal to do with President Bush's decision to go [to Somalia] in the first place, and, I will tell you equally frankly, I was one of those two or three that [*sic*] was strongly recommending he do it . . . ."

He continues: ". . . and it was very much because of these starving kids, substantial pressure from Congress that came from the same source, and my honest belief that we could do this, do something good at not too great cost and, certainly, without any great danger of body bags coming home."[17]

Despite Eagleburger's imputation that media were a big factor in his decision, academic work that traced U.S. commitment to the Somalia relief effort (prior to Operation Restore Hope) found that the United States was rather significantly engaged before the press became at all interested. Instead, it became quite interested later. While one may be tempted to accept the conclusion of the policy-maker over the academic, it should not be forgotten who has the wider, empirical, and nonpartisan view.

In any event, which images was Eagleburger referring to anyway? At what point did he make the recommendation? In response to what exactly? Eagleburger also admitted to sending troops for a reason no one would ever suggest was a bad *motivation*. In a word, his analysis itself was actually a positioning move that made the White House seem sympathetic. Are we to take this at face value? And so here too the issue becomes clouded.

Former White House press secretary George Reedy described the familiar reality about government–press relations in the following way:

> You don't come out to the podium in the White House and say, "Amongst the factors that were considered when the President was try-ing to make up his mind what he wanted to do about 'X' was how folks are going to react in New Hampshire, and besides that we got the folks on the Hill and they're worried about where they are going to get this carrier refurbished." You don't talk about that.[18]

The memory of policymakers, combined with their angle of vision (more like a soldier on a battlefield than a general with a map) and their personal concern for how they and their political allies are perceived and remembered makes widespread interviewing about "influence" rather a sketchy endeavor. Additionally, few politicians or carrier civil servants properly retire. Most who are not in office are still "in play" unless they are very old or very discredited, and thus will invariably prefer certain interpretations to others. Something more systematic, explicable, and transparent is needed before we can test for media impact and understand how and when it may be manifest—if ever.

The use of a positioning approach to examining inter-institutional conversations, as between media and government, is therefore a means of going beyond memory, testimony, arguments that may be "tainted," and sheer rhetorical talent based on anecdotal experience. It is a way to look at the documented records of social interactions and find in them evidence that reputational authority has been challenged, and in turn, responded to in the media–government relationship.

The next section takes this approach to conversational analysis and examines specifically the nexus at which conversation takes place. Once we can identify different types of episodes we can code them, distinguish them from other forms of talk, and then measure their occurrence.

A Typology of Episode Types

The give-and-take of media–government interaction is a conversation that impacts one's position in a moral universe, made all the more significant in security policy in liberal democracies because of the need to maintain coalitions to sustain policy longevity or viability. But for empirical analysis of these conversations, we now need to move beyond metaphor and create real tools of analysis.

The first step is to appreciate that *a conversation is a theoretically determined thing*. It is perfectly reasonable to question whether two people are engaged in a conversation, as in, "Excuse me, are you listening to me?" or to qualify the idea of conversation in the form of a report, as in "We were talking, but we weren't really having a conversation."

Speaking in turns, therefore, is not a guarantee of a conversation any more than flipping television channels between two stations makes what is seen a program. Instead, conversations are understood theoretically as being composed of a series of utterances comprised of "episodes," which Harré and Secord explain as being any sequence of happenings in which human beings engage, which has some principle of unity. In conversation per se, we are interested in not only unity but a narrative continuity to the exchange, which can in turn be called a storyline. A way to think about this is to note that every conversation is about something (or at least one thing). As such, each episode is also about something. Sometimes, conversations shift from one topic to another, using such devises as, "that reminds me of," or, "funny you said that, because," etc. Such transitions are evidence of new storylines (though aspects of the old can always form a thread in the new). Whether we choose to view the new storyline as a new conversation is here deemed to be arbitrary, the only necessity being internal consistency to the analysis and transparency in the method.

The evidence of a storyline is one important criterion by which we determine whether a principle of unity exists in what we suspect may be an episode. Therefore, an "episode" will be the primary analytical unit in an analysis of conversation.

But what is a storyline? How can a researcher know that the subject being followed has not inadvertently slipped into another story altogether, thereby making measurements of media attention to a storyline utterly meaningless or self-serving? The reason this is important is because a lot of research that now passes for "content analysis" is either a simple search for keywords used in newspapers, or else the subjective and unsystematic reading of a bunch of articles that is subjected to an analysis that is non-replicable because we don't really know what the researcher did.

Key words, I regret to say, are not helpful. Evidence for this comes forcefully in chapter 5, but the key point here and now is that one cannot determine media attention through simple algorithmic protocols like searches and tallies of location names, proper nouns, or the like. A story is *about* something, and meaning requires comprehension. One helpful place to look for clarity about story characteristics is John Gardner who was a novelist and a teacher. His classic book *The Art of Fiction* is known to most every student of fiction writing. Gardner explains:

> By definition—and of aesthetic necessity—a story contains profluence, a requirement best satisfied by a sequence of causally related events, a sequence that can end in only one of two ways: in resolution, where no further event can take place (the murderer has been caught and hanged, the diamond has been found and returned to its owner, the elusive lady has been captured and married), or in logical exhaustion, our recognition that we've reached the stage of infinite repetition; more events might follow, perhaps from now till Kingdom Come, but they will all express the same thing—for example the character's entrapment in empty ritual or some consistently wrong response to the pressures of his environment.[19]

Gardner defines the term "profluence" (which comes from Aristotle) as, "[o]ur sense, as we read, that we are 'getting somewhere.'"[20] He goes on to explain,

> . . . the conventional kind of profluence—though other kinds are possible—is a casually related sequence of events. This is the root interest of all conventional narrative . . . . What the logical progress of an argument is to non-fiction, event-sequence is to fiction. Page 1, even if it's a page of description, raises questions, suspicions, and expectations; the mind casts forward to later pages, wondering what will come about and how.[21]

The central idea of a story, then, is the narrative progression of events that all are causally linked through argument, or event sequence, and are unified around some central, unresolved tension that creates curiosity in the reader or listener. What this in turn implies is that "the story" is best identified by looking not at its characters or scenarios, but by *the unresolved tension that functions as the unifying theme of all that transpires.* In chapter 4 on the Iraqi Civil War, we find numerous themes (e.g., should U.S. troops come home? should Saddam be brought to justice? what is the nature of the ceasefire? has the ceasefire been violated as a result of the civil war and suppressions? etc.) but the one that interests us—and is the central tension around which all storytelling progresses—is "what is to be the Western role in the future of Iraq?"

Identifying a storyline is not an exact science. It is achieved by taking an abductive approach that looks at numerous articles and tries to find the most refined unifying elements. One might start by identifying the storyline as being, "what should be the future of the Middle East?" but will soon find that this criterion—though encompassing all the stories of interest—is too broad, because it also includes many stories of no interest. Then, one might refine it to ask, "what should be the future of Saddam Hussein?" but soon find that many stories of interest cannot be included. The researcher can settle on a central question once that question allows for the inclusion of all interesting stories and exclusion of all those of no interest. This can only be done through the hypothetico-deductive process of making a proposal and testing it against each piece of new data—in this case, by reading or watching the selected news items. The entire news data set will need to be read prior to settling on a central tension. This, by the way, is what we tend to do naturally, the way historians will read vast amounts of material and start to see a pattern and structure emerge from the records. In this case we make the added effort of being explicit in our search for a common storyline that we will follow in our media analysis.

In early March 1991, when the Shiite uprising began, the first media attention did not carry with it a moral element of responsibility. As will be seen, this was in large part due to both the optimism of the press, the Iraqis, and the Western politicians alike that the rebellions—unplanned, but still portentous—would work and overthrow Saddam. Only later, in the third week of March, when the scale of the slaughter became apparent, the rebellion tipped back in favor of the Iraqi armed forces, and General Norman Schwarzkopf made some statements that effectively said the United States was duped and was partly responsible for the deaths, did the media then settle on a moral tension of Western responsibility for the future of Iraq. Here, the moral onus shifted, but the central tension selected for the study remained sufficiently broad to encompass the pre-shift period, and sufficiently narrow to limit the inclusion of such items as soldiers' return home after the war, parades, and the like. These were all stories related to Iraq and the war, but not about the uprising and the fate of the nation.

What also becomes clear is that when the question of Western participation in Iraq's future is no longer in doubt, and there is no tension about this potential role, this storyline—and with it, *all* media attention—ends.

* * *

Once the story for the period is selected, the media–government conversation about that central tension needs to be mapped, measured, and explained. The problematic here is determining the initial "principle of unity" in the media–government dialogue, and not simply using this as a metaphor for analysis. Simply put, how do we know that the media and government are engaged in a conversation? In interpersonal conversation, the principle of unity can be determined with some ease (if we know what to look for!). We can see body language, indexical cues, eye contact, and emotional shifts that are responsive to the conversation's development. In inter-institutional conversation, however, there are far fewer cues and a lot more ambiguity. Most of it isn't face-to-face. For an empirical study of a conversation, as between the media and government, we need to *know* that the media and government are reacting or self-positioning themselves in relation to one another. The crux of the problem lies in episodic unity, and overcoming what I'll call *episodic ambiguity*.

Four distinct types of episodes exist in inter-institutional conversation. They overlap with interpersonal conversation, but that is of limited concern here. Each implies a different level of confidence in whether to treat a series of statements as a conversation or what we'll call merely "talk." Figure 3.2 details a typology of conversational episodes.

A familiar type of inter-institutional conversation is a reporter–executive dialogue. Here, the two people see and hear each other;

	Contiguous (i.e. turn-taking is immediate)	Non-contiguous (i.e. turn-taking is separated by time, space, or other complications)
Referenced (i.e. uptake is clear)	Face-to-face conversation (strong coding)	Distant conversation (strong coding)
Non-referenced (i.e. uptake is unclear)	Face-to-face talk (moderate coding)	Distant talk (weak coding)

Figure 3.2 A typology of conversational episodes

they are speaking on behalf of institutions; they are mutually responsive; and they engage the central storyline being created through the talk. For matters of determining the property of episodic unity here, we start with the observation that the utterances by each conversationalist are *contiguous*, meaning that the turn-taking of the participants was immediate and in that sense "touching." One spoke, and then the other responded. The second criterion is that the response was also *referenced*. This means that the unity of the episodes was demonstrable by indexical cues in the utterances of the conversants, or else by the continued existence of a discernible storyline.

Contiguity (or non-contiguity) is important because the separation of one speaker and another by time or distance can, at times, make indeterminate the perlocutionary force of the first speaker. In face-to-face conversation where turn-taking is always contiguous, we can witness the effects of the first speaker on the second, and through response, we can see how the second speaker understood him- or herself to be positioned, and also whether that positioning was acceptable. These effects, or "Act-Action" as Harré calls it, take place immediately, and the statement–response turns are contiguous insofar as nothing separated one from the next. This does not imply that storylines will not change, only that the observer has confidence in being witness to a conversational episode.

But in non-contiguous conversation, the second speaker is always coming *to* the conversation as an act of will from a point that is *away*. Though silence as a response in a face-to-face conversation is certainly possible, it is always a turn in an episode that can be immediately challenged, as in, "why haven't you said anything?" This line of inquiry can go on as long as the two conversants so choose, generally giving greater rhetorical power to the one who chooses to speak.[22] This, of course, until the first speaker realizes that the other person *isn't* there and in which case it never was a conversation and the speaker truly was just talking to himself.

In non-contiguous conversation, however, the second speaker has always made some kind of choice to engage in the conversation. The separation of time—though possibly space as well—opens the range of possible responses by the second conversant. The essence of this freedom to maneuver is derived from the possibility of *denial* by the second conversant to ever having heard the words of the first. This is effectively impossible in face-to-face conversation unless something interrupts the conversation (e.g., a passing truck or the whirling blades of Air Force One), which according to the definition here immediately places the conversation in the "distant" category.

Conversation requires people to talk *about* something. In that talk, people refer to certain features or characteristics of the world, and also to each other. These verbal or written cues may be called "referents," and conversational episodes that contain referents are in turn "referenced."

The need for referencing is increased as time, distance, or other interruptions degrade confidence in the unity of episodes. In face-to-face conversation, these referents are not always apparent, in large part because they are not much needed. In cases where we are not engaged in face-to-face talk, however, the speaker needs to (re)integrate him- or herself into a narrative. Here, the use of referencing is common. Examples of referencing include, "Regarding that book you owe me . . ." or, "Remember when we were talking about going to Bermuda?" Here, the storyline of a book or about going to Bermuda is reawakened by referring to it, so that the conversation can be engaged, and the central tension resolved or else fall into logical exhaustion.

A specific type of referent that has received a good deal of attention is the "indexical." "Indexing" refers to the taking or assigning of responsibility for actions by making use of the locative power of pronouns as indicators.[23] Harré explains that "[t]he way that latitude and longitude are used to index names of cities, lakes and so on with their positions on the abstract geological grid is not a bad analogy for the function of pronouns as indexicals."[24] Note this is a very different use of the term "index" from W. Lance Bennett's, in which he uses *indexed* synonymously with *pegged*, meaning hooked on to, or linked up with. As Harré explains, in order to evoke an aspect of a social act, one needs to "locate" that act through the use of some noun or pronoun in the utterance. An indexical is a specific type of referent.

Why be so concerned with indexical expressions and whether episodes are or are not clearly referenced? The short answer is so we can determine "uptake" and hence know for certain that a conversation is taking place—and we aren't simply imputing unity where none really exists. And this is really the heart of the problem when we want to know whether the media and government are actually in conversation, and hence the media's utterances are actually having a direct influence on the government. Failing to determine whether this is happening is the most common mistake made by the casual media observer and we hear it nearly every day on the news by "talking heads." We always hear that someone made a statement and someone else "reacted," but how do they know? It is knowable and obvious in the case of face-to-face conversation (as at a press conference), but not in some other settings.

Natural scientists who ignore cause-and-effect relationships would be thoroughly discredited in their own fields. While cause-and-effect isn't mechanical in social relationships, unity in social episodes either does or does not exist, and once a theory of episodic unity is posited, the subsequent research may be judged on the soundness of the theory and the validity of its findings in the context of the theory itself. To raise our own standards in political communication we must make the effort in both cases. I've done so here and hope it provides a valuable foundation on which to improve both our theoretical stance and our means of measurement.

*   *   *

Rom Harré and Luk van Langenhove cautioned readers to remember that positioning is generally an unconscious act in interpersonal conversation, and flows naturally with conversation; however, in this section, the caution to readers is exactly the opposite when confronting inter-institutional discourse: one does not become the president of the United States or prime minister of Great Britain without understanding how the use of certain phrases and expression opens and closes possibilities for discussion, or positions oneself as responsible or not. If by chance it does happen, the naïveté does not last. One can comfortably err on the side of assuming that people such as George Bush, John Major, or any other politician in a Liberal democratic system knows exactly what it means to speak to another state, a media organization, the head of a rebel group, or any other type of exchange. This brings about the next major difference in inter-institutional discourse, namely, *positioning in inter-institutional conversation is generally a deliberate act.*

In some cases, specifically because of the power of institutional discourse, institutions and states will make use of ambiguous talk in order to avoid making direct reference to other actors so that denial remains a viable tool in the future. This feature is highly characteristic of diplomatic language. One example is public statements made at the UN, where countries often make subtle references to other states on sensitive matters without being deliberately provocative and thereby causing a diplomatic or international incident or insult that in turn effects a positioning response by another state. The diplomatic record on human rights, for example, is littered with formal protests from states to the Sub-Commission on Human Rights complaining they have been "singled out" for special condemnation, which is deemed an undiplomatic act. The practice of using ambiguous phrases such as, "some people" or "certain countries" sometimes serve as indexicals insofar as we "know" we are witnessing a conversation, but uptake and episodic unity are also ambiguous, allowing for denial, even if the meaning is generally obvious to those who understand the intentions of a speaker. Even when we see a "response" by another actor, we are often witness to equally vague utterances that lack clear indexicality to the first speaker.

The Ubiquity of Security Coalitions in Liberal Democratic Statecraft

The last part of the Positioning Hypothesis to discuss, before delving into British and U.S. policymaking during the Iraq Civil War, is the question of security coalitions. A coalition is the temporary cooperation and coordination of two or more actors, each of independent will and capacity, working toward the same initiative. This cooperation may be motivated for any number of reasons. Commonly, it is due to genuine agreement between the partners, or else some form of political expedience. The third motivation has to do with legal requirements, which makes coordination a requirement for action.

Insofar as each of the participating actors has some power over the direction of the coalition's policy, then the active maintenance and cohesion of the coalition becomes a requirement for the successful fulfillment of the policy itself. Because the Positioning Hypothesis grounds its argument on the power of words to undermine reputational authority and the coalitions that reputation cements, it needs to be demonstrated that coalitions are a normal and ubiquitous feature of the political environment in liberal democracies. Though there are many ways to analyze coalitions, focus is placed on two issues: that of formal powers (usually meaning legislated relations between or among the executive and other actors), and that of behavioral realities, or the observed practice of how things are done.

The general claim here is that security policies—even in times of strong executive dominance—are nevertheless the product of coalitions and bargaining between actors in coalitions. This is a general claim for both domestic politics, particularly in democracies, and for international politics insofar as extended security operations (i.e., those policies put into effect involving a foreign actor) require the implicit or explicit support of other foreign actors, thereby making all such action dependent in some form on coalition relationships broadly defined.

I don't suspect this claim is terribly contentious, so my defense will be mercifully brief.

*   *   *

In neither the United States nor the United Kingdom are coalition actors always inclined to affect the policy advocated by the executive, despite their power to do so. In the United States, references to oppositional voices with formal powers means either the opposition party (in modern times, either the Democrats or Republicans) or the Congress. The legislative branch can form a constraint on action, but is generally not a coalitional player. In Great Britain, and numerous other parliamentary systems, despite their differences, this generally means the opposition per se and the shadow cabinet, neither of which is part of the "government"—a term in Britain that traditionally refers to the executive members of the ruling party.[25]

The textbook definition of parliamentary government usually emphasizes the idea that "in parliamentary government the executive must be supported by a parliamentary majority," but as Elijah Ben-Zion Kaminsky points out, "any workable distinction [between presidential and parliamentary systems] must be based on actual behavior rather than legal prescriptions."[26] As Kaminsky explains it (though not referring to Britain specifically), "[p]arliamentary government is a democratic regime in which the executive and the legislature ultimately *must* agree on policy. The two branches are synchronized, so to speak, like two gears that mesh. If the two branches are out of 'synch,' something will be done to compel policy agreement between them."[27]

Temporary failure to agree leads to a short-term crisis, and could end by numerous means, the most extreme being a vote of no confidence and the walk-out of the opposition, especially if that walk-out brings down the government itself. This is a behavioral, not a constitutional or structural, definition. It is how the political actors behave rather than their constitutional, partisan, or parliamentary environments that sets the definition of parliamentary government.

Kaminsky's concern was with the comparison of presidential and parliamentary systems from a methodological perspective, and therefore rather provocatively dismisses the need to appreciate formal powers. Our own analysis, however, can make use of both approaches to appreciate that behavioral and formal structures alike make coalitions a ubiquitous and permanent part of the democratic landscape.

To what extent is Congressional support necessary for the conduct of executive action in the international security arena in the United

States? The answer would appear to be, as necessary as the Congress itself determines it should be. A look at the historical record of the latter half of the twentieth century quickly reveals that Congress has asserted itself very differently at different times in U.S. history, and not because the laws have changed so radically.

In 1955, for example, U.S. Democratic Senator Mike Mansfield—later the chairman of the Foreign Relations Committee—introduced a resolution calling for a joint oversight committee to oversee the operations of the newly formed Central Intelligence Agency.[28] Gregory Treverton quotes Senator Leverett Saltonstall—the ranking Republican on the Armed Services Committee—as responding to the resolution, saying:

> It is not a question of reluctance on the part of the CIA Officials to speak to us. Instead, it is a question of our reluctance, if you will, to seek information and knowledge on subjects which I personally, as a Member of Congress and as a citizen, would rather not have, unless I believed it to be my responsibility to have it because it might involve the lives of U.S. citizens.

Treverton tells us that in April 1956, the resolution was killed by a vote of 59:27. Here, the formal powers of Congress relented to what has been called the "imperial presidency" from the 1950s through the early 1970s. This was not imposed by the president, but decided—by vote—by the Congress itself.

There are other times, however, when formal powers of the opposition members of a coalition do manifest themselves very differently from a behavioral perspective. In the *International Herald Tribune* on 27 April 2000, for example, we read that:

> In a stinging attack on President Bill Clinton that could rattle U.S. arms negotiating efforts, the chairman of the Senate Foreign Relations Committee vowed Wednesday to block any treaty changes the administration negotiates with Russia while Mr. Clinton remains in office.
>
> "This administration's time for grand treaties is clearly at an end," Jesse Helms, the conservative North Carolina Republican, said on the Senate floor. "We will not consider any new, last-minute arms control measures that this administration negotiates in its closing months," said Mr. Helms, long an unabashed critic of Mr. Clinton's.

The constitutional powers of the U.S. Congress to ratify any and all treaties of the United States *de facto* makes Congress a coalition member of the executive in treaty-making foreign policies. In this case, circumstances such as Jesse Helm's dismissal of then U.S. president Bill Clinton seem to have contributed in part to a rise in Congressional action to obstruct executive policy. The same was observable as well in the U.S. Congress rejection of the Comprehensive Test Ban Treaty in 1999.

Congress control of the purse is likewise a significant formal power, and to a great extent is one that must be considered in any executive move to undertake a humanitarian operation. If and when U.S. troops are deployed on such operations, their movement becomes subject to the *War Powers Act*, which makes the executive accountable to Congress within sixty days of the deployment to seek funding approval. Though the *War Power's Act*, at the time of writing, has yet to be evoked by Congress, the legislated possibility remains.

Congress also has the uniquely vested authority to declare war—a power that is increasingly irrelevant in the modern era when war is never declared, and the laws of war themselves are under profound revision in the face of international terrorism and its highly contested responses by the United States and United Kingdom in particular.

In all these cases, Congressional support is formally necessary, or at least enough congressional support to prevent the *War Powers Act* from being implemented or legislation of a "cease and desist" variety from being passed.

In Great Britain, as Kaminsky explained, parliament and government necessarily must operate as a moderately united unit, otherwise opposition can arise in the House of Commons to challenge the policy of the executive and even conceivably pass a vote of "no confidence," bringing down a government and forcing new elections. But it is generally understood in the British system that, barring large disparities in party power, relations between government and opposition are absolutely vital for the continuance of policy. National security policy, in particular, remains a "hot topic" in parliament, in part because of Britain's significant role in the post–World War II international security structure, including its strong alliance with the United States, its status of a nuclear weapons state, its permanent position on the UN Security Council, and its nearly unique record of not having lost a war in the twentieth century. As Martin Shaw also explains, "British policy debates on global crises have not merely a general but also a national dimension."[29]

The United States and Great Britain are by no means alone, however, in having national security policy determined by coalition forces. Looking at all of democratic Europe from 1945 through 1999, only Spain and Great Britain have had single party governments (and we can include Greece for most of this period).[30] All states in Western Europe experienced highly significant periods of formal coalition governments during the latter half of the twentieth century.[31]

An interesting question I can't address here is whether formal coalition governments, such as those in Germany, France, or Italy, have a more difficult time maintaining international security policies over extended periods than countries with more concentrated power. As France in particular is an assertive international player in security affairs, with a permanent seat on the UN Security Council, maintains a nuclear arsenal and large standing army, and is also a state with an extremely high rate of coalition governments (over 80 percent in the last fifty years), it may prove a highly interesting and informative case of possible media influence over policymaking. The fact that French policy has generally *not* been claimed to be influenced by the media makes it that much more interesting, enabling work to be done on what counterforces may exist in French political life that would retard the proposed mechanisms of media pressure and influence.

Regarding coalitions in international relations, Glenn H. Snyder remains informative.

> Alliances and alignments are surely among the most central phenomena in international politics. Yet we have no theory about them that remotely approaches the richness of our theories about war, crisis, deterrence, and other manifestations of conflict. What might explain this? Perhaps it is their ubiquity, given their informal as well as their formal manifestations, and consequently the difficulty in isolating them as objects of study. George Liska, in the opening sentences of his *Nations in Alliance*, which after nearly three decades remains the only comprehensive theoretical treatment, put it this way: "It is impossible to speak of international relations without referring to alliances: the two often merge in all but name. For the same reason, it has always been difficult to say much that is peculiar to alliances on the plane of general analysis."[32]

Snyder reminds us of the ubiquity of alliances in international relations, and introduces the more flexible term "alignments" to broaden the possibility of analysis and to cast light not only on the formal (or contractual) alliances between states, but on the issue of "expectations held by policymakers concerning the question, 'who will defend whom?' or, more broadly, 'who will support whom and who will resist whom to what extent and in what contingencies?'"

Coalitions appear to be a growing rather than decreasing in international security affairs. If so, then the power of the media to affect those policies will increase as well, in the absence of learning how to control it at the state level.

CHAPTER 4

The Iraqi Civil War and the Aftermath, 1991

The period from March to July 1991, just after Operation Desert Storm came to an end, is the period of the Iraqi Civil War, the Kurdish refugee crisis, and the largest humanitarian relief operation in modern history.[1] In relation to the period's significance to contemporary policy in the Middle East, it has received little attention. As noted by Martin Shaw in 1996, "[c]overage of the Kurdish refugee crisis . . . has been much referred to but—unaccountably except in terms of the inability of researchers to adapt to unexpected events—has not been closely studied."[2] The same can be said of the Shiite uprisings, of which even less has appeared in print. With the discovery in Iraq, in June 2003, of some 10,000–15,000 bodies in mass graves (with many more likely to be found), the lack of attention to these events is unnerving.

While the daily and weekly press covered the events and the aftermath in various grades of detail, no books have been written and no proper case studies have been produced on this period. Even those writers who focus on the region have generally only written of the civil war as something of an afterthought to the Gulf War itself, or else as a bridging period between the end of the Gulf War and the resumption of Saddam Hussein's consolidation of power.

Consequently, all records remain scattered, and the political players themselves have relegated the events to a few lines or pages buried within their memoirs or reflective offerings.[3] Various scholars in international relations often aim toward "policy relevance," and when doing so, will often define relevance by the vigor of political discussion on a given topic. The trouble with this approach is that policymakers generally do not talk about things of which they are ashamed. As there is great reason for shame about the policies taken during this period, it stands to reason that the period has disappeared from elite discourse, and hence from contemporary history.

This regrettable formula might help explain why the crisis of the post–Gulf War period has simply not appeared on the academic or policy agenda in now over ten years and there is no indication that interest is gathering. The terrorist attack on the World Trade Center in New York in September 2001 should only reiterate that it is essential for national security in the United States and Great Britain, and indeed many other countries as well, to know what happened after the Gulf War, what decisions were made that left Saddam Hussein in power, what events led to that result, and what the memories are of the people who lived through it all.

There are other reasons for attention as well. U.S. and British troops have maintained no-fly-zones (Operation Northern Watch and Operation Southern Watch), and a full-time, heavily armed presence in live-fire zones in both northern and southern Iraq since the end of the Gulf War and the initiation of Operation Provide Comfort in April 1991 through 2003.[4] These controlled regions have acted as *de facto* Kurdish and Shiite safe havens and have, without interruption, been a source of military conflict, regular bombings of Iraq sites by American and British forces, and political dispute among coalition partners that have strained U.S. relations with NATO and Europe, and British relations with its European Union (EU) partners. Hundreds of millions of dollars—by the United States alone—have been spent on operations in the region.[5]

The history of this period produced in this chapter is unfortunately limited in its scope and does not exhaust the primary source material available. Not all media coverage has been examined; and surely helpful Arabic, Farsi, Hebrew, and Turkish sources have not been consulted outside of a few translations from the Foreign Broadcasting Information Service (FBIS). A rigorous, day-by-day chronology has not been produced, although efforts have been made to examine the primary decision junctures with some care.

Thus far there have only been three public studies of any detail on this postwar period. The most directly relevant to our concerns came from Martin Shaw, who produced a history of the period by "examining key elements of British television coverage of the revolts in Iraq, their repression by the regime and the consequent refugee crises, together with responses by Western states and civil societies."[6] His work focused only on the period of March and April, and only on the writing and broadcasting of the British press.

The other highly noteworthy study was an unpublished dissertation produced by Gordon William Rudd for Duke University in 1993 entitled *Operation Provide Comfort: Humanitarian Intervention in Northern Iraq, 1991.* Rudd was the official field historian for Provide Comfort to the U.S. Army, and wrote the dissertation at the request of General Harold Nelson, then chief of the U.S. Army Center of Military History. Rudd never published his findings, which is unfortunate, other than through UMI Dissertation Services. His work was relied on here for better understanding the military aspects of Provide Comfort, for establishing time lines for field operations, and for getting a better sense of how much lead-time field commanders had to prepare for policy shifts as directed by Washington. Rudd was not focused on the Washington or London decision-making processes or the geopolitics of the decision making, but rather on the humanitarian relief efforts themselves and is therefore of little direct use here. But some of his observations dovetail perfectly with this study. For example, on 6 April, the day after President Bush said that the United States would start dropping aid to the Kurdish refugees and Resolution 688 was passed, Brigadier General Richard Potter would go to the operations section of US European Command (EUCOM). There, he was briefed by Admiral L.W. "Snuffy" Smith. Rudd explains that, "for Jamison [another field commander] and Potter, the operation kicked off with no notice. The political guidance was to assist the refugees. There was no operation plan available to activate for such an operation, nor was there any formal doctrine for humanitarian assistance."

Along with other evidence explored later, it becomes clear that the Bush administration had no intention of becoming involved in the refugee crisis until 5 April after the UN resolution was passed.

The final piece is a chapter in the book *After Such Knowledge, What Forgiveness*, by Jon Randal, a long-time reporter with the *Washington Post* and a war correspondent during the Gulf War. Randal's work is helpful in providing insight, a sequence of events, and first-hand experience of the major actors and their relations. It is not an empirical study or detailed history, and some of his conclusions about possible media influence appear contradictory. Nevertheless, it is an important contribution and should be consulted when this period is examined.

This chapter is broader and uses a different focal point from Shaw's, Rudd's, or Randal's studies. The intention here was not to look at issues of representation or operational problems and successes but rather to track and organize the decision-making steps and processes of the United States and Great Britain during the first three months of the civil war and its aftermath and analyze how those decisions were reflected in the media. To ascertain the accuracy of media records, it was necessary to look beyond them. The primary sources for that independent story were generally the White House itself and all its public statements and press conferences as well as the House of Commons records (HANSARD). At times, the press conferences of the State Department and Pentagon were consulted as well. Further, the media stories were compared against one another—across countries and formats—to try and get the story straight, or, at the very least, site the major junctures of contention. The format of this section was therefore to follow the records of the media coverage of the executives, political opposition, and international actors and events to create an accounting of the major decisions of the period, and the U.S. and British responses to them. Whereas the role of international organizations and other major political players, such as the UN, European Commission, France, and Turkey, will be discussed, their own inner workings are not followed. Rather, their own stories are incorporated when their storylines influence those of the United States and Britain (and ultimately Iraq).

The time scale of this review is also wider than Shaw's, covering the period of 1 March to 2 June 1991, although the detailed case history ends around the beginning of May.[7] Operation Provide Comfort I ended on 24 July 1991 in striking fashion: It was met without a single mention on any television network or newspaper in either country.[8] In fact, media interest was found to have tapered off to a mere trickle by the end of May and on this finding the time horizon of the study was determined.[9]

Like Somalia and Bosnia, the Kurdish refugee crisis of 1991 has been identified as a clear case of media influence over foreign policy in the United States and Britain respectively. The more recent material, in fact, the more axiomatic the argument becomes, despite the fact that no empirical studies exist that are either comparative in nature, or seek alternative explanations for either U.S. or British policymaking. What we observe when examining the conclusions drawn about these events is that conventional wisdom is becoming increasingly assertive in its conclusions in the absence of any new information.

As early as 26 April 1991, while the relief effort was well under way, Victoria Brittain wrote an understandably bitter editorial for the

Guardian in which conventional wisdom about agenda-setting was already beginning to cement. She wrote:

> For every Kurd wretched on the mountains of northern Iraq there are nine Africans threatened with hunger and starvation. But the ratio of media interest has been far more than nine times over in favour of the Kurds, with the excellent result that US sources say within days they will have enough food to keep them alive.
>
> International reaction to the two tragedies says much about the relationship between media and Western interests, and how television's priorities set agendas. Many of the Kurds can well articulate their crisis for Western television. Africa's starving are peasants, often in areas unreachable by outsiders, and with a language and culture barrier which precludes a television soundbite.

Years later, all evidence suggests that the idea of television agenda-setting on government policy toward the Kurds was to be all but permanent. Warren P. Strobel writes,

> Western reporters and camera's already in the region to cover the Gulf War dramatically captured the Kurd's plight. The video and still images they showed to the world—mother's burying son and daughters on the rocky mountainside, children burned by napalm, miles-long lines of refugees snaking up the snowy mountains—were critical to Bush's policy switch, according to news accounts at the time and subsequent statements by the president's top aides.[10]

Philip Seib concludes in his brief look at this period that, "[George Bush] had no interest in becoming embroiled in Saddam Hussein's ongoing battle with the Kurds living in northern Iraq. But news reports, particularly those with vivid television pictures, were a major factor in Bush's decision to change his policy."[11]

Seib also quotes Deborah Amos of ABC news as writing that, "[p]ublic reaction was swift and strong, and governments were scrambling to fashion a policy to stop that slaughter and stop the pictures on the evening news . . . . It was a moment when the power of television journalism was at its height."[12]

Martin Shaw, who has done the most thorough job to date of looking at media coverage of the Kurdish crisis in the British press and subsequent foreign policy decisions in that country, also concluded that the Kurdish case was "the only clear cut case, of all the conflicts in the early 1990s, in which media coverage compelled an intervention by the Western powers."[13]

Susan Carruthers would both echo and amplify Shaw's argument by writing, "the Kurdish case therefore appears as a classic case of television-led intervention to serve humanitarian ends," although she does note the observation by Minear, Scott, and Weiss that Thatcher was putting pressure on Major domestically as well.[14]

Not mentioning the media per se but rather public opinion more generally, Lincoln Bloomfield argued, "[i]n response to public outrage, the victorious coalition moved inside Iraqi territory and established protected aid channels to 'Kurdistan,' although not to the South where the regime was busily crushing Shiite dissidence."[15]

Finally, Daniel Schorr, in the most congratulatory piece about media influence, began an article for the *Columbia Journalism Review* called "Ten Days that Shook the White House" with, "Score one for the power of the media, especially television, as a policy-making force. Coverage of the massacre and exodus of the Kurds generated public pressures that were instrumental in slowing the hasty American military withdrawal from Iraq and forcing a return to help guard and care for the victims of Saddam Hussein's vengeance."[16] He referred to the period of 2–12 April 1991.

This study provides a different reading of this history than the prevailing conventional wisdom by revealing a starkly different series of events than those concluded by the authors mentioned. It provides a first attempt to answer the following questions about the history of the events generally: How did the civil war begin? What was the international response to the war and how did those responses change as events unfolded? What was the logic behind coalition action and how widespread was support for those policies? What were the major changes to coalition policy, and how were they implemented? Why was Saddam Hussein left in power by the coalition? Was it possible to have removed him? What were the factors that led Western leaders to allow it to happen? And finally, why was Operation Provide Comfort launched, and what pressures were brought to bear on George Bush and John Major to encourage the operation?

A Historical Overview of Events

Phase 1: Non-Engagement

On 2 August 1990, Iraq invaded the neighboring state of Kuwait, occupying the country and then annexing it. On 16 January 1991, less than a day after a UN deadline for Iraq to retreat from Kuwait, an international coalition of states led by the United States and operating under the resolutions mechanisms of the UN, launched a counterattack against Iraq from bases primarily in Saudi Arabia and off-shore sites in the Persian Gulf. The mandate of the operation was the liberation of Kuwait from Iraq and the restoration of the Kuwaiti government. Following an initial air campaign designed to neutralize Iraqi defenses, the coalition then launched a massive ground assault at 4 a.m. local time in Iraq on 24 February.[17] The counterattack inflicted massive, though formally untallied, casualties on Iraqi forces and met little organized, sustained resistance.[18] On 28 February at 8 a.m., U.S. President George Bush called a unilateral ceasefire following the successful liberation of Kuwait and shortly after a brutal military attack on armed, retreating Iraqi troops along the Mutlaa Pass. Under 200 coalition forces were killed by the end of hostilities and Iraqi casualties are generally estimated at upward of 50–100,000 men, though no one knows for sure.[19]

For the next forty-eight hours, Iraq was quiet. Troops deserted to American and allied forces in the south or else made their way home in disheveled, ad hoc convoys.[20] But the postwar silence was short-lived. On 2 March 1991, Iraq would explode in a full-fledged civil war for control of the dictatorial state, and casualties—which can only be estimated from news reports—would mount into the tens of thousands.[21] This was no mere revolt or opportunist grab for power; it was a new and brutal war to determine the future of Iraq and the outcome was far from certain.

* * *

Peter Galbraith in his Congressional testimony describes the initial events leading to the southern uprisings:

> On March 2, two days after President Bush halted the ground war, a surviving Iraqi tank driver in the southern city of Basra halted his tank before one of the 2-story high portraits of Saddam Hussein that hang everywhere in Iraqi cities. Through the portrait he fired a shell. This shell ignited a spontaneous rebellion that raged, like a nearby Kuwaiti oil fire, through the Shi'a-dominated cities of Southern Iraq.

Yitzhak Nakash, in his book, *The Shi'is of Iraq*, places the earliest revolts during the war itself.[22] He writes:

> In its origin the insurrection of March 1991 was spontaneous and disorganized, but its spread in the Shi'a south and later in the Kurdish north was stimulated to a degree by foreign countries as well as by the Iraqi opposition groups in exile. One of the earliest reported incidents

which preceded the Shi'a insurrection is traced by the media to 10 February. On that day, a crowd of Iraqis in the predominantly Shi'a town of Diwaniyya, 110 miles south of Baghdad, protested Saddam Husayn's refusal to relinquish Kuwait. Shouting anti-Saddam and anti-Ba'th slogans, the protesters killed ten officials of the ruling Ba'th party. Five days later, U.S. president George Bush made his first explicit call for the Iraqis to topple Saddam.

The fighting after Desert Storm, however, started in Basra, he writes, and then "spread . . . to a string of other predominantly Shi'i towns in the south, most notably Amara, Nasiriyya, and Kut."[23]

According to Majid Khadduri and Edmund Ghareeb, however, the uprisings began neither in Basra nor—necessarily—were they spontaneous or disorganized.

> The "popular uprising," as it was described, began on March 2nd when a group of armed men from Suq al-Shuyukh, a town under the control of US troops, arrived at Nasiriya and organized hundreds of deserters to attack government headquarters in the area. Nasiriya lies on the edge of the marshes where Iraqi deserters from the war had taken refuge along with Shi'i opponents of the regime.[24]

Each of these accounts can be separately confirmed, to some degree, by British news reports thereby further complicating the matter.[25] The *Daily Telegraph* on 2 March appears to support Galbraith's account and reported that "Mr. 'Abdullah Jabir al-Badran, 24, a student from Kuwait, said that at 9am [on 2 March] an Iraqi tank fired three or four shells through a giant portrait of Saddam wearing military uniform in the center of [Basra] next to the Ba'th Party and Popular Army Headquarters."

The British broadsheet the *Independent* on the same day seems instead to back the Khadduri–Ghareeb account:[26] "The rebels say they are followers of Mohamed Bakr al-Hakim, a long-standing opponent of President Saddam. His group, the Tehran-based Supreme Assembly of the Islamic Revolution in Iraq, issued statements in Lebanon claiming control of Nasiriyah, a strategic city on the Euphrates, of nearby Souk al-Shuyukh, al-Tar and al-Fuhoud and parts of al-Amarah."[27] There is evidence that Iran supported this group in an effort to influence the Shia uprising, but none as yet available to make one suspect that Iran either prompted it, or did anything more than contribute some material support and general propaganda on behalf of the southern rebels in the event they unexpectedly succeeded. Notable, however, is that even by 4 March, the *Independent* was still so uncertain as to the reasons or cause of the events in Basra that a front page article would only describe the scene as "chaotic," shying away from classifications such as "rebellion" or even "revolt."

Several reasons exist for the conflicting stories. First, Western news services were receiving most of their material from Pentagon, State, and White House briefings, which were not particularly helpful, largely because they too appear to have been quite uninformed, as will be discussed.[28] Their other sources of information were foreign, unconfirmed news coming out of Iran and Syria particularly. Second, there were no reporters south of Kurdistan or north of Safwan—the "truce" village just north of the Kuwaiti border where Schwarzkopf met the Iraqis to issue American demands during the unilateral ceasefire. Not until 5 March would journalists such as Robert Fisk of the *Independent*, Martin Woolacott of the *Guardian*, and Jonathan Randal of the *Washington Post* make their way into the conflict zones outside of the American controlled regions. They would not be there long.

What these conflicting reports appear to indicate is that there was no single "start" to the rebellions because they were not a unified effort that was jointly initiated. Rather, there were "starts," soon to become widespread and opportunistically fuelled by numerous players and factions, including Iran and the Badr Brigade, in an effort to harness wide-ranging, and unfocused dissatisfaction into some form of unified political movement.[29] Khadduri and Ghareeb reach a similar conclusion. "These events [in the south] were a spontaneous anti-regime reaction that exploited the weakness of the Iraqi army caused by its haphazard and bloody with drawl from Kuwait."[30] At the conference in Damascus in mid-March, numerous opposition leaders would also confirm that the uprising was unplanned and disorganized.[31]

A number of observations might be made about the nature of the uprising and its leadership. The uprising seems to have occurred in areas where the people and civil infrastructure were not equipped to handle the large number of troops and equipment that were retreating from Kuwait. Further, the uprising began as an expression of the state of anarchy in a Basra that was crowded with huge numbers of heavily armed soldiers who were still reeling with bitterness from the military defeat and the sheer weight of the coalition's attacks by planes, ships, missiles, and laser-guided bombs as well as from hunger resulting from the economic sanctions. It is clear that the uprisings did not come about as a result of a well-planned action that was able to offer a political program or alternative vision for the future.

One story never properly explored in the coverage of the period was the question of what other countries—beside the United States—may also have promoted the uprisings, or more broadly, what *else* other than the United States may have prompted it. Tehran Radio, for example, is known to have been broadcasting in the south, as well as the BBC. In the north, five Kurdish radio transmitters were located on the Turkish side of the border in Cizre.[32]

U.S. reaction at this stage was summed up by then-secretary of defense Dick Cheney, who said, "[a]t this point I'm not certain that there's much that can be done about it, other than to make certain that we provide for the security of Kuwait, for example, that that kind of unrest and turmoil that we now see developing in parts of Iraq hopefully won't spread over into other areas in the neighborhood."[33]

International reaction to the rebellion was varied, depending on individual state interests, but other than some direct support from Iran, the revolts were contained within Iraq itself, and no evidence is available to suggest that the rebels were being militarily supplied with arms or funding from the outside. This was not a regional war, but a true civil war, with few cross-border arrangements for support for either side.[34] Because the uprisings in the south were over within two weeks at the outside, and there was no thus-far-determinable preplanning of hostilities, there was little opportunity to supply the revolts had international actors even wanted to—not to mention complete coalition domination of the airspace.[35] There was also the complicating facts that all bridges across the Tigris and Euphrates had been destroyed by allied forces, and the southern portion of the country—including all access roads from Saudi Arabia and Kuwait—were guarded by hundreds of thousands of foreign troops. With the possible exception of minor provisions of small arms from Iran, the rebellion must be viewed as internal, contained and without international aid of any kind.

Viewed militarily, the lack of an organized command and control system among the Shiites; the unorganized distribution of weapons; the inability of rebel forces to concentrate fire on selected targets; a general lack of training among fighting men; the need of combatants to hold ground in order to protect their families rather than press an attack on the enemy; the almost complete lack of heavy weaponry and the superior firepower of the Iraqi military; the ruthless willingness of the Iraqi forces to massacre any and all civilians; and the lack of material support from outside nations for the reasons just mentioned, all but doomed the rebellion from the moment it began. A Kurdish spokesman, when it was all over in mid-April, would look back and draw similar conclusions. "We lost because we were lightly armed and they had heavy weapons, because our people were starving and because we simply could not marshal the large numbers of people who had joined in the uprising."[36] These very unsolvable problems—evident at the earliest stages by those versed in military matters—likely were considerations in the calculations of countries such as the United States and Britain and helps explain why even a sympathetic and opportunist Iran hedged its support.[37]

Coalition and non-coalition states alike issued numerous statements and aired broadcasts that all carried the same basic message: no one wanted to get involved in supporting the uprisings, and all states publicly called for the maintenance of the territorial integrity of Iraq. One of the first voices was that of the French Foreign Minister Roland Dumas, who said on 3 March that France would "not participate in whatever expedition there may be to depose Saddam Hussein."[38] Morocco issued a statement on 5 March, saying that, "[t]he latest developments inside Iraq are cause for serious concern about this sisterly state. In this regard, the ministry's spokesman reaffirmed Morocco's attachment to Iraq's territorial integrity and reiterated that even if there are problems among segments of the Iraqi people, and despite their potential for such problems, Morocco affirms the territorial integrity of Iraq."[39] On the same day a statement came from the small Gulf state island of Bahrain that warned against any possible "dismemberment" of Iraq. As Bahrain has traditionally functioned as a vassal state to Saudi Arabia, it is likely that this call represented the views of the Saudi government as well, as neither was keen on the Sunni Arabs losing power to the Shiite majority in southern Iraq.

At the White House, policymaking was focused on extricating U.S. troops from the Middle East. Over 500,000 troops remained in the region. The objective in early March was to draft a permanent ceasefire agreement (a peace treaty was unnecessary as there was no declaration of war) and to return the troops home. At a speech to the Veteran's Organization at the Old Executive Office Building in Washington on the afternoon of 4 March, Bush explained that,

> [o]ur goal remains what it's been all along: Iraq's complete and unconditional compliance with all relevant United Nations resolutions and its implementation of all the requirements to be found in Security Council Resolution 686, passed overwhelmingly late Saturday afternoon, just this past Saturday. This would allow us to move beyond the current suspension of military operations to a more permanent and stable cease-fire.[40]

In the White House there was a "wait-and-see" attitude toward the uprisings, and according to the same newspaper report, the American administration believed that nine out of ten possible outcomes of the civil war would be positive for the United States.

Peter Galbraith calls this the "no contacts" policy and does not mince words about how detrimental this policy was to U.S. interests or for the future of Iraq. He writes:

> The United States was unprepared for the peace that followed the gulf war. It did not comprehend the depth of popular anger inside Iraq at Saddam Hussein and therefore did not anticipate the uprisings either in the south or the north. The administration in its policy assessments seemed to mischaracterize the positions of the Kurdish and Shi'a rebels. As a result, an opportunity to overthrow Saddam Hussein in mid-March may have been lost . . . Being caught by surprise may be directly traceable to a policy of no contact with the Iraqi opposition.

The policy of no contact may have been a short-sighted policy, but it was not altogether unreasonable, because of the absolute value placed on maintaining the coalition long enough to establish ceasefire conditions favorable to U.S. interests. It was a tactical decision that followed logically from what was a primary flaw in the U.S.-led war: a failure to plan for a postwar Iraq. The mistake was allowing the coalition to be threatened by an action that was integral to long-term policy needs rather than short-term coalition needs.

President Bush made his first major address since the ceasefire went into effect on 28 February. The audience was a joint session of Congress. Speaking to the Senate, the House, the American public via live television, and the world as a whole, he began by thanking the Speaker of the House, Thomas Foley, and described the world after Desert Storm as one "blessed by the promise of peace."[41]

> From the moment Operation Desert Storm commenced on January 16th until the time the guns fell silent at midnight 1 week ago, this nation has watched its sons and daughters with pride—watched over them with prayer. As Commander in Chief, I can report to you our armed forces fought with honor and valor. And as President, I can report to the Nation aggression is defeated. The war is over.

Once again blaming Saddam Hussein personally, as he had for nearly six months straight, Bush described the situation in Iraq without making any reference to the civil war:

> Tonight in Iraq, Saddam walks amidst ruin. His war machine is crushed. His ability to threaten mass destruction is itself destroyed. His people have been lied to—denied the truth. And when his defeated legions come home, all Iraqis will see and feel the havoc he has wrought. And this I promise you: For all that Saddam has done to his own people, to the Kuwaitis, and to the entire world, Saddam and those around him are accountable.

The speech served many functions. It praised the troops, its leaders, and the American people for standing by them, all in terms that so mirrored the Vietnam experience that the pride felt by the audience must have been proportional to the shame felt about Vietnam; it was applause for heroism in both wars. Beyond the epideictic quality to the speech, the more practical matters were to lay out a four-point plan of action for postwar Iraq. Quoting Bush, these were:

1. First, we must work together to create shared security arrangements in the region.
2. Second, we must act to control the proliferation of weapons of mass destruction and the missiles used to deliver them.
3. And third, we must work to create new opportunities for peace and stability in the Middle East.
4. Fourth, we must foster economic development for the sake of peace and progress.

Other than oblique comments about how Saddam was "walking in ruin" and hopeful terms about how his returning legions will rise up against him, the four-point plan of the administration, which listed otherwise very significant U.S. security interests, nevertheless gave no hint at how the continued threat of Saddam Hussein would be handled or how the civil war would be engaged so as to *promote* these stated U.S. interests. The reason for this lack of policy detail was that Bush and the administration were far more concerned about what they would not do than what they would. In short, there was no plan of action for Iraq itself, only hopes that Saddam Hussein would be overthrown.[42]

To find an explicit administration theory behind the inaction, one needs to jump ahead to a brief statement made on 26 March at a presidential press conference, and then to a rather innocuous Arbor Day tree-planting ceremony on 25 April—long after the civil war had ended and Operation Provide Comfort was under way. On 26 March, the president was under severe pressure from the press to explain what seemed a profoundly contradictory (as opposed to unpalatable) policy, and was trying to understand what logic might possibly hold it together. Bush was asked, "Did you say before that you don't expect Saddam to last much longer?" His response was the first glimpse of the theory that underpinned American non-action.

> We, I didn't say much longer, but he will not—he will not—with this much—put it this way, with this much turmoil it seems to me unlikely that he can survive. People are fed up with him and see him for the brutal dictator he is. They see him as one who tortured his own people. They see him as one that took his country into a war that was devastating for them. And this turmoil is not completely historic unrest; it's historic unrest plus great dissatisfaction with Saddam Hussein. So—

After planting a tree at a "photo op" a month later, Bush fielded a few questions with reporters. Though details about media coverage and executive relations will be discussed in the next section, suffice to say that even at this comparatively late date when pressure by the media had largely subsided, most reporters were still uncertain about what Bush's Iraq policy was and still occasionally fielded a few questions on the off-chance Bush might take the bait and explain what he had in mind. On this particular day the gamble paid off. The rather open question was, "what's going to put him [Saddam Hussein] out of power?" Bush, rather frustrated that the questioning of the past two months simply would not end, responded with this theory:

> That fact that he's been whipped bad in the military. His aggression— he's been forced to do that which he said he would never do. His people don't like him and it's only terror that's keeping him in power. And some day history will show you these things manage to take care of themselves. And I hope it happens soon because we want him out of there. And we don't have any fight with the Iraqi people. I've said that from day one. Go back and look at the texts back in August, September, October. Our fight is not with the Iraqi people. Our objective was to repel aggression and we did it. And the American troops deserve enormous credit and they're getting it every single day they come home. But beyond that, this internal matter has been going on for years—years and years. And I'd like to see it ended. And one good way to end it was to have somebody with a little more compassion as president of Iraq. But that's—let them worry about that problem. I worry about it because there won't be normal relations until he's gone. But history has a way of taking care of tyrants.

On 7 March, Saddam Hussein expelled all journalists and Westerners from Iraq, thereby ending all television coverage and virtually all firsthand, on-the-ground knowledge for Western observers of what would come to pass in the civil war. Two days later, Lee Hockstadter of the *Washington Post* wrote with unfortunate foresight, "[m]any of the journalists say the [Iraqi] government's decision to eject them is a signal that President Saddam Hussein's crackdown against Kurdish rebels in the north and Shiite Muslim fundamentalists in the south may enter a new and more ruthless phase that the government does not want witnessed by outside observers." He was absolutely correct.

Saddam Hussein's move to eject foreign journalists from the country and to assign Majid to put down the uprisings was not met with any direct policy changes in the United States or Britain. In the former, attention was focused on three primary concerns. The first was the extrication of U.S. combat troops from the region beginning with all nonessential personnel. The second was the preparation and signing of a permanent ceasefire agreement. The 28 February ceasefire was a unilateral declaration by George Bush acting on behalf of the coalition. It was not an agreement between the United States and Iraq, or even the UN and Iraq. For this to come to pass, Iraq needed to agree to and abide by the terms of the ceasefire as negotiated by Schwarzkopf and the Iraqis at Safwan. The United States generally imposed the conditions, and there was some discussion and some concessions made to the Iraqis— perhaps the most unfortunate and well-known being the license to fly helicopters (but not fixed-wing aircraft) over their own territory. Without this permanent ceasefire agreement in place, Bush did not have the minimum conditions necessary to effect a full withdrawal.[43] The third consideration was the development of a comprehensive Middle East peace plan.

The idea was pervasive in Washington that the victory of the Allies, the respect the Arabs were assumed to have for the Americans at that moment, the debts owed the United States—by Saudi Arabia and Kuwait at the very least—and the general unification of actors traditionally on opposite sides of conflict, such as the Syrians and Israelis, made this a unique window of opportunity for forcing a peace plan onto the otherwise belligerent parties. In Israel, Yitzhak Shamir— known for a hard-line stance against the Arabs generally—was expecting to come out of the conflict with the upper hand over the Palestinians. Israel had, albeit reluctantly, sat out the conflict during some forty days of Iraqi missile attack without returning fire. This was an uncharacteristic move by Israel and undoubtedly accompanied promises by the United States beyond the concerted "Scud hunt" during the opening days of the air war.[44] The Palestinians, meanwhile, had managed to snatch defeat from the jaws of political victory by siding with Saddam Hussein during the Gulf War, an act followed by Jordan due to the 60 percent Palestinian population of the Hashemite Kingdom, thereby weakening their position to such an extent that even supportive publications would conclude that, at the very least, Arafat was doomed as their leader.

For the White House, this formula of admiration, debt, and political positioning signaled that a rare moment had come to launch a peace initiative for the entire Middle East that was conducive to U.S. policy interests and would be palatable to the Arabs and Israelis. To assemble this peace plan, Secretary of State James Baker III was dispatched to the region on a "secret" mission to usher in this New World Order.[45] Although Baker had a clear objective in mind, the trip was described as one "without a blueprint" for peace.[46] The characterization was accurate, and was the product of George Bush's own personal means of governance. Since first coming to office, and perhaps learned from his earlier career as a diplomat to the UN, Bush liked to "work the phones" to such an extent that sometimes even the State Department became nervous or felt left out.[47] Bush would regularly pick up the phone and personally call foreign leaders, make deals and promises, and form coalitions. If he was unable to do it, he would send someone in his stead to conduct affairs in a similar manner. In this case, that someone was the secretary of state, who had an open and standing order to make peace in the Middle East. He was given ten days.

While Baker was in the Middle East, the Shiite uprisings were by most reports quelled; the Kurdish revolts gained ground; the United States ushered in a major policy shift on 13 March by effectively issuing an unenforced ban on Iraqi helicopter gunships and use of chemical weapons; the British government would break ranks with the United States for the first time on a substantive policy by opening direct contact with the Iraqi opposition as well as Kurdish leaders.[48]

President Ozal of Turkey, by 12 March, was still under significant domestic pressure for supporting the coalition during the Gulf War. During the war, Ozal chose the bold path of brushing aside a seventy-year Turkish legacy of limited, or even noninvolvement in Middle Eastern politics. Ozal's motivation—according to a close associate—was his determination to be "at the victory banquet and not on the menu," when the war finally came to an end.[49] Since the end of the war, Turkey's political policies continued to evolve in rapid fashion in response to the fluid circumstances of the Iraqi Civil War and its repercussions. Ozal, for example, agreed in principle to local autonomy in Iraq for the Kurds as well as the use of their own language in Turkey itself.[50]

Perhaps even more significant was that the Turks publicly met with Kurdish leaders for the first time in sixty years. This thawing—if not actual warming—of Turkish–Kurdish relations may have been viewed by France and Britain as an opening: both had been having contact with the Kurds for some time now, but following the Turkish move, they increased their public support of Kurdish autonomy and denounced Iraqi military atrocities.

Part of the trouble, however, was that U.S. policy toward the opposition—though understandable from a geopolitical perspective—was baffling from the point of view of political maneuvering and common sense. The stated US policy was that Iraq should maintain its territorial integrity because of coalition stated goals and because of the legally binding nature of the UN resolutions. As the latter has a long and tainted history of being used to advance the less-than-altruistic objectives of like-minded states on a given topic, it must have struck the opposition as being inconceivable that the "real reason" for the lack of U.S. support was its firm adherence to international law and the collective will of the coalition within its UN authorized mandate.[51] Although Bush and Major would eventually bend some rules, particularly when it meant moving the Kurds off the mountains and into Iraqi territory around Dohuk, it must be mentioned that the rules established by the UN were in fact adhered to, and were considered a significant consideration in the later refugee crisis.

France that day called an emergency meeting of the European Community (EC) to discuss the situation inside Iraq, with Britain in attendance. But while the EC meeting provided evidence of concern for the rebellion, no decisions were made about actual support, and neither France, Britain, nor the United States was yet of any mind to engage the civil war. According to the *Independent*,

> All this is merging in a common criticism of America. All agree that the United States has been equivocal in its support for a fully democratic solution in Iraq, and, unlike Britain, has had virtually no contacts with the opposition. The US Secretary of State, James Baker, has no plans to see anyone from the Iraqi opposition when he passes through Damascus tomorrow, while the British Foreign Office minister, Douglas Hogg, who is there at the same time, will be meeting a group of opposition speakers.

The British policy was officially to speak to the opposition but not to grant it any official mandate. As was often echoed through Whitehall, "We recognize states, not governments."[52]

Amidst the political repositioning in Europe and the first signs of an opening Euro-American fracture in policy approaches, Iraq was dropping napalm on civilians and revolutionaries alike in the southern region, with a few surviving stragglers crossing the American positions to the south with obvious burns, confirmed by local military medical personnel.

Phase 2: "Operation Desert Calm" and the Banning of Helicopters and Chemical Weapons

The first major policy shift since the conflict started came on 13 March, and the reasons for it are not obvious. The reason for the confusion and the flawed communication policy of the White House to explain its actions was quite evident from the subsequent theorizing of the press and the confusion the policy shift created among coalition countries and among the combatants in Iraq themselves.

The statement that Bush made, which would soon be viewed as a major policy shift by the United States, came during a news conference in Ottawa where Bush was meeting with the prime minister of Canada then, Mulroney. The press conference covered a range of issues, and the subject of the Iraqi Civil War did not figure prominently. The exchange that entered the United States into a new phase of foreign policymaking seems by all measures to have been made totally off-the-cuff, taking the White House—the United States with it—into new territories of commitment and international hostility.

The exchange was as follows:[53]

> **Q**: What is your assessment, please, of where we [the United States] stand on the achievement of a permanent cease-fire and how it might affect the ability of U.S. troops to be pulled out of southern Iraq?
>
> **The President**: One, I'll restate my view that I want our troops to come home as soon as possible. I've just been elated as I've watched the troops come home and the warmth of the welcome and all of that. There are some details to be worked out on the cease-fire—the return of all the prisoners, accounting for those who have not been accounted for. I must confess to some concern about the use of Iraqi helicopters in violation of what our understanding was. That's one that has got to be resolved before we're going to have any permanence to any cease-fire. And so there are several details remaining out there.

Q: Generally, are you satisfied with the progress, or do you think the Iraqis could do better?

The President: I'm very much satisfied with the progress that has been made since General Schwarzkopf met in the tent, but there are still some very important things to be taken care of, including the fact that these helicopters should not be used for combat purposes inside Iraq.

The question addressed to Bush was rather open and vague. It was a typical question that politicians generally like because any probe for one's "assessment" allows any form of response. Bush's confession that he was concerned about the Iraqi use of helicopter gunships being used to put down the rebellions could not, therefore, be seen as an extracted confession. In the next sentence, Bush makes the far more powerful statement that, "[t]hat's one has got to be resolved before we're going to have any permanence to any cease-fire. And so there are several details remaining out there."

On 13 March, Marlin Fitzwater—the White House press secretary—made the following statement:[54]

Saddam Hussein has a track record of using his military against his own population. We have received information over the past week that he has been using helicopters in an effort to quell civil disturbances against his regime. We are obviously very concerned about this. President Bush expressed his concern at the news conference. This behavior is clearly inconsistent with the type of behavior the international community would like to see Iraq exhibiting. Iraq has to convince the world that its designs, both against the international community and its own population, are not military and aggressive.

Fitzwater's statement, read with scrutiny, is wholly different from Bush's statement to the reporters and is an attempt to back-peddle. Bush was not simply expressing concern at the news conference as Fitzwater described, and the impetus was not on Saddam Hussein to "convince the world" of his peaceful designs. The *New York Times* saw through the ruse and reached a similar conclusion in the front-page story the following day. "By raising the issue, Mr. Bush further involved himself on the side of anti-Government factions in Iraq battling against forces loyal to President Saddam Hussein. That also means that the United States military forces will stay until the rebellion issue and others are resolved."

The period from 13 March until 5 April is an extremely tangled story characterized by an absence of unified leadership from either the coalition as a whole or from the United States itself—a demonstrable failure to recognize the continued importance of political communication to the general public as a means of galvanizing support for even a flawed policy and a failure to "get the story straight" among the U.S. administration's key players in their conversations with the press. Partly as a result of unclear information coming from the White House, there was often poor reporting about U.S. policy actions in the U.S. papers and particularly on the major networks.

John Major met with Bush in Bermuda on 16 March mainly to discuss the finalization of the UN permanent ceasefire that would eventually be signed on April 5. Britain was, by then, far more actively involved with its European allies and the Kurdish rebels than its American counterparts. In a phrase that encapsulates the value of analyzing political communication through the lens of the Positioning Hypothesis, one British official said the day before the Bermuda summit that Britain and the Allies were looking on at Iraq's destabilization with "helpless concern," a description that in two words positions the Allies as non-agentive, and thus not responsible, but morally engaged.[55]

Outside the British government, the opposition in the House of Commons was so complacent during this otherwise complicated and ambiguous time that it is perhaps not going too far to say they resembled scolded children, asking submissive questions and waiting for the day when their opposition to the Gulf War might fade sufficiently as to allow them to return to parliament.

On 21 March, for example, numerous questions were asked about defenses issue and the Gulf. The word "rebels' or "rebellion" or "helicopters" didn't make the HANSARD records, but this probing question about camels was given place of prominence:

> **Mr. Flynn**: To ask the Secretary of State for Defence what information he has on the number of camels (a) killed by allied bombing raids or ground attacks in Iraq and Kuwait and (b) that have died of asphyxiation from smoke from the burning oil wells in Kuwait.

The answer was "none."

Despite its general complacency, Labour was not completely silent. Until 28 March, Corbyn, Coombs, Fyfe, Graham Churchill, and Campbell-Savours posed a few questions during parliamentary sessions about the fate of the Kurds, the possibility of the use of chemical weapons, and whether the government had any plans on taking action. But these questions received no sustained discussions, answers were quick and often perfunctory, and not until the recess did articles begin to appear with any frequency about the efficacy or morality of British policy.

All told, the questioning of government by opposition was timid. Early in the month of March, concerns or simple inquiries were about returning troops, support groups for veterans, war costs, POWs, and the Kuwaiti oil fires. No questions were asked about the uprisings until 12 March when Mr. Corbyn (MP) asked the secretary of state for Foreign and Commonwealth Affairs: "what meetings have been held with representatives of Kurdish political parties from (a) Iran, (b) Iraq, (c) Syria and (d) Turkey; what support has been offered to them; and what is Her Majesty's Government's policy towards demands for Kurdish self- determination?" Mark Lennox-Boyd (parliamentary undersecretary of state for Foreign and Commonwealth Affairs) answered and set the policy that the government would stick to until early April. "We believe," he said, "that the Kurdish people should enjoy proper representation and respect for human rights in all of the countries in which they live. But as a signatory to the treaty of Lausanne of 1923, which established the present boundaries in the area, we cannot seek support for the establishment of a separate Kurdish state within these boundaries."[56]

Between 3 March and 27 March, roughly 1,200 words were spoken on the topic of the Kurds, Shiites, rebellions, or the immediate future of postwar Iraq. By the end of May, the total would be roughly 51,000. To say parliament came to the debate rather late would therefore be something of an understatement.[57]

The government was in fact meeting with Kurdish dissident groups, unlike their American counterparts. Mr. Sillars (MP) asked the secretary of state for Foreign and Commonwealth Affairs, "pursuant to his answer to the hon. Member for Liverpool, Mossley Hill (Mr. Alton) of 5 February, Official Report, column 82 , when Ministers last met representatives of the Kurdish nation." Lennox-Boyd replied that the minister had "met representatives from a number of Iraqi opposition groups, including a Kurdish representative, on 7 March." This was near the very beginning of the uprisings. These meetings kept questions about British policy alive in the House of Commons, but may have implied to the opposition that the government was informed, and that its policies were therefore based on sufficient information, thereby effectively silencing opposition as well.

The central tension that concerned the White House—but was not evident in their public statements or military actions—was the withdrawal of American troops. With the president's statement that the matter could not be accomplished until the helicopter problem was resolved—and his refusal to either retract the statement or explain it sufficiently—made the extraction of the troops deeply complicated from a public relations perspective. For the Bush administration, the future of Iraq would either be handled through clandestine support for an American supported coup—for which there is, as yet, no proof—or by some form of popular uprising, such as what was taking place at the time. Either way, the war was over, troops were to come home, and as explained earlier, Bush assumed the situation would take care of itself. What seemed like escalations for the benefit of the rebellion, therefore, can in fact be better understood as increased action *to support the withdrawal of U.S. troops.*

On 22 March, a U.S. F-15C shot down an Iraqi SU-22 over northern Iraq. On that same day, in a separate incident, another U.S. pilot intimidated the pilot of an Iraqi PC-9 (or possibly PC-7) to eject. The *Washington Post* saw all this as further proof of American support for the insurgency—which had no air force or surface-to-air defensive capability—and framed the story in this manner. The White House again denied that the incidents had anything to do with support for the rebellion and claimed that the existence of airborne Iraqi combat aircraft was a threat to U.S. ground forces. The problem was that the newspaper and television accounts that were following the America-supports-rebels storyline, forged earlier for lack of a clear alternative, were now able to incorporate exactly the same episodes into their analysis as the America-defends-and-withdraws-troops storymakers at the White House. *Both storylines were equally plausible based on exactly the same social episodes, but only one story had a compelling moral narrative.* As discussed earlier in reference to John Gardner's lessons about fiction writing, all stories need tension and profluence. Moral concerns, or matters of life and death, are the life-blood of the market-driven media.

On 22 March, a UN report on the status of Iraq after the war was published at an awful time for American public relations. It described the state of Iraq as "near-Apocalyptic" with the country relegated to a "Pre-Industrial Age."[58] This becomes one of the catalysts for the soon-to-escalate discussion of whether American use of force was proportional to the extent of the threat posed by Iraqi forces. The ensuing debate was met with furious opposition by military personnel who tried to explain that just because the coalition had won did not mean that it was predestined to have won, and that the overwhelming use of force was the reason for the success in the first place—along with superior strategy, training, doctrine, and deception techniques. The also tried to explain that the use of the term "overwhelming" only makes sense in retrospect anyway. This military argument, which was rather sound and is supported here, gained no purchase with those who saw nothing but a U.S. and allied refusal to account for Iraqi casualties and the present suffering of the Iraqi people. The Allies, in an Orwellian *volte face*, were now being blamed publicly for the consequences of Hussein's gambit to conquer the Arabian Peninsula.

The White House, however, was not budging on actual action against the helicopters, and its public pronouncements only added to confusion and helped keep the story alive. The typical reply of the White house to the questions about whether the helicopters were being used by the Iraqi military to murder vast numbers of civilians was generally to deny knowing whether it was actually happening. For example, at a press conference with Marlin Fitzwater, the White House spokesman, he was asked whether "[the Iraqis] continue to use those choppers to attack their own people . . ." to which Fitzwater replied, "I don't know the exact status of the helicopter use." This positioning move—to present oneself as not having information, and hence non-agentive, and therefore not responsible for action or inaction—was used regularly and to great effect by the White House. The one unanswerable question for the historian is why no reporter ever thought to follow up with, "well, why don't you please find out for us and tell us tomorrow?"

On 24 March, the explicit order *not* to engage the helicopters came down the chain of command.

The newspapers and television alike were now starting to ignore White House explanations about the events in Iraq and forge their own interpretations—the White House logic being too outlandish and incommensurate with what everyone was observing. The White House itself, probably on 20 March, realized that it had a communication strategy problem. As evidenced by the change in tone and answers from the spokesmen at the press conferences, the following observations were undoubtedly made: (1) the president and his staff were being grilled on the ambiguity of their Iraqi policy after the war particularly regarding the helicopters, (2) the media were relentlessly seeking some clarity to the matter and were drifting toward the conclusion that the White House was the last place in which that clarity could be found, and (3) the president knew he was not going to change his policy, but he did not want to say that because it would seem to contradict the statement he made in Ottawa about the helicopters. So the White House decided to embrace the ambiguity *as* the policy. The word that became the mantra was "murky."

Pete Williams would answer a question for the White House press corps on 21 March with, "[i]s our policy somewhat ambiguous? Yes."[59] "Murky" would make its lexical debut on 26 March. Fitzwater's characterization of U.S. policy toward the shooting down of helicopters as "[m]urky, murky, murky" did function to bring the matter to some rhetorical closure but only, as John Gardner would have it, through means of logical exhaustion, and then only once the refugee crisis began and the question of the helicopters became moot.[60]

And yet, the media could not accept the absence of a storyline because of their need to peg their stories to a central tension within an explicable policy. As one editorial phrased it, "[n]otwithstanding presidential disclaimers of interference, Washington is insisting that Iraq not use aircraft (or chemical weapons) against insurgents, enforcing its edict by shooting down errant aircraft and moving around heavy armor ominously. These gestures favor the insurgents."[61] It was precisely for this reason that the executive order not to shoot down the helicopters came as such a shock to the media and only just before it was implied to be a sucker policy by a war hero.

Brit Hume said that the "sudden" controversy concerns, "just what Joint Chiefs' Chairman Powell was told in this Oval Office phone call with General Schwarzkopf on the day the President called a halt to the fighting."[62] Schwarzkopf's comments alone could have been easily contained by the White House spin doctors, but it was just what the U.S. press needed, a split on the home front that allowed the confused reporting on and in Iraq to shift inward to the very topic of whether America was doing the right thing by staying out of the conflict.

Meanwhile, across the Atlantic, 26 March was again a magical day for the flow of events, because that day the BBC managed to get a reporter into the north of Iraq, in the Kurdish-held areas. The news item, however, was only reported by telephone, with no accompanying images, and the story only came fifth in the line-up.[63] Martin Shaw notes that from 26 March, "the crisis of the Kurdish rebellion and the issue of Western responsibility rose rapidly up the news agenda" in Britain. It would not be until 28 March, however, that the House of Commons would have anything meaningful to say on the matter.

From 26 March until the end of the month, refugees flowed southward, the southern fighting ceased entirely, and the Iraqis moved an estimated 150,000 troops to the north and retook the entire territory. Roman Popaduik, the White House press spokesman when Marlin Fitzwater was elsewhere, told reporters that there was confirmed use of the Iraqis using phosphorous bombs against "dissidents" in northern Iraq, which certainly meant combatants and civilians alike.[64]

Until 28 March, the word "helicopters" would not appear in HANSARD with reference to the rebellion. No voices would encourage British participation in the rebellion, and few would even bring up the subject. As Ann Clwyd explained:

> [i]t is an indictment of the House that, while the Gulf war was raging, we had almost daily statements on the conduct of the war, but since the perceived end of it, there has been not one statement on the situation inside Iraq or on the great troubles caused to its people. Were it not for the squalid maneuvering of the Government over the past few days, rushing through legislation which they think will bring them electoral gain, there should have been a statement on that situation.[65]

Clwyd would be sent to Iraq for a five-day fact-finding mission for the Commons. Her experience was hard and her conclusions lucid, but her less controlled moments revealed the extent of her frustration. On 16 April, she addressed the Commons: "Saddam Hussein is still killing, killing, killing in Iraq. This must be genocide, and it must be up to the international community to deal with it."[66]

On 28 March there was the first and in many ways only potentially influential discussion of the subject in parliament. Dale Campbell-Savour (MP) was the first to address the topic and the helicopters, and his arguments were built on and tied directly into the American domestic debate taking place in the media and press conferences:

> My principal and most immediate aim in raising this debate is to ask the Government to press the coalition forces to issue a statement at once insisting that the terms of the ceasefire are complied with, that those terms include the requirement that all Iraqi combat aircraft, whether fixed -wing or helicopters, are grounded and that, if Saddam Hussein does not immediately comply, those aircraft will be shot down without further notice.
>
> I remind the House that, in an interview broadcast last night the allied commander in the Gulf, General Schwarzkopf, told David Frost that Iraq was given permission to fly its helicopters only for civil, humanitarian and internal administrative purposes and that he had been lied to and "suckered" by Iraqi ceasefire negotiators as to their use.

The summation of his comments was presented in the following manner: "[w]e have the proven capability to stop these atrocities. If we fail once again to act, we cannot help but be implicated in Saddam Hussein's massacres. The coalition fought the war that made the uprising possible. President Bush himself called for the uprising. We cannot now wash our hands of the consequences."

Britain, however, could not have acted alone by this date even had it wanted to. According to Hella Pick, "British forces were the first to be taken out of the Gulf, and are now [16 April 1991] virtually all gone. The Americans too are leaving as rapidly as organization allows. There could still be isolated action to make good the warning against Iraqi helicopters and aircraft to operate north of the 36th parallel."[67]

Discussion continued for several hours on the matter of British policy toward the Kurds, Shiites, and the Iraqi people in general as they now suffered the consequences of a devastated infrastructure. The government stressed that it appreciated the concerns, but the absence of a UN Security Council resolution that specifically addressed the internal matters of Iraq prevented the government from any action on behalf of the rebels within Iraq. The most concise statement that day was made by Mark Lennox-Boyd (MP):

> The hon. Gentleman referred to the helicopter gunships that appear to be being used in Iraq in breach of the ceasefire. The terms of the present de facto ceasefire—we have not had the UN resolution—relate to the conflict with Iraq over Kuwait. It does not relate to the internal situation in Iraq. However, the coalition made it clear in the terms of the de facto ceasefire that fixed-wing aircraft should not be allowed to fly. As the hon. Gentleman knows, action has been taken to ensure that fixed- wing aircraft do not fly. However, while we deeply deplore the use of helicopter gunships, we have to accept that there is no Security Council resolution or mandate to deal with the action that the Iraqis have taken with helicopters. It is not a part of the ceasefire and it is not a part of a United Nations resolution. However distressing it is for me to say this to the hon. Gentleman, and however distressing it is for him to hear it, I think that he will accept that all of us have to recognize that a mandate from the United Nations is essential to underline and to give support to any hostile actions in the Gulf.

The opposition voices, while needling the government into blunt statements of amoral policy, were otherwise consistent in their inconsistency. Some raised the historical injustices done to the Kurds, others the suffering of innocents in Iraq. Others suggested that more immediate humanitarian aid should be sent everywhere. But there were no unified calls for British intervention, there was no unanimous party call for British action in the civil war. It therefore cannot be argued that parliament in any way was a strong pressure on John Major's government to intervene in the civil war. Likewise, because parliament would be in recess until Operation Safe Haven (the British name for Provide Comfort) was well under way, parliament as an institution was not an actor pressuring the government for the relief effort, though members of Parliament would make very public statements during the recess period.

In the United States, Democratic criticism of Bush's policies came very late as well. George Mitchell was on *Face the Nation*, a television program, on 31 March saying the United States should shoot down the helicopters. Al Gore appeared on CBS on 3 April opposing the lack of support to the rebels. But on 23 March his name was already being mentioned by the Democratic National Committee as a possible candidate, and two days later the *Guardian* would write, "[s]o far, Democratic leaders have supported President Bush in his balancing act. Senator Albert Gore, a possible Democratic presidential candidate, expressed his support yesterday for the continued presence of US troops for a 'limited amount of time to increase the chances of a structured peace.'" His later change in policy came at such a moment when his concerns could not possibly have been put into effect, considering the civil war had been lost and the refugee crisis had begun.

It is of more than passing interest that whereas the House of Commons seems fully informed about the American press—television images and programs, and the major U.S. papers are regularly referenced—the U.S. Congress makes virtually no references to non-American papers at all unless trying to make weak arguments about "world opinion." This was unfortunate if for no other reason than the British were often first with information about Iraq both on television (CBS regularly relied on Britain's ITN) and in print (Martin Woolacott, again, being one of the first into the north to report on the Kurdish rebellion for the *Guardian*).

Further south, where the killing had ended and troops were simply bored, the mood was different and the newspaper accounts told a different story. One article said,

> the prevailing sentiment can be seen in soldiers' T-shirts that read, "If I Were An Iraqi POW, I'd Be Home By Now," or the "Free Kuwait" signs on which the name of the liberated emirate has been crossed out and replaced with the phrase, "US Servicemen Trapped in Saudi Arabia." Airmen "lampooned a new safety slogan—Not One More Life—by scribbling on their billet doors, Not One More Day."

Lt. Col. Robert Purple, a base commander, was asked if they should get involved in the fighting. His answer summed up the thoughts of many in the southern region. "The world can't make up its mind, so why should a serviceman at Kharj want to? . . . We're in 'Desert Calm,' waiting for political acts by the United Nations and others."[68]

George Bush took this moment to go on vacation. Though well-earned, the timing was inauspicious at best and the setting could not have been better scripted by Democrats in Hollywood. Like the ill-fated election of Gary Hart in 1984, who was photographed with his mistress on a boat ironically named the *Monkey Business*, journalists went on immediate metaphor alert when George Bush smiled and waved from a fishing boat actually named the *Backlash*.[69] On his way to Florida, a reporter asked his response to Mitchell's call for shooting down the helicopters: "Always glad to have his opinion. Glad to hear from him."

Beyond the domestic politics and the moral considerations, other actors were making major policy moves that the American newspapers noted but did not rely on to tie the threads of U.S. policymaking together. The UN Security Council was now in session trying to negotiate among themselves a permanent ceasefire agreement that would bring the war to an end. It involved the drafting of Iraq's responsibilities in return for the ceasefire, such items as destroying its weapons of mass destruction, denouncing its claims on Kuwait, and allowing in weapons inspectors—all actions that Iraq would subsequently thwart in the years to follow.

France and Turkey were taking the lead, by 2 April, by proposing a resolution in support of Kurdish refugees. Turkey's overwhelming concern was that they neither enter nor come to reside in Turkey itself. France's motivations are less clear, but Jonathan Randal suggests that it was the result of the prime minister's wife, Danielle Mitterand, who personally championed the cause of the Kurds to her husband.[70] Be that as it may, the next day, Britain and Belgium would also sign on to some kind of proposal on behalf of the Kurds. This left the United States in an awkward position of effectively refusing to support a resolution backed by its major coalition partners and three NATO allies. In the end, Resolution 688 was sponsored by Britain, France, Belgium, and the United States, and passed. It mentioned the Kurds for the first time ever in a UN document, and was the first (and at the time of writing, remains the only) resolution by the Security Council to authorize humanitarian assistance within the borders of a country without its permission, in order to promote international peace and security.

Just before the resolution was passed, Bush would say, "[y]ou haven't seen the call for any . . . incidentally from any of [the coalition partners] for the United States to go in and use this superior military might to try to sort out this civil war."[71] True enough, none of the countries now pressing for some aid to the Kurds and Shiites had made such calls earlier, when the tide of battle might, ostensibly, have been altered. Whereas the diplomatic moves still did not press for military support of the rebellion, as Bush said, the Western coalition partners, including Turkey, were now changing their position on "internal intervention" into Iraq. This major diplomatic change, coming as it did during the height of the negotiations that would allow U.S. troops to return home—the administration's highest priority—did not receive a fraction of the attention that "pressure from the media" was beginning to garner as the explanation for the changes in U.S. action that were to come about in only two more days.

In Britain, while John Major was out of the country but paying close attention to the events and the political winds alike, pressure began to mount for military action from an all-party group of MPs, who jointly condemned President Saddam's "brutal massacre" of the Kurds. The MPs said the British and American governments should stop standing "idly and callously by."[72] As the *Guardian* reported it: "The MPs called for the UN Security Council to discuss the plight of the Kurds. All humanitarian aid possible should be rendered through the UN, and Turkey should open its borders, subject to guarantees of help from the UN. Allied forces should announce their intention to shoot down any Iraqi aircraft."[73]

Major's position as prime minister was not yet politically solid, having come to the position after a Tory-led political coup against Margaret Thatcher, and he came to the Gulf War late, taking over after Kuwait had been invaded. One headline in the London *Times* described Major as "still an uncertain political product, putty ready to be shaped."[74] An all-party group of MPs might well have been able to further upset that uncertain position. And soon enough, Margaret Thatcher herself would begin to needle him.

That spilt in the Conservative party itself, now under pressure from both the Labour and an all-party group of MPs, came on Wednesday 3 April when Thatcher said that the Kurds "need help and need it now." John Major's response was unfortunate: "'I do not recall asking the Kurds to mount this particular insurrection," he replied. This exchange among Tories, rather than from opposition Labour leaders, came at a highly coincidental moment.[75]

The refugee crisis was now reaching startling dimensions, the complete collapse of the rebel forces in the north were only days away, and the UN permanent ceasefire was being finalized. It is important to remember that the end of the civil war was in no way connected to the signing of the permanent ceasefire. That the rebellion collapsed a few days before the signing of the UN resolutions being passed was *sheer coincidence*. Had the fighters had the capability, they would certainly have fought longer. This coincidence had a striking illusionary effect over the reporting of policy changes. After the resolutions were signed, Western support for the refugees, but not the fighters, quickly materialized in response to domestic pressures for John Major, and international pressure on George Bush. Because of Britain's key position of being a member of the Security Council, a strong ally of the United States, a member of the European Community, and also suffering from a fragile leadership, minority voices in Britain—backed with wide media coverage of the refugee crisis and the human costs of non-action—changed not only British policy, but strongly influenced the Bush decision to act on a humanitarian basis for the Kurds.

From now through the 15 April decision to deploy ground troops, Thatcher's voice would only rise to fill what some in Britain were beginning to consider a moral power vacuum. "It should not be beyond the wit of man to get planes there with tents, with food, with warm blankets. It is not a question of legal niceties. We should go now—it is a real mission of mercy." It may not be going too far that the implication was that Major was both witless and merciless.[76]

Phase 3: Airdrops and Aid

The rebellion was crushed, and now the refugees were fleeing the approaching Iraqi army and taking refuge deep in the Turkish mountains in the north and the Zagros mountains in Iran. As with the civil war itself, the coalition and the international organizations were caught completely unprepared. The entire situation from 3 March through 5 April was summed up well by an Iraqi opposition leader: "Everyone was counting on a palace coup and when that didn't materialize, we were abandoned," said Talib Shibib. "No one was prepared to support a popular revolt." Why the coalition expected the palace coup to begin with remains the biggest mystery of the post–Gulf War story, and remains a central concern about intelligence gathering and covert operations regarding present day Iraq.[77]

A poll was taken by Gallup that unfortunately was conducted from 4 to 6 April, and therefore straddled the April 5 announcement by

Bush that the United States would start initiating airdrops, which very likely skewed their findings. With an alleged margin of error of 3 percent, they nevertheless found that 78 percent of 1,002 people surveyed favored "providing food and medicinal supplies to the rebels" (the term refugee was not used for some reason); 57 percent favored "using US aircraft to shoot down Iraqi helicopters and other aircraft being used against the rebels"; 51 percent favored "using US aircraft to destroy Iraqi tanks and artillery being used against the rebels"; 40 percent favored "providing guns and military assistance to the rebels"; and 29 percent favored "using US ground forces to fight Iraqi military forces being used against the rebels." Bush's approval rating had now fallen from 92 percent (in a poll taken from 28 February to 2 March) to 78 percent. And 56 percent of Americans polled said that the United States should have pressed the fight to Baghdad and removed Saddam Hussein; 36 percent disagreed.[78]

When the refugee crisis began, Turkey immediately closed its borders. Recalling their experience in 1988, when thousands of Kurds had fled into Turkey and then remained there—causing trouble via the Kurdistan Worker's Party, or PKK, and draining the Turkish economy—Ozal now wanted no part of the million or more Kurds now dragging themselves up the mountains. The catch phrase that would emerge at the White House, in Britain, in Senate reports, and in the newspapers was that Turkey was "unable or unwilling" to take in the refugees beyond the thin border area.[79] Ozal wanted international aid for them, a relieving of Turkey's financial burden, and the repatriation of the entire population. He was not going to allow the Kurdish "problem" in Anatolia to be exacerbated.

The importance of Turkey's needs in the refugee crisis as being even greater than the needs of the refugees themselves is supported by the fact that by mid-April, almost twice as many refugees were entering Iran as were entering Turkey, and yet the scale of support to the latter group was vastly larger.

On 5 April, the day of the decision to begin Operation Provide Comfort, Bush, Colin Powell, Dick Cheney (the secretary of Defense), and Brendt Scowcroft (the National Security advisor) were all at a hotel in California attending the fiftieth anniversary of the USO with Bob Hope.[80] They were informed that Resolution 688 was passed by the UN Security Council and was path-breaking. On that day, Bush made a policy announcement that by all accounts was not well prepared, although it was not the off-the-cuff comment made on 13 March about the helicopters. After consultation with his advisers,

Bush would address the nation and state that the United States was now undertaking a new operation and a new policy:[81]

> I have directed a major new effort be undertaken to assist Iraqi refugees. Beginning this Sunday, U.S. Air Force transport planes will fly over northern Iraq and drop supplies of food, blankets, clothing, tents, and other relief-related items for refugees and other Iraqi civilians suffering as a result of the situation there. I want to emphasize that this effort is prompted only by humanitarian concerns. We expect the Government of Iraq to permit this effort to be carried out without any interference.

Numerous scholars, as indicated earlier, have suggested this was a reversal of prior U.S. policy statements by the White House. That is not my reading of the record. By 5 April, several events coincided that made a policy change logical and explicable without resort to blaming media pressure. By this date, a permanent ceasefire had now been signed providing the possibility for an exit of U.S. troops from the region. The UN, under whose auspices the Desert Storm was con-ducted, had now officially ended that operation with the supposed consent of Iraq. Furthermore, the civil war in Iraq was effectively over, though reports of some fighting—what are euphemistically called "mop-up" operations—were being conducted by the Republican Guard. The consequence of the failed uprisings was the refugee crisis of some two million people pouring into neighboring Turkey, which was keeping its borders closed, or else keeping the refugees on a thin strip of Turkish land high in the mountains along the Iraqi border. With the backing of France and Great Britain, Turkey was pleading with the Americans to resolve the crisis, and it was becoming clear that only the Americans had the airlift capability to provide relief.

With the ceasefire signed and Resolution 688 passed, Bush contacted the military and provided a clear objective, but one that had not been planned prior to the ordering of the operation. Dubbed Operation Provide Comfort by the Americans, this airlift and later ground-supported mission would be the largest humanitarian mission ever launched. Colin Powell described Bush's stated political objec-tives of Operation Provide Comfort as being: "an interim measure designed to meet an immediate, penetrating humanitarian need. Our long-term objectives remain the same—for Iraqi Kurds, and indeed, for all Iraqi refugees, wherever they are, to return home and to live in peace, free from oppression, free to live their lives."[82]

During the Kurdish uprisings, Colin Powell was in almost daily contact with General John Galvin who was the commander-in-chief

(CINC) of the U.S. European Command based out of Germany, whose operational orbit includes the Middle East. According to taped interviews with both Powell and Galvin, Rudd noted that they "maintained a dialogue on the possible consequences [of the uprisings]" as the Kurdish revolt 'flared and failed."[83] Galvin initially chose General Jamerson of the U.S. Airforce (USAF) as the first commander of the task force who was then deployed to Turkey in early April, making it appear that "the Air Force would be the key player in the operation and his primary officers were all Air Force Officers."[84] Later—presumably after 16 April—Galvin assigned an army general to assume control of the task force as U.S. special forces were the first ground troops involved in the humanitarian relief operations. Notable was that Galvin, though in regular contact with Powell prior to the 5 April decision by Bush, nevertheless was operationally unprepared for the initiation of the humanitarian relief operation, lending credence to the conclusion that Bush had not prepared the military for this contingency and that the possibility arose only in early April.

This would imply that the media pressure that evidently mounted prior to 5 April was not a major consideration on Bush's operational plans for the region, as no military preparations were made during this period.

The events that led to the 5 April decision to begin Operation Provide Comfort began not in the United States but in Europe. According to the journalist Hella Pick, the British policy evolved in the following manner:[85]

> There were suggestions yesterday that the notion of emergency measures to help Iraq's Kurdish population had been hatched up by officials while the war was still on. Persecution of the Kurds is said to have been predicted. With the realisation that Turkey could not cope with a huge influx of Kurds, an area of flat land in northern Iraq had been identified.
>
> But while this may have been on a Downing Street file, the Prime Minister first came to grips with the idea on Sunday. It came not from his own staff or the Foreign Office, but from Turkey's president, Turgut Ozal.
>
> Towards last weekend, as Washington and London realised that Saddam Hussein was chasing hundreds of thousands of Kurds out of Iraq, Mr Ozal received a series of messages from President Bush and Mr Major insisting that Turkey must keep its frontiers open.
>
> President Ozal insisted that Turkey could not cope. Then, on Sunday [7 April], he declared on American television that the only solution was to create an enclave in northern Iraq, where the Kurds would be safe.

A private message was sent to the Prime Minister. The essence of President Ozal's concept was that the Kurds must be able to go back to their homes in Iraq. Turkey appears to have assured Britain that it was prepared to join any enforcement action authorised by the UN Security Council.

On 8 April, the European Community collectively called on the UN to create a haven in northern Iraq to protect the Kurds from repression.[86] The UN Security Council then took up the plan the next day and Britain's representative, Sir David Hannay, said the idea won "a lot of support," and U.S. representative Thomas Pickering told the UN that "the general idea, including a safe haven or area of tranquility" is one that "matches our hopes."

By the middle of the second week of April, the EC, the UN, the United Kingdom, France, and Turkey were all now pressing for further concerted action on behalf of the refugees, if the means was still unclear. Far from this being pressure on a reluctant U.S. military, the U.S. armed forces were starting to become aware of what this operation really involved and were starting to develop a consensus that what was needed was ground force intervention. This recommendation by the military to the White House effectively removed the administration's concern of a Vietnam-like situation where the military would be dragged into a new job through "mission creep." Instead, the military requested to go.

According to Rudd, "General John Galvin, Commander of NATO and all American forces in Europe (US European Command) stated that he perceived the need for intervention almost from the beginning of the operation. After several phone conversations with General Colin Powell, Chairman of the Joint Chiefs of Staff, a consensus developed among the senior American military leaders that intervention was necessary."[87]

This did not prompt an order from the top to prepare for the operation. Rudd explains that, "when it became obvious early in April that relief supplies parachuted to the refugees in the mountains, could not correct the causes of the refugee flight, senior American military leaders reviewed the situation and made recommendations to the civilian leadership."[88] However, when the decision was made on 16 April to send in ground troops, military leaders had little time to prepare for the action, although they reached some consensus that it would be needed very early in the operation.[89]

Rudd explained the problem:[90]

Shalikashvili would have to maintain air superiority over northern Iraq; sustain an airlift of supplies,; support the relief workers, soldiers and civilians in the mountains; supervise an intervention; refurbish the civil infrastructure in northern Iraq; and balance the support for everyone. It was a task of multiple dimensions taking place simultaneously with virtually no planning or preparation. There was also little precedent for such an undertaking. As Potter prepared to move the refugees from the mountains, Garner had to create a place for them to go.

With public support for the idea at home, Congressional support, lingering criticism over Bush's prior non-actions, military support, and the *de facto* result of a unified Iraq under Hussein's leadership, Bush would have had to go *against* every significant actor in American and international coalition politics *not* to have ordered the ground intervention.

France originally prompted the meeting of the EC to discuss its failure to respond forcefully to Iraqi invasion of Kuwait, and during that time, the EC countries began to formulate the idea of support for the Kurds. Interestingly, the *New York Times*, having now offered domestic political explanations for American and British action, nevertheless felt inclined to then say that all the European countries themselves chose to act because of "enormous pressure" in the previous ten days from "intense coverage of the plight of the Kurds" that has "brought the problem to the top of the agenda."[91] The myth of media power, though not created here, was being further fueled in the crucible of coincidence.

Later that day at the UN, Washington expressed lukewarm support for the safe haven idea; USSR and China were also hesitant. Iraq, calling it a "'European conspiracy," flat out rejected any establishment of such a region. The EC countries thereafter scaled back their suggestions, but continued to maneuver for a humanitarian solution. The primary concern of the United States was that the safe haven would become a sort of Gaza Strip—a permanent refugee camp sowing discontent and becoming a base for operations against Turkey and Iraq. In the words of Neil Kinnock, the Labour leader, the plan carried a risk of creating "a permanent refugee enclave, of which there are already so many in the world." The Americans clearly agreed, and Major maintained the concept but shifted the legal rhetoric.

When the policy decision was made on 5 April, Robert Kimmitt, undersecretary of state for Political Affairs, and other State Department officials met with the French and Turkish ambassadors to coordinate UN relief efforts and specifically to urge Turkey to keep the border with Iraq open.[92] On 7 April, Saddam Hussein declared victory in the civil war, which he earlier described as the "[g]ravest conspiracy in [Iraq's] contemporary history"[93] and then ridiculed the Western relief effort as being an "ostentatious dropping of crumbs." Iraqi Foreign Minister Saadun Hamadi said, "outsiders were fabricating and exaggerating the refugee problem." ABC News—in a tortured attempt at objectivity—chose not to report this as a propagandistic lie but rather that "Mr. Hamadi has apparently not been to the Iraqi border with Iran where ABC's Forrest Sawyer has been today."[94]

Though Saddam had already declared himself victor of both the Gulf War and civil war, the killing didn't stop. "Kurdish and Shi'ite rebel spokesmen accused President Saddam Hussein's troops of using helicopter gunships to attack all escape routes to the Turkish and Iranian frontiers, killing or wounding thousands in a new massacre."[95] The position of the United States and Britain, however, was as firm as ever that neither would be drawn into fighting in the country. "We have no intention of sending any combat forces into Iraq. We are in the process of pulling out of Iraq once the resolution, cease-fire resolution is implemented."

Phase 4: "Operation Major Triumph": The Introduction of Ground Troops

On 16 April, George Bush announced that the United States would send ground troops to the refugee zone to aid in the relief effort and to resettle the Kurds in their homes in Iraq. The policy announcement was made at 18:04, from the White House briefing room. Bush made the following statement about their motives:[96]

> The Government of Turkey, along with U.S., British, and French military units, and numerous international organizations, have launched a massive relief operation. But despite these efforts, hunger, malnutrition, disease, and exposure are taking their grim toll. No one can see the pictures or hear the accounts of this human suffering—men, women, and most painfully of all, innocent children—and not be deeply moved.
> It is for this reason that this afternoon, following consultations with Prime Minister Major, President Mitterand, President Ozal of Turkey, Chancellor Kohl this morning, U.N. Secretary-General Perez de Cuellar, I'm announcing a greatly expanded and more ambitious relief effort. The approach is quite simple: If we cannot get adequate food, medicine, clothing, and shelter to the Kurds living in the mountains along the Turkish-Iraq border, we must encourage the Kurds to move to areas in northern Iraq where the geography facilitates rather than frustrates such a large-scale relief effort.

It was a needed political victory for John Major and an obvious victory for the Kurds. The *Guardian*'s Andrew Rawnsley would call the Tory rally of support "Operation Major Triumph" as the party hurled accolades at their party leader to shore up political support.

The decision came after telephone exchanges with Major, Presidents Kohl and Mitterand, and other key allies, which delighted Downing Street as the prime minister had appeared isolated earlier as a result of insufficient enthusiasm for his safe haven idea.[97] " 'We nudged and nudged the Americans, and suddenly, on Tuesday, they came like a rocket,' is how a British diplomat described it."[98] Earlier that day, the British war cabinet had been convened for the first time since the ceasefire, presumably to discuss British troop deployments.

What was driving this fervent round of international policymaking was a fear that these refugees would permanently reside in Turkey, create massive political upheaval within Turkish politics, and would eventually become a politicized entity possibly seeking statehood in parts of NATO-member Turkey. Thousands of lives were being saved, and the United States does deserve recognition for doing what no one else could have done. However, the successes of the operation still did not make this a morally driven policy initiative. The decision was buttressed by Bush's position now as a "bad guy," the unity of the international coalition to "do something," the Congress, even by the U.S. military's pressure to act, and the geopolitical necessities of action that did not run against the moral arguments being made. Had moral action been *contradictory* to other U.S. interests, and no other superior explanation for U.S. policymaking were available, and if the Bush administration had in fact *changed* its policies rather than created new policies to affect new realities *without* leaving the old policies in place to manage the old realities, we may have been able to argue for a CNN Effect. But this did not happen.

Major, meanwhile, was being absolutely badgered by conservative members of his own Tory party and was receiving jabs from the Labour opposition for his inaction in the face of the Kurdish crisis and his seemingly aloof responses to Kurdish suffering. The *Guardian* reported the Tory assault that began the first week of April and was now redoubling its efforts:

> The Prime Minister last night came under an unprecedented and ferocious attack from a fiercely pro-Thatcher group over his handling of the continuing Gulf crisis. The Bruges Group, which includes several Conservative MPs and which supported Mrs Thatcher's anti-federalist approach to the EC, accused him of 'gesture politics' and claimed that he was wobbling in his approach to the Kurdish refugees' plight." "Was the price for the overthrow of Mrs Thatcher paid for with the blood of thousands of innocent Iraqis?" the Bruges Group said in a statement.[99]

Thatcher herself, though publicly criticizing Major's policy, did not back the rather slanderous comments: "I had no knowledge of the statement issued by the Bruges Group and I thoroughly disagree with it. I loyally support President Bush and Prime Minister Major in their task," Mrs Thatcher said.[100] All the same, accusations of "wimp" and spiritlessness were splashed in various newspapers that often revelled in their propensity toward literary hooliganism. Though the Bruges Group came under extreme abuse from very senior Tories and in some manner backfired, if measured by their reduced standing following the mud *fest*, the panicked response by the Tories to some of their own having gone too far was indicative of something else. The something else in question was the concern over whether Major could hold the party together and survive the next election.

The aid effort was now going, but was not going well. Rough estimates during the first two weeks of the refugee crisis put the daily death rate for the Kurds at 20 per 10,000—somewhere between 900 and 1,600 people per day, with perhaps 80 percent of them children. By the week of 11 April, researchers for Doctors Without Frontiers said the figure had dropped to 13 per 10,000. At the end of April, the group said the toll was down to 3 to 6 per 10,000.[101] The most vulnerable, the children, were the first to die, many not far from television cameras. In the first week of April, camera crews and journalists, hungry for pictures largely denied during March, traipsed across the hills of Cukurza. The Turks were regularly cited for less-than-hospitable activities toward the Kurds, and few minced words about how they felt about the swell of sudden concern for the refugees. "You Westerners are so romantic," said one Turkish field commander. "First it's the whales, then the turtles, and now the Kurds. I told an American soldier: 'You threw bombs on these people in Iraq and killed them. Now you throw aid on them and still kill them.'"

The comment was sadly true, though the people were not the same. American and British aid pallets were landing squarely on the Kurds and crushing them to death. The senior Turkish army commander, who was not unsympathetic but rather quite frustrated, told a *Guardian* reporter, "'I am a soldier. You cannot drop heavy pallets on a mountainside crowded with starving, exhausted people and not expect casualties. We gave the Americans the co-ordinates, the locations, and they ignore them. They drop the aid where they see people.'"[102]

Where the Turkish soldier saw arrogance, Rudd saw operational complexity. Their observations, however, were identical.

Airdrops to the Kurds met the most immediate need of delivering food and blankets, but if it was the expedient method it was also inefficient and inflexible. Parachute drops are difficult to target under the best of conditions and the rugged, steep mountains along the Iraqi border combined with high winds and changing weather patterns of the region hardly qualified as the best of conditions. The bundles often missed their intended landing areas, water bottles ruptured, and occasionally refugees were hit causing injuries and several fatalities.[103]

There were more problems. American servicemen, in a time honored tradition from World War II, handed out chocolate Hershey bars to Kurdish children as an act of kindness. Kurdish children, however, had been taught by their parents that one should always return an act of kindness in kind. Having nothing to give the servicemen, the kids scoured the countryside for gifts. What they found was hand grenades, landmines, and cluster bombs. U.S. personnel, after the first incidents, were instructed to end the charity immediately.[104] The number of children killed or maimed from this practice is uncertain, but causalities were often reported.

The Hershey bar episodes were a metaphor for the problems Operation Provide Comfort was having. In aggregate, people were being saved. In the overall assessment, it was a brilliant military campaign and achieved its goals. However, not unlike a work of French Impressionism, the closer one looked at the picture, the less harmonious it appeared. While the press was generally helpful, which was also the opinion of field officers at all levels who believed the media presence aided the relief effort, they also illuminated the inexperience of the international community and the military in handling the problems. Tents were positioned in traditional "diamond" configurations to make the best use of space and resources, but the Kurds moved them to accommodate family structures and social organization. "Three seater" latrines were dug, but the Kurds refused to use one while someone else was in an adjoining unit, leading to a waste of up to two-third of the resources. Beyond starvation level, Kurds refused to eat many of the foods being sent, including corn—which was considered a food for animals, akin to cat food—and most pork products common to "MREs" or "meals ready to eat." Aid, generously donated by well-meaning people globally, often complicated the distribution system, which needed specific things at certain moments. Rudd described it as a "push" system whereby the field receives what headquarters wants to send rather than a "pull" system, whereby the headquarters provides what the field requests. Fights broke out regularly among the Kurds for resources, and in the eyes of U.S. and British soldiers, men sat around doing nothing while the women collected food and water though in ill health. Turkish soldiers were accused of abusing the Kurds and looting aid. As one U.S. soldier put it, "If you haven't got a strong man in your family, you're finished."[105]

At 13:29 in the early afternoon of 11 April, Bush stood at the South Portico of the White House with EC Council President Jacques Santer and Commission President Jacques Delors to hold a press conference. Bush's concern over coalition fragmentation was evident, as was his obvious dissatisfaction that the U.S. media was not drawing a distinction between the relief effort and support for the Kurdish insurrection.[106]

> We're going to do what we need for humanitarian relief. And there is no difference between the United Kingdom and the United States, and there's no difference between the EC and the United States, and there's no difference between the UN Secretary-General and the United States on this question. So, I hope that you will understand that . . . . And P.S., I am not going to involve any American troops in a civil war in Iraq. They are not going to be going in there to do what some of my severest critics early on now seem to want me to do. I want these kids to come home. And that's what's going to happen. And we are going to do what is right by these refugees, and I think the American people expect that, and they want that. But I don't think they want to see us bogged down in a civil war by sending in the 82d Airborne or the 101st or the 7th Cavalry. And so, I want to get that matter cleared up.

On 21 April, the British Royal Marines, fresh from northern Ireland and trained in low intensity conflict (LIC), entered Silopi in Turkey. Two days later, they would be joined by troops and doctors from Belgium, Canada France, Germany, Italy, the Netherlands, and New Zealand. Once fully initiated, the aid effort was a multilateral operation aided by France and Britain at the initial stages and led by the United States. At the height of the operation, at the end of April, the mission was composed of over 23,000 troops, all from Western countries (see figure 4.1).

While approximately 500 refugees a day were still dying in the Turkish and Iraqi mountains, Jalal Talabani met with Saddam Hussein to discuss the "democratization" of Iraq, a subject that had been going on for several weeks since Hussein promised that Iraq would become a democratic society.[107] It was then taken as arrant nonsense by the White House and Whitehall alike—a conclusion borne out in the subsequent decade. Though claims to install a democracy were

Service	US military participation	Troops
Army		6,119
Air Force		3,588
Marine Corps		1,875
Navy		734
Total		**12,136**

Country	Coalition partners' participation	Troops
Australian		75
Belgium		150
Canada		120
France		2,141
Germany		221
Italy		1,183
Luxembourg		43
Netherlands		1,020
Portugal		19
Spain		602
Turkey		1,160
United Kingdom		*4,192*
Total		**10,926**

Figure 4.1 Troop deployments for Operation Provide Comfort, 1991

clearly absurd, the indication that Hussein may have been willing to make major concessions was not entirely outside the realm of possibility. According to the KDP spokesman, Hoshiar Zebari, the Kurds took the offer because they did not see any clear evidence of U.S. policy leading to Saddam's replacement by "a more decent regime."[108] To take his offers at face value without international guarantees, however, was naïve. Talabani did his cause few favors by physically embracing Saddam Hussein like a brother before the cameras, and making such statements as: "I have never seen in all these times such a kind of spirit . . . positive spirit, as of the kind of positive climate and positive ground for negotiations between Kurdish people and the Iraqi government."[109] In the Middle East, such statements are intended to generally communicate the attitude of the participants at a moment in time and to signal a willingness to negotiate. In the West, however, such statements are taken as analytical descriptions of events and carry implications about future action. To a

Middle Eastern ear, it was a statement of hope and possibility, but to the Western ear the statement sounded like sheer lunacy.

The plummeting media coverage, coupled with record low pressure since the refugee crisis began at the beginning of the month, demonstrated that the media had collectively decided that now—whatever the prior fault of the Americans and British—it was their problem.

Phase 5: The Expansion of Kurdish Safe Havens

The first week of May saw a dramatic reduction of refugee deaths along the Turkish border and a general stabilization of the relief effort. Nevertheless, there remained two major political problems and two logistical problems. In the first camp was the muted conflict with the UN, which insisted that Iraq's permission was needed before the people could be resettled. The UN High Commissioner for Refugees (UNHCR) was critical of the intentions of Operation Provide Comfort because they viewed the efforts to return the Kurds to their home as a form of "refoulment" or the forced return of refugees. Likewise, it was illegal to establish a security zone for the Kurds unless Iraq—meaning Saddam—gave his permission. The second political problem remained Turkey. Ozal was not going to accept a million Kurdish refugees into Turkey and he was not going to accept the permanent settlement of a "Gaza Strip" refugee zone, which would inevitably become a base for terrorist operations against the country. The Kurds needed to be resettled, but there was no international mechanism to do so.

Then there were the logistical concerns. Though the Kurdish leadership was supportive of resettlement in principle, they had political motives of their own for encouraging a permanent coalition presence to protect them against Iraqi aggression. The Iraqis still had four under-strength divisions in the region, and scattered reports of fighting and killings continued. Such cover would provide them with negotiating power with Saddam and would strengthen their standing among the population. That population, meanwhile, was quite reasonably scared about possible massacres by Iraqi troops once the Western forces left. They wanted guarantees. The trouble was, the UNHCR had 2,000 personnel worldwide, and Provide Comfort fielded 23,000 troops, many of them well trained and with vast resources. The UN was simply incapable of providing for those people. "We have become part of a great gamble," explained Sadako Ogata, head of the UNHCR. "We have been drafted in as heroic partners, without financial assurance and without physical back-up." Prince Sadruddin was even more succinct: "The allies have passed the buck to the UN without taking into account the costing and the logistics of providing relief for the refugees."[110]

The operational questions then became, how would the coalition coax the Kurds out of the mountains on the one hand, and how would they provide for their protection and safety on the other. It was a complex problem and had never been faced before.

One of the keys to the riddle was Dohuk. Dohuk was the northernmost capital of the three Kurdish provinces of Iraq. Thousands of the refugees were from there. It soon became clear that without taking Dohuk and securing it, the refugee crisis could not be solved. The trouble was it was below the 36th parallel and the effective control of Provide Comfort. Taking it would require the occupation of a much larger part of Iraqi territory and an executive policy decision.

On 7 May, Major General Jay Garner had two Marine battalions closing in on Dohuk. Generals Corwin and Abizaid were in command. "Garner, having confidence in his men, wanted to take it," said Rudd.[111] Rudd explained that General Shalikashvili, in charge of all troops in northern Iraq, while recognizing the operational possibilities, also knew there were larger strategic considerations. Shalikashvili therefore had U.S. Colonel Naab talk to the Iraqi colonel in charge of forces in Dohuk. Rudd reports that Naab concluded that the Iraqis' number one consideration was getting allied troops out of Iraq and would do whatever it took to make that happen, including repatriating the refugees. It was a further insult to Iraq for the allies—whom they could not possibly repel—to take another large section of the country. Shalikashvili discussed taking Dohuk with General Galvin, who in turn brought it up with General Colin Powell in Washington.[112] Powell explained that the National Security Council didn't understand the operational aspects of what was happening and that it was they who called a halt to the southern expansion.

This decision to halt, which came from Washington, was a problem. It signaled weakness on the part of the coalition and hesitation. On the next day, Iraqi Colonel Nashwan handed a note to Naab saying, "the Iraqi government would view any effort to enter Dohuk as dangerous and a threat to Iraqi authority."[113] There was now a crisis in Dohuk largely created by the National Security Council.

By 7 May, Rudd writes, "[U.S. Lieutenant Colonel] Abizaid cautiously maneuvered his companies closer to Dohuk and by 7 May, [General Jay] Garner had two American battalions closing on the town. with the full confidence of Corwin and Abizaid, Garner wanted to take it." Recognizing that Dohuk was a major regional center with political significance, Shalikashvili discussed it with his commander, Galvin, who in turn contacted Powell in Washington.

At that moment, not one but two possible scenarios had been prepared to take Dohuk by force. It was the last major, planned military action, point of political contention, and possible moment for battle fatalities. Iraqi forces reoccupied Dohuk on 10 April and reinforced positions outside the town. Saddam Hussein then went on Iraqi television and stated that Iraq would fight to defend Dohuk. The Iraqi rejection of a coalition presence in Dohuk forced Perez, the UN secretary general, to call for a UNSC resolution to handle the matter.[114] All this made some people in Washington uncomfortable with Jay Garner, who was treated as bringing on the crisis. However, it was not Garner who was to blame for the predicament, but the National Security Council for reining in the military before they were able to take the necessary action for fear of a political fallout. The irony was they succeeded in creating the problem they wished to avoid by demonstrating their hesitancy to the Iraqis.

During the operational "pause" the Iraqis moved armor and artillery into the town. The new strike scenario, drafted by Whitehead, started with air superiority and suppressing fire on Dohuk, which was intended to render the Iraqis 80 percent ineffective within forty-five minutes. The ground forces would then move in. The possibility of military confrontation was clear and present, but the press was uninterested.

In the end, Naab was the person who managed to finesse the problem by successfully playing on the ultimate Iraqi desire to see the coalition leave. Dohuk was eventually taken without force, the refugees were resettled, and Operation Provide Comfort began to end. The UN, though generally unprepared for the task, was forced into taking it over with its limited staff based out of Geneva at the UNHCR, and the troubles in northern Iraq began to fade.

The Iraqi Civil War was never engaged by the coalition forces, and the relief effort began only after the Turks pressured the British and French into taking up the Kurdish case, which in turn brought the Americans around. The United States, being the only force on earth with the logistical capability of making Provide Comfort, took up the responsibility reluctantly, and it was the U.S. military that took the lead once they appeared on the ground. It may never be possible to know the proportions of anger and gratitude the Kurds may have felt about those who came to their aid so late. But the media chose their ending. As coverage drifted off to a thin memory, pressure evaporated, and the eye of the media turned their gaze elsewhere, what was needed was a moral ending. It was provided by a Kurd named Ahmed.

"We saw in our lives only bad people," he told one newspaper on 29 May, "the terrorist men of the Baath Party. When we see kind people like the Americans, we are very surprised. We see there is humanity in the world. We will not forget this," he said. "We will never forget."[115]

REFLECTIONS ON THE EVENTS

The Iraqi Civil War and the refugee crisis that followed is among the most important and under-studied events in the Middle East since the end of the Cold War. Iraq was nearly overthrown by two distinct internal rebellions that might have had serious consequences for the entire region. No one knows just how many people were killed and murdered during this period, but even conservative estimates run to tens of thousands. Saddam Hussein's Iraq was constantly involved in high-stakes international relations since that time including an attempt to assassinate George H.W. Bush. Likewise, it is impossible to argue—as the George W. Bush administration has attempted to do in recent years—that the breakdown of law and order in Iraq, the upsurge of sectarian violence, or the profound difficulty in holding and securing a completely occupied Iraq was somehow beyond the knowledge or experience of the U.S. government. In fact, if George W. had merely paid more attention to his father's experience in Iraq much of the operational and planning weakness experienced in Iraq after 2003 could have been well avoided. What is utterly unclear is how Dick Cheney—then secretary of defense—could have forgotten the lessons of this period and proceeded with an Iraqi invasion plan that did not account for what was predictable based on his own professional background. It will be up to historians to follow this thread.

The period 1 March–2 June was a complex period by any accounts. A careful review of the available documents challenge some of the earlier—and still prevailing—histories of the period. The civil war began as an uncoordinated series of spontaneous attacks on the Baathist regime that were soon encouraged and marginally supported by Iran. There is no available evidence to suggest, however, that the Iranians coordinated or prompted the uprisings in the south among the Shiites, nor that they provided much by way of material support although the inclination was certainly there. But even symbolic rhetoric was restrained and came to an end once the tide of battle had turned in favor of the government.

The international response to the uprisings was *universal ambivalence* from state governments. No state wanted Iraq to lose territorial integrity and all states that had been members of the coalition against Iraq called for withholding of support for the Kurds and the Shiites. The reasons were numerous, but the end result was that the rebellions were unsupported and in many ways even unwanted.

Though states did not coordinate a response, a few generalizations are reasonable about why the events unfolded as they did. A Shiite regime would have challenged the prevailing order in the entire Middle East for many different reasons. Among the Arab countries, a Shiite regime would have threatened the superior position of the Baathists and socialists in Egypt and Syria. Though Saddam Hussein was hardly a stabilizing force in the region, the generally secular character of the dictatorial regime aligned Iraq more closely with the non-theocratic regimes of the Middle East and North Africa. A religious state with some allied goals to neighboring Iran would have changed that prevailing order. Likewise, a Shiite state was objectionable to the Sunni regime in Saudi Arabia which has strained relations with the Iranians. For the Turks, a successful rebellion would have meant either a Kurdish state in the north of Iraq or else a region with sufficient autonomy to allow PKK attacks into its territory. Being a NATO country, this too would have put strain on the alliance as a whole, which would also prefer its eastern flank to have a settled border lest it embroil the entire alliance in conflict.

At no point did these policy goals change. Five different policy phases were determined from the viewpoint of U.S. and British policymaking, however, no policy shift challenged the conservative goal of maintaining a status quo Middle East. Implicitly agreed by all relevant powers, the only real change to the status of the region was to be the liberation of Kuwait and its restoration as an autonomous state, and some efforts to encourage dialogue among the Arabs and Israelis.

Coalition policy did not change regarding these issues for the entire period examined. What did change was the decision to aid the refugees *once that support did not challenge these prevailing goals.* That moment came on 5 April when the Permanent Ceasefire was signed and the civil war was, coincidently, over.

The decision to leave Saddam Hussein in power is slightly more complex, and more historical material is needed to bring the picture to light. It remains unclear how much support was provided to internally placed Iraqis who might have attempted a palace coup. There is enough reason to suspect this was attempted and that U.S. support of one type or another was on hand. There is every reason to suspect this was the outcome the West expected.

CHAPTER 5

Measuring Coverage

Media coverage is a measure of the time or space allocated to an existing news hole on a given storyline. This chapter details a method used in measuring media coverage. It provides an analysis of media coverage during the case study period in both countries. The chapter begins with an account of the measurements used, and provides net-assessments for the period. White House press conferences are also examined to create another comparable measure of media interest. The second section provides time series data on media coverage during the case study period. Once the measures are provided and explained, we then disaggregate pressure from coverage to create an entirely new form of measuring media activity in its relations with foreign policy makers.

TYPES AND MEASURES

The News Sources

For the United States, I looked at the *Washington Post* and the *New York Times* on a daily basis and subjected them to detailed measures of both coverage (or attention) and pressure. To complement the record, I used *Newsweek, US News and World Report*, and *Time Magazine* on a weekly basis to prepare the case histories but did not measure their coverage. On television, I examined the official transcripts of ABC, NBC, and CBS nightly news broadcasts and coded them for coverage in terms of minutes.[1] Congressional debate and Congressional hearings were followed as they appeared; secondary academic sources were examined as they were available; and random pieces gleaned from various sources (FBIS and others) were consulted to flush out the history of events.[2]

For Great Britain: I read the *Independent* and the *Guardian* daily and subjected them to detailed measures for coverage and pressure; *The Economist* and the *New Statesman* were examined weekly though were not coded for measurements; and debates in the House of Commons—as recorded in HANSARD—were tracked daily. Other magazines and newspapers such as the *Daily Telegraph*, the *Times*, and the *Observer* were consulted periodically for material, but were not followed in as systematic a fashion.[3] Notes on the British television broadcasts as viewed by Martin Shaw were helpful because the footage from 1991 was inaccessible.[4]

* * *

All news outlets—such as newspapers, television, or radio—have a "news hole." The news hole is the amount of news-related material that can be disseminated (i.e., published, broadcast, etc.) during a given news cycle.[5] The news cycle, in turn, is determined by the dissemination rate of a news product by an organization. The news hole is determined by two factors. The first is the time or space at its disposal. The second is the subjective decision of the news organization about how much of the available space or time it will devote to a given type of news. This is generally not a matter for section editors, but for the publisher and the senior management. It is not to be confused with the daily editorial decision of how to fill the news hole.

Media coverage can be measured quite successfully as times series data. The information gleaned from a time series provides comparative knowledge about relative interest *within* that organization on a particular subject over time, assuming, that is, one follows the same storyline successfully throughout the period and standardizes the coding techniques to differentiate among, and hence follow, stories.

Because the news holes for different newspapers are all different, raw information about "words written" or "paragraphs published" cannot be used to determine comparative interest *across* news organizations on a given subject. Fifty stories in the *Independent* and forty-five in the *Washington Post* does not necessarily mean that the former had more interest in the subject on a given day—tempting though it is to use these measures.[6] Likewise, the *Guardian* does not have a Sunday edition, which makes the comparison of the raw paragraph counts by week completely spurious. Concerns about relative interest would need to consider the overall available space for the two papers (i.e., measuring the news hole) and then create a percentage by dividing the paragraph or word count of the actual story into the available news hole itself.

That percentage would become a comparable figure across news organizations of the same medium (print, broadcast, etc.).[7]

This, however, was not done because our concern is with fluctuations of interest in a given organization over time in response to events on the ground, not in producing comparative data across organizations. However, changes in interest within one organization (such as a 45 percent drop in news coverage as measured against its previous levels) is comparable to fluctuations in interest in another organization.

The first step in determining media attention was to identify a single storyline (for all news outlets) and track it across the period examined. In Iraq the central tension in the storyline was, "what is to be the Western role in the future of Iraq?" The question used to track media attention is in accord with the media's own criterion of storytelling.

Newspaper Coverage Measures

Four measures were used for all newspapers at all times. These were: (1) story counts; (2) paragraph counts; (3) editorials; and (4) opinion pieces. It should be noted that the different measures were not combined to produce weighted measures, as such an exercise presented no obvious benefits to this study.[8] The four measures are as follows:

Story Counts
Counting the number of articles about the Western role in Iraq was found to be insufficient for producing measures of pressure (in the next section), and were also found to be inferior to paragraph counts for accuracy. The reasons are explained below.

Paragraph Counts
This process was selected as the best measure for tracking media coverage because it was most representative of the editorial decision to allocate resources from the news hole to a particular topic than story counts and was also manageable unlike word counts. Figure 5.1 shows that the *Independent* in Britain ran over twice as many stories as did the *Washington Post* during the most intense week of coverage, 15–21 April. If story counts alone were used, it would have been inaccurately concluded that the *Independent* provided more coverage than the *Post*. In fact, the situation was reversed. Story length varied greatly in different periodicals; American papers tended to have longer stories on average. Total figures of coverage by stories and paragraphs shows that the *Washington Post* provided the greatest

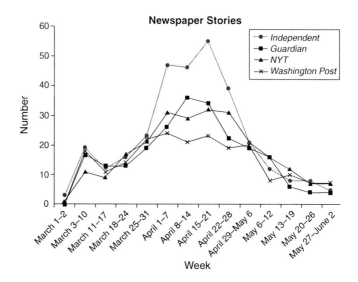

Figure 5.1 Newspaper coverage in the United States and Britain by story count

	Total stories	Total paragraphs	Average story length in paragraphs
Washington Post	205	4,838	23.6
New York Times	244	4,812	19.7
Guardian	230	3,771	16.3
Independent	314	3,201	10.3

Figure 5.2 Comparative aggregate newspaper coverage

coverage of events (as measured by space), and the *Independent* the least (see figure 5.2). The reason the measure of paragraph counts is considered more valid than story or article counts is because the paragraph count is a direct proportion of the news hole, and therefore a highly accurate measure of the editorial decision to allocate limited resources. It should be noted that word count could also have been used to achieve similar results, but the process is exceedingly

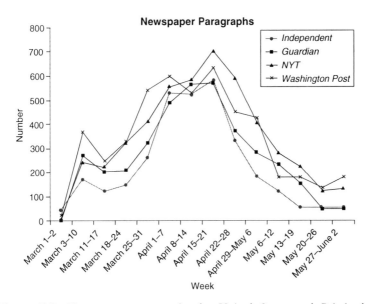

Figure 5.3 Newspaper coverage in the United States and Britain by paragraph count

tedious; over case study periods of several weeks or months, it is considered very unlikely to produce more accurate results because differences in the word count per paragraph will likely average out over any extended period. (See figure 5.3.)

Not all paragraphs from a story were always counted. Quite often, news stories are divided into subsections. This is done because the main part of the story may be worthy of a headline but there is not enough information available to the journalist to produce a full-length piece. In such cases, other subjects with a broader, perhaps regional, focus will comprise the next third or half of the article. In these cases, all paragraphs in demarcated subsections were counted, even if the majority of that section did not discuss the subject that concerned us. Paragraphs were never counted outside the parameters of a subsection. For discussion purposes, the existence of a coding indicator—for example, "Kurdish refugees"— is called a *mention* in the newspaper. This technique produced a consistent, if slightly generous measure for assessing interest.

Editorial Frequency
Editorials were counted as units. Paragraph counts were not used because all editorials are around the same length by design. Later,

when looking at pressure, we will look at these editorials for what they had to say. In measuring attention, however, it was only considered relevant whether an editorial appeared because the decision to dedicate the space to that subject, of all other options available to the newspaper, was noteworthy.

British newspapers do not use the same vocabulary as their American counterparts. The British run what is called a "lead article," which is similar in practice to an American editorial in that both are clearly pieces expressing the opinions of the newspaper on some highly relevant matter of national policy (i.e., any situation in which the national decision makers have an ability to effectuate a change in national or international events). The average lead article length is five paragraphs or 550 words. Also interesting is that the lead article will not necessarily appear in the same place on the front page. Whereas the American formatting process is more rigid, the British practice is more rhetorical in that it uses placement as a rich device for adding emphasis to articles. Newspaper editorial frequency was found to be a good indicator of whether an event was considered both pressing and seemingly unresolved. (See figure 5.4.)

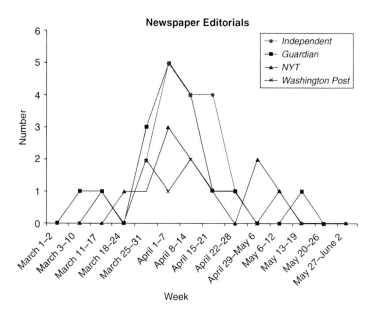

Figure 5.4 Newspaper coverage in the United States and Britain by editorial count

Opinion-Piece Frequency

The fourth measure was *opinion articles*. They are usually found on the Op/Ed page of U.S. papers, where they are called "opinion"; they are usually called "commentaries" in British papers (see figure 5.5). Opinion pieces are distinguished from editorials in being signed. Editorials represent the views of the newspaper as an organization. Opinion pieces, though obviously selected by the newspaper, are nevertheless officially representative only of the author's own point of view. Opinion pieces are also more numerous. Each day, a newspaper may run up to half-dozen or more pieces. On 5 April 1991, for example, the *Independent* published an astonishing nine opinion articles and an official editorial about the British and U.S. air drop initiative for the Kurdish refugees along the Turkish border.[9] Opinion pieces are only printed about an on-going story with an unresolved outcome, and where the determination of some aspect of policy still appears to be pending. Like editorials, these pieces are therefore a good indication of the level of media interest and the peaks of tension that the media has recognized in its own storyline and theme.

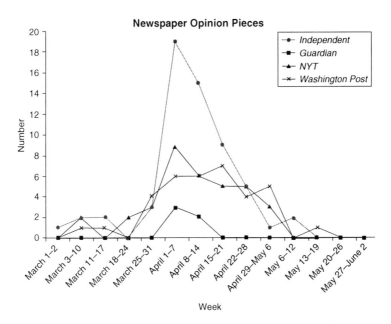

Figure 5.5 Newspaper coverage in the United States and Britain by opinion pieces

Television Attention Measurement Techniques

American television data was drawn from the TV News Archives of Vanderbilt University, available on the worldwide web (http://www.tvnews.vanderbilt.edu), and culled from the complete manuscripts of the broadcasts, as downloaded on Lexis/Nexis. The Vanderbilt archives are the most comprehensive and accessible archive of American television news broadcasts since 1968. From the material available online, story counts and numbers of minutes of coverage were determined. Storyline selection criteria were the same as for the newspapers. The news summaries available were sufficient to determine: (1) number of segments (i.e., stories); (2) length of segments; (3) order of segments; and (4) general subject of the stories. The summaries, however, were not sufficient for in-depth content analysis, and comparisons of the transcripts to the on-line summaries demonstrated a level of "politeness" or political correctness that actually distorted the story tensions and made the summaries unusable for our needs.

In producing the data sets, all Vanderbilt University archives were downloaded for every day of the period examined. The minutes of coverage were rounded to the nearest ten-second block of time. Each ten-second block was converted to a percentage of a minute for easier calculations later, as figure 5.6 demonstrates.

In some cases, an entire story was on the topic of Iraq, and so the figures provided by Vanderbilt for the length of the story were used. In other cases, discussions of Iraq were only mentioned in parts of the segment, just as only some parts of newspaper stories were dedicated to the relevant matters in Iraq. In these cases, estimates were produced instead of counting the entire segment length to better approach the real coverage time. This was rare, however, and was only done in five instances in a total of 459 days of coverage (153 days for

Seconds	Percentage conversion
10	0.17
20	0.34
30	0.5
40	0.67
50	0.83
60	1

Figure 5.6 Conversions from seconds to percentages of a minute

three news networks).[10] All time estimates erred on the side of more coverage.

Lead Stories

The first story of the news cycle is rhetorically presented as most important. The more frequently the central storyline appears as the first story of the day, the more attention the story is receiving over the course of a week, and hence is a reasonable proxy measure for media coverage. Lead stories in all three U.S. news programs were similar, with ABC News leading with the matter of Iraq more than the other two news organizations (see figure 5.7).

The number of lead stories—over the course of a month—was also highly correlated to the number of minutes dedicated to the story (see figure 5.8). As a consequence, counting lead stories on a *monthly* basis

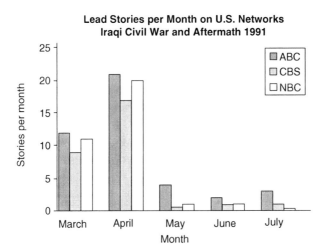

Figure 5.7 Lead stories per month in U.S. TV networks

	ABC	CBS	NBC	Number of days with no news
March	12	9	11	ABC-1, CBS-5, NBC-0
April	21	17	20	ABC-0, CBS-3, NBC-0
May	4	0	1	ABC-0, CBS-2, NBC-0
June	2	1	1	All data
July	3	1	0	All data

Figure 5.8 Count of lead stories per month on U.S. TV networks

would have proved a useful proxy measure for television attention, had this level of generality been needed. This study, however, is an intensive examination of only three months and hence needed a more refined process. Note again that no efforts were made to value the quality of the reporting in terms of detail, evidence, or other such indicators.

Minutes of Weekly Coverage
All television broadcasts on the three U.S. networks were downloaded from the Vanderbilt archives. Each file was the read for stories about Iraq or U.S. relations with Iraq based on its relevance to the central storyline being tracked for all media reports in both countries. The summaries themselves were usually detailed enough to make this judgment. Other times, however, the transcripts were consulted. The transcripts for ABC News and CBS News were available on-line and were read and coded each day, but CBS News was not. In chapter 6, only the two former stations were analyzed for media pressure because the Vanderbilt files were not sufficiently detailed, as will be explained. In the end, a generous measure was produced for TV coverage. All stories where the revolts or refugees were mentioned were included, even if the reference was included within another story, and no single segment was devoted to the subject. Also, all time estimates err on the side of

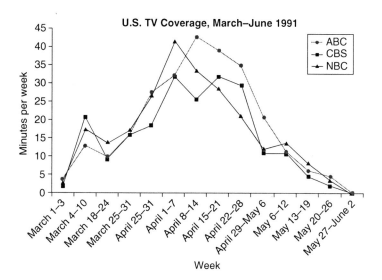

Figure 5.9 Minutes of news coverage per week on U.S. TV networks

more media coverage if the exact number of minutes was unknown, or the time period fell between ten-second increments. (See figure 5.9.)

Absence of the British Television Data
In the case of Britain, material was more difficult to come by. Unlike in the United States, the United Kingdom does not have an archived depository of news footage that is publicly accessible. The BBC has not yet made electronic transcripts available, and practical limitations prevented stays in London to view archived footage for three months of coverage. Martin Shaw, in 1996, gained access to BBC footage from Leeds University in the United Kingdom, which maintains a video archive of Gulf War material ending in April 1991. That material, however, is only available on the site. Professor Shaw did not archive his extensive notes from the viewing sessions, making them unavailable for analysis here.[11] The BBC has not yet established a public archive for the transcripts of its material.[12]

US Press Conferences
In trying to isolate media pressure, as will be done in chapter 6, it is necessary to find data sets that are to the greatest extent possible:

1. Complete for the entire period under examination.
2. Provide evidence of executive "uptake" of media utterances so that episodic unity in the media–government conversation can be determined with strong verifiability. This means preferring face-to-face conversation and distant conversational episodes to either face-to-face talk or (worse) distant talk. It also requires an ethnographic appreciation for the rules of conversation in a given community and the function of questions and replies.
3. Attributable to sources that have the legitimate authority to speak on behalf of the executive.
4. Appear regularly and at regular intervals so that measurement can be made evenly and in close correlation to actual foreign policy–related events such as policy changes.

In the United States, the White House press conferences, or press briefings, have been selected as serving as a useful data source.

The selection of a data set for other countries should follow the four rules above. In Great Britain, the House of Commons question period functions as a proxy media pool. The analogy should not be pushed too far, but MPs regularly cite newspaper and television coverage when introducing questions, as these sources function as a surrogate intelligence agency for the parliamentarians, which is *open source* and therefore can be cited without revealing state secrets.[13] In the case study, the House of Commons was not in session for most of March 1991, and therefore another proxy media corps had to be used. Though unorthodox, the *American* press was selected due to the deliberately close coordination of Whitehall and the White House during the crisis and the very deliberate alignment of U.S. and British policy during the immediate post–Gulf War period. (Cautions for false positives in coding are explained later.)

Press conference coverage can be measured in a similar manner to newspaper or television coverage, with some notable differences in coding techniques. In the case of the United States, the first step in converting the press conference material to data was to tally the number of questions fielded at each conference for each day of the case study.[14] This is not a strictly mechanical process. Although the official transcripts list a "Q" for question and "A" for answer, counting the number of "Qs" is insufficient because the "Q" appears each time a journalist *speaks*. The total number of "Qs" is *the sum of questions asked and answered*, combined with *the sum of question asked that could have reasonably been answered*. The second type is dependent on

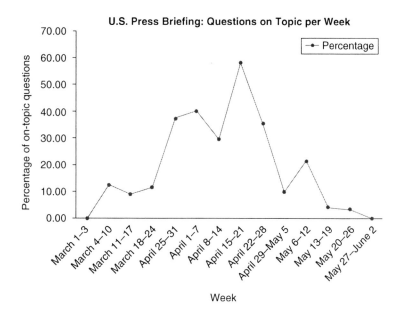

Figure 5.10   Media questions fielded at US press conferences on the topic

the judgment of the researcher and therefore provide a greater margin of error, but the benefits outweigh this cost. The process of selection is important, because sometimes there will be a volley of questions with only one selected by the White House for response. It is more accurate to count the volley as media interest than the single question actually answered. The second step is to review all questions asked that day on every topic and then code each question as either being inside or outside the identified storyline of the media—or "on topic" and "off topic" as I called it (see figure 5.10).

Net Media Coverage

In aggregate, 612 days worth of news coverage, 991 stories, 16,607 paragraphs, 55 editorials, 134 opinion pieces, and 143 photographs were all manually counted—and would later be counted a second time to code for media pressure as a subtotal of coverage, as seen in chapter 6. In the United States, the *Washington Post* yielded 204 stories on the Iraqi Civil War and the Kurdish refugee crisis, 4,822 paragraphs of coverage, 9 editorials, 35 opinion pieces, 34 front page photos relating to the subject, and 29 other photos located at different places in the paper. The *New York Times* produced a remarkably similar pattern of coverage with 244 stories, 4,812 paragraphs of coverage, 11 editorials, the same 35 opinion pieces, and 24 front page photos. The *Times*, however, published nearly four times as many non–front page photos (114) as the *Post* (see figure 5.11).

In Britain, the *Independent* produced 314 stories of 3,201 paragraphs, 18 lead articles, and an extraordinary 59 opinion pieces or letters to the editor. The *Guardian*—which only comes out five times a week—had 229 articles but substantially more raw coverage than the *Independent* with 3,757 paragraphs. Seventeen lead stories were published along with only five opinion pieces (see figure 5.12).

For television, the same 612 days worth of coverage was measured resulting in 768.5 minutes (12.8 hours), and 103 lead stories. Unlike the newspapers, where the news holes are all different due to

	Stories	Paragraphs	Editorials	Opinions	P. 1 photo	Other photos
Washington Post	204	4822	9	35	34	29
New York Times	244	4813	11	35	24	114

Figure 5.11 Weekly totals of U.S. newspaper coverage, 1 March–2 June 1991

	Stories	Paragraphs	Lead articles	Opinions
Independent	314	3201	18	35
Guardian	229	3771	17	35

Figure 5.12   Aggregate totals of U.K. newspaper coverage, 1 March–2 June 1991

	Total minutes	Lead stories
ABC News	291	42
CBS News	224.8	28
NBC News	252.8	33

Figure 5.13   Aggregates of U.S. TV news coverage during the case study period

formatting, typefaces, and other considerations, television news holes are almost exactly the same in the United States, as the same number of minutes is allotted to advertisements. For this reason, media attention can be properly compared across stations. ABC did not consistently provide the most coverage on a weekly basis, but did provide significantly more coverage during the weeks when the story was highly regarded by all stations—as during the first three weeks of April, for example.

Coverage on television followed a remarkably similar pattern to coverage in print. During 4–10 March, just after the rebellions began, coverage reached a moderate level, as optimism rose about the possibility of Saddam Hussein being overthrown. The absence of pictures combined with little information from the government, and most importantly, no opposition to governmental policy, meant a quick downturn in coverage. Like newspapers, attention rose rapidly in the last week of March (see figure 5.13).

Levels of Media Interest

Weekly correlations between news outlets were remarkably high. These correlation coefficients were not only high (i.e., over 90 percent) among like-media within countries, but even *across media between countries*. For newspapers, correlations ranged from a low of 0.90 between the *Independent* and *Washington Post* (the two papers with

	New York Times	Washington Post	Guardian
Independent	0.92	0.90	0.96
Guardian	0.95	0.91	-
Washington Post	0.93	-	-

Figure 5.14 Correlation coefficients among weekly newspaper coverage

	ABC News	CBS News	NBC News
ABC News	1	-	-
CBS News	0.92	1	-
NBC News	0.93	0.95	1

Figure 5.15 Correlations between network coverage

the greatest differences in the number of stories and paragraph length, as explained earlier), to a high of 0.96 between the two British papers (see figure 5.14).

For television (in the United States only), the overview looked quite similar. A correlation of 92 percent was the *lowest* between CBS and ABC news during the case study period, with a high of 95 percent between CBS and NBC (see figure 5.15).

Most remarkable was the high correlation of coverage across media types and between countries (see figure 5.16). The lowest correlation in coverage was between NBC news and the *New York Times* at 85 percent during the case study period. U.S. television was no more closely correlated in coverage to American newspapers than they were to British. The highest recorded was ABC News and the *New York Times*, at 95.7 percent over the three-month period.

What accounts for this? I believe the answer comes definitively from Ron Scollon who writes that "primary social interaction . . . is among journalists and such subsidiary personnel as producers, directors, or printers . . . At the same time I argue that the primary social interactions which involve reading/watching are among readers and viewers who, as observers of this posed spectacle, make a variety of uses of it, ranging from disattention . . . to other more focal social activities such as watching or reading or making commentaries. In any event, I argue that the primary social interaction

Television station/newspaper	Correlation (%)
ABC/*NYT*	95.7
ABC/*WP*	90.9
ABC/*Independent*	93.7
ABC/*Guardian*	95.3
NBC/*NYT*	85.0
NBC/*WP*	89.3
NBC/*Independent*	90.8
NBC/*Guardian*	92.0
CBS/*NYT*	91.6
CBS/*WP*	90.0
CBS/*Independent*	91.3
CBS/*Guardian*	92.7

Figure 5.16 Correlation coefficients across media types and countries

is not between the producers of the spectacles (journalists) and the observers (readers/watchers)."[15]

In short, media producers are primarily concerned with their social interaction with other media producers and not with the consumers of their products. This is profoundly important because it means that journalists are looking to other news agents for stories, for guidance, social standing, reputation, justification, ethical insights, and other cues about how to be a "social actor" in the world of media. Not surprisingly, therefore, they tend to converge in their social practices, which in turn yields similar stories and "gut instincts" about what makes something "newsworthy." This aligns perfectly well with Herbert Gans's 1979 observations that newsmakers do not poll the population to learn what they would like to know.

While this is bad news for democracy, it is good news for researchers because the high correlation among news coverage in general—always over 85 percent—allowed for a single scale to be used for newspaper and television attention levels. On measuring the intensity of newspaper coverage in both U.S. papers (i.e., the level of coverage during a period of time), four levels of media attention were noted, based on the practice of expanding coverage and maintaining numerous story tensions. The divisions between categories are estimates and are labeled minimal interest, moderate interest, strong interest, and feeding frenzy (see figure 5.17).

Paragraphs per week	Level of interest	Definition
0–200	Minimal interest	Maintaining story thread
201–400	Moderate interest	Probing for story escalation
401–600	Strong interest	Story has "legs" and is a feature of daily coverage
600+	Feeding frenzy	Central story of the nation

Figure 5.17 Scale of media interest by paragraphs of weekly newspaper coverage

Minimal interest constituted 0–200 paragraphs of coverage per week and was notable as being the effort of the newspaper to maintain the story thread. From this low level of interest, stories were in a sense waiting for something to happen.

Moderate interest constituted 201–400 paragraphs of coverage per week and was notable as being the effort of the paper to probe for story escalation. Here, the paper is looking for new angles, new story ideas and spin-off storylines, and probing for scandal or dissent at the governmental level.

Strong interest is when daily lulls in events or governmental statements do not affect the coverage the following day, as sufficient "momentum" had gathered for the papers to drive their own discussions of events and produce new story ideas. In journalistic lingo, the story has "legs."

More than about 600 paragraphs a week constituted a feeding frenzy (!) by the press where the subject at hand becomes the central story for the entire nation. This figure might be lowered slightly for the British press. As seen below, these categories for newspapers corresponded well with similar practices and experiences in television coverage, and could also be seen—not surprisingly because they were often the same journalists—at the press conferences in the United States. During periods of feeding frenzy, press conferences are absorbed by the central story at the exclusion of other possibly important stories. For example, on 29–30 April 1991, a cyclone in Bangladesh killed 90,000–120,000 people. This was near the end of the peak of media coverage on the Operation Provide Comfort. This horrible event, and the deployment of U.S. troops to help with the humanitarian relief effort, barely made the newspapers or television.

British newspaper coverage appeared to follow the same general trend as the U.S. papers, and as a first pass at the matter, the same scale

Minutes of TV Coverage per week	Level of interest	Description
0–10	Minimal interest	Story thread is being maintained
11–20	Moderate interest	Media is probing for story escalation
21–30	Strong interest	Story has "legs"
31+	Feeding frenzy	The central story of the nation

Figure 5.18   Scale of media interest by TV coverage per week

Percent of media queries at press conferences	Level of interest	Description
0–10	Minimal interest	Story thread is being maintained
11–30	Moderate interest	Media is probing for story escalation
31–50	Strong interest	Story has "legs"
51+	Feeding frenzy	The central story of the nation

Figure 5.19   Media interest by queries to White House per week

can be used to discuss coverage there as well. For a proper cross-paper comparison study of coverage, raw paragraphs must be converted to a percentage of the space available in the news hole for international news. This was not done; hence, graphs and data can only be used to compare relative changes in each paper over time. Graphs displaying more than one paper show that the changes in coverage were highly correlated over time.

For television, the levels were similar (see figure 5.18). An identical assessment was made of the White House press conferences and the same logic applied (see figure 5.19). As an estimate, I found that 0–10 percent of questions constituted minimal interest; 11–30 percent moderate interest; 31–50 percent strong interest; and more than 51 percent was a feeding frenzy. The highest recorded was 89 percent on 29 March 1991—a truly bad day to be the White House spokesman.

Understanding Trends in Media Coverage, March–June 1991

Britain did not publish an official policy statement about the Iraqi Civil War and the newspapers in that country interestingly paid more attention to American policy than that of their own government. On the front pages of the *Independent* and the *Guardian*, attention was focused on the events in Iraq and the American responses to them. The BBC was reiterating that "conclusive information on what is happening in Basra is impossible to obtain," and like the newspaper reports, it was unable to obtain any visuals or confirmation of reports. Shaw notes that on 3 March, the BBC was "reduced to quoting from Teheran radio, and noting that the 'US military, privately hoping for Saddam's downfall, today had little publicly to say.'" [16]

On 4 March, the *Washington Post* reported on the front page that the Iraqi cities of Basra, Nasiriyah, Amarah, Suq ash-Shuyukh, Tar, Fuhoud, and Ali al-Gharb had all been taken by the rebels in the south. Interviews with a motley assortment of local leaders produced a consistent flow of rhetoric about how they wanted an Iranian-style state. Confident that this was the plot to the events and the relevant narrative thread, the paper would confidently describe events in the south as "a fundamentalist Islamic uprising" the next morning, although substantiation was weak and speculative.

Reports in the *Independent* that same day quoted American intelligence officers as having no human intelligence in Basra. Robert Fisk wrote:[17]

> For information on events in Basra, the US is relying on satellite photography. "We don't have anybody in Basra," an intelligence officer said. "All I can tell you is the town has traffic that's chaotic, it's everywhere. What we're seeing is a lot of people milling around all over the place. Cars parked on the side of the road chaotically, not in any kind of normal pattern. I don't attribute it to some kind of large-scale civil disobedience. There does not appear to be good civil control of the populace at the moment, or of the military that's there. The military doesn't seem to be going through the town in a very organized kind of way. It's almost as if they're leaderless."

This lack of field officers was implied two days earlier on BBC 1 when the U.S. military said that aerial photographs "show a total breakdown of control [in Basra], but no sign of revolt."[18]

Two days later, the *Wall Street Journal* published an account that again corroborates the seeming lack of human intelligence in southern Iraq. "Senior pentagon officials in Washington," the report stated, "said conflicts were under way in at least six southern Iraqi cities, with aerial reconnaissance showing buildings and vehicles on fire and military checkpoints set up at strategic intersections."[19] Lieutenant General Thomas Kelly, then director of operations for the Joint Chiefs of Staff said that in Basra, Iraqi army T-55 and T-72 tanks appeared to be involved in the fighting, but he was not clear which side the tanks were on. He reportedly told the *Washington Post* that "reconnaissance planes had photographed a large crowd gathered near 'one of the holy places' in Basra, indicating that some 'anti-regime resistance' was under way. He said the regime in Baghdad was trying to quash the uprising."[20] Such confusion would be a logical consequence of analysis that relied heavily or solely on aerial imagery.[21] On 7 March, the *Washington Post* reported that "[i]n contrast to Tuesday's fighting in the southern city of Basra, when dissident Iraqi armor forces and loyalist Republican Guard tanks squared off and exchanged fire, opposing sides 'no longer have tanks pointed at each other,' said a US official in Riyadh, the Saudi capital."

The continued references to visual cues to make arguments point at dependence placed on visual intelligence, and hence aerial or satellite imagery. This does not prove that the United States had no further intelligence information. It may point to limited channels of information to the press, for example. And there were some clues that more detailed information may have been available, as when the *Guardian* quoted a Pentagon intelligence specialist (presumably at the Defense Intelligence Agency, DIA), saying the person "predicted that President Saddam Hussein would succeed in quelling the unrest, as loyalist Republican Guards were reportedly fighting from house to house in a bid to regain control of Iraq's second city of Basra."[22]

This, however, may have been observable from aerial data as well. The level of detail (i.e., the magnification and image correction technology) is top secret, but is well known to be exquisitely precise as even the unclassified images during the Gulf War make clear. The observation remains, however, that the wide range of U.S. and British publications that were interested in the topic, the fierce competition among the newspapers to get information about the insurrection, and the absolute consistency in information from all sources reviewed here indicate either exceptional secrecy on the part of the intelligence community or else an utter lack of any substantive information about the civil war other than aerial imagery.

The suspected early lack of proper intelligence information about the civil war was of limited discernible interest to American officials—which perhaps explains why so little existed in the first place. They had already decided what they thought would happen and how.[23] According to Richard Haass, "[s]enior Bush Administration officials expected that surviving Iraqi troops would return home in March 1993 [*sic*] and, together with their fellow citizens, rise up against the government of Saddam Hussein. Things did not work out that way."[24]

These concerns were of no consequence in the United States. Jeff Greenfield, reporting from the Senate for ABC News, described the reaction to the speech:

> Listen. Listen to the sounds of exultation. Yes, the Congress always cheers the President, but when was the last time you heard cheers like this? By every measure, a torrent of praise from across the spectrum, celebrations in print and in public, poll numbers of record proportions, the swift, total victory in the Persian Gulf has given the President a stature unequalled by any president in decades, a stature especially remarkable for a political figure of limited eloquence or charisma.[25]

In stating the conflicting goals of the administration, Colin Powell said, "I think the interest of the region would be best served with Saddam Hussein out of power, and I think the interest of the region would be best served if Iraq remains a single country."[26] Such a wish, however, could only have been achieved had a new strongman toppled Hussein and *then* put down the insurrection in much the way Hussein did. William Safire, the conservative commentator who would emerge as one of Bush's harshest critics and a champion of the Kurdish cause, would later say that Bush was expecting the Tooth Fairy to perform the coup.

Much later, on 15 April, Fouad Ajami, writing in *US News and World Report*, concluded rightly that, "[t]he American reluctance to be drawn into Iraq's affairs springs from many sources. We didn't trust our knowledge of that country and its ways and sects. Nor did we trust the rebels and their intentions. We are haunted by the specter of Lebanon; we didn't want to see Beirut by the Tigris." In short, what was missing was sufficient strategic intelligence about the society.

Coverage changed its tone during the second week in March. During 11–17 March, there were no journalists operating in the conflict zones because Saddam had now thrown them out. The absence of images and information—and yet the knowledge that there were media-worthy events afoot—necessitated a turn inward to domestic news sources to fill the image and content gap. Luckily for the media, President Bush made a policy shift just a few days after Saddam pulled the plug on media coverage in Iraq, which had clearly led to a drop in coverage from the second to third week of March. Marking the beginning of Phase II, at a news conference on 13 March, one quizzical journalist followed up Bush's off-the cuff reference to the use of helicopter gunships against civilians in southern Iraq. The question was:

> **Q**: What helicopters were you speaking about, sir? On the rebels?
> **The President**: The use of helicopters—yes.
> **Q**: Against the rebels?
> **The President**: Yes. Warning them, do not do this.

This final statement, perhaps made too casually, was nevertheless a direct threat by the president of the United States against Iraq after having described the situation as being of vital importance to the removal of U.S. troops. James Baker, on returning from the Middle East, would meet the press in early April and be asked about Bush's helicopter policy. According to the *Washington Post*, "Baker did not answer a question about why Bush issued a warning to Baghdad not to use helicopter gunships against rebels if he was not prepared to act on the warning. 'Well, that's a question you can address to him,' he said, referring to Bush."[27]

A look at the flurry of questions that were to follow in the next few days, and the inconsistent responses by the administration to account for Bush's policy formula strongly supports the thesis that all subsequent White House communication on this matter was a post hoc attempt by the spin doctors to reconcile Bush's statements with the continued intention of the administration to not interfere in the civil war. Bush took his staff by surprise, drew the United States into a new phase of policy, and by failing to act as promised, brought all future criticism of U.S. policy on himself.

A half-hearted effort was made to gloss over the statement by the president. On moral grounds, it could not possibly be retracted. On the basis of the positioning arguments made earlier about agentive and moral authority, Bush could neither retract a presidential statement— for fear of seeming uncertain—nor suggest that, on second thought, Saddam could kill as many people as he wanted with helicopters. However, having had no intention to enforce this threat, the White House was at loss to explain its policies. With no journalists covering the actual events, cameras naturally turned to the White House to see what the new policy was all about. This is confirmed by both newspaper coverage and television coverage in the United States, and interestingly, newspaper coverage in Great Britain as well.

What the White House actually feared is uncertain. Returning to the points made earlier about security coalitions, the United States was now embedded in a complex international coalition of unlikely states. The president was the central leader of that coalition, and any statements that made the United States look uncertain or morally inept *may* have been a problem to coalition actors. The word "may" must be underscored, however, because the cultural factors that assign rights and obligations within one community may say nothing about how they affect another, and a statement that might cause offense in the United Kingdom, for example, may have limited if any significance in, say, Syria. Nevertheless, Bush's aids must have decided to finesse the matter as much as possible in the hopes it would go away, and in doing so, miscalculated. When the cameras are at home and American policy is in doubt, the cameras have nothing better to do than find flaws in senior policymaking.

The *New York Times* saw through the spin by the White House and reached a similar conclusion in the front page story the next day. "By raising the issue, Mr. Bush further involved himself on the side of anti-Government factions in Iraq battling against forces loyal to President Saddam Hussein. That also means that the United States military forces will stay until the rebellion issue and others are resolved."

The *Washington Post*, on 15 March, had also taken Bush's statements to be a major policy shift, but cast some doubt as to whether the rest of the administration knew it had happened. "After Bush first raised the helicopter issue on Wednesday in Canada," the paper wrote, "top advisers scrambled to decide how to explain what the president meant. Several hours later, a carefully worded statement was issued by the press office that spoke less to the details of the alleged cease-fire violation and more to the issue of Saddam's future."

The period immediately following the 13 March announcement of a discernible policy by the White House about how to extract U.S. troops from the region and what to do, if anything, about the civil war, was a period of extensively increasing media coverage. No more firsthand information was coming out of Iraq than before, but now it was possible for the media to get information from *this* side of the Atlantic. And that allowed the story, finally, to escalate.

Following two days of unsuccessful spin doctoring about Bush's new policy analysis and direction, the United States made a militarily logical but publicly baffling move that falsely signaled to everyone watching that the United States was stepping up pressure on Hussein and that the former was coming to the aid of the insurgents in a bid to rid Iraq of the man Bush often called "worse than Hitler." What the media saw was U.S. troops moving thirty miles deeper into Iraq to reoccupy positions in the Euphrates valley that they held at the war's end, but then abandoned. As the *Guardian* explained, this meant that the troops from the 101st Airborne and 1st Cavalry divisions were now able to block important communication routes in southern Iraq, which could affect Hussein's ability to put down the rebellion. It seemed to be a clear move of rebellion support, and after the statements about the helicopters and the chemical weapons, it seemed logical to the press. With no more compelling explanation coming from the White House, it was the story they ran with.

David Martin, reporting for CBS News, began a report on 14 March saying, "[d]espite [Bush's] repeated calls for Saddam Hussein's ouster, President Bush today insisted the US has no intention of intervening in the fighting now going on inside Iraq." This was indeed U.S. policy, and Bush was then shown, saying, "We are not in there trying to impose a solution inside Iraq." However, American military moves would not be isolated from support for the rebels in the television coverage. Martin goes on to say immediately afterward, "[however] the Bush administration is doing everything it can short of intervention to help the Iraqi people get rid of Saddam. Today, the president said there would be no permanent cease-fire and no final withdrawal of allied troops from southern Iraq, if Saddam continues to use helicopters against the rebels."[28]

The press's confusion deepened. On 15 March, Bush made a new statement saying that any fixed-wing aircraft (i.e., not helicopters) that were found airborne would be immediately shot down. The *New York Times*, the next day, seeing what appeared to be an evident trend in the past few days, suggested that the United States was stepping up support for the rebellion. CBS News came to the same conclusion. As Jim Stewart reported, ". . . there have been other violations. Iraqi combat helicopters have continued to fly, even after last Sunday's meeting between US and Iraqi commanders, where Iraq was specifically warned that any Iraqi aircraft in the air would be viewed as a threat." All the pieces were in place to make the story plausible, and seeing as no other explanation was coming out of the White House other than denials about aiding the rebellion—and the fact that still no journalists were reporting from *inside* Iraq—the newspapers and television alike assumed that the United States government was concerned with the future of the rebellion. They were wrong.

The newspapers were not attuned to the extremely limited U.S. objective of a ceasefire agreement and troop withdrawal because they could not reconcile what Bush had said about the helicopters—and the refusal of the administration to withdraw the comments—with

American and allied unwillingness to shoot them down along with the planes.

After the policy shift and the forward deployment of troops, events started to move very quickly, and with them increased media attention. However, part of the reason was that the story was able to shift from Iraq to the United States, or in other words, from where information and access was unconfirmed and limited to where information (and opinion) were readily available.[29]

On 24 March, Robert Zelnick, for the *Washington Post*, explained that, "the restrictions imposed by the United States on Iraqi combat aircraft were believed to have applied to helicopters as well, but the commander of U.S forces in the gulf, Gen. H. Norman Schwarzkopf, today told reporters that US pilots patrolling over Iraq have been told not to shoot down helicopters unless they approach allied forces or somehow pose a threat to them." Such explicit statements, however, were very hard for journalists to figure in the face of statements as that by Colin Powell, a day earlier, to the effect that "I don't think we're trying to use our military force to influence events inside Iraq." Journalists such as Zelnick can certainly be forgiven for making certain assumptions, if not for overselling the limited facts. After all, if Colin Powell wasn't certain what the policy was, who could be?[30]

On 26 March, CBS would go so far as to call this a reversal of policy. As Dan Rather introduced the story, "[i]n an apparent reversal of policy, President Bush today gave Saddam Hussein what amounts to a green light to use helicopter gunships against Iraqi rebels. Military sources say the choppers may turn the tide in the civil war Saddam's way."[31] This is a starkly clear example of how professed objectivity in media coverage in no way prevents the possibility of media pressure on the government.

The term "slaughter" is emotive, and is generally not reserved for academic or even journalistic accounts of events. However, the term is also specific and in this case accurate. The killings that took place in Iraq—often committed by the rebels as well in the initial stages—were so creatively sadistic they could have been driven by pure hatred. Reports were available that Republican Guard troops were systematically rounding up and executing all boys aged thirteen and older—the age of manhood in Islam. Children far younger were regularly found by U.S. forces in the south shot at point blank range (evidenced by powder burns on their chests), as bodies were carried to allied lines. An American intelligence officer told the *Independent* that there were "credible reports of public beheadings in Nasiriyah." Children under ten years old were found with throats slit, and helicopter gunships emptied magazines into villages and in pursuit of unarmed, fleeing civilians. In the Shiite south, villagers were often hanged, tied to tanks as human shields, and dropped out of helicopters into public squares. Women and children who could not account for the whereabouts of their brothers or fathers were killed on the spot. An Iraqi student, desperate at a U.S. southern checkpoint, told a soldier, "[i]f you withdraw from Iraq, they will massacre us all. The things we have seen are making us lose our faith in God."[32]

This was not "collateral damage," an unfortunate but defined term for those who are killed as a consequence of military actions against a legitimate military target. Bob Drogin, reporting from Ur, explained:

> Saddam Hussein is offering a cash bonus to his troops to kill the families of Shi'ite insurgents in southern Iraq and has turned tanks on refugees, according to deserting Iraqi soldiers. The PoWs said they get 250 dinars to kill babies and women and up to 5,000 dinars for adult males, said Captain Rhett Scott, aged 28, at Checkpoint 5 Alfa, southwest of Nasiriyah and the most advanced American post on the main road west to Baghdad. "They can kill up to 100 a day. That's the limit."[33]

The question was put to Schwarzkopf if he thought the coalition should have pressed on to Baghdad and if, perhaps, Bush had called an end to hostilities too soon. To the consternation of the White House, Schwarzkopf admitted that this was exactly what he thought, and that he made that very suggestion to Bush. This is not to say, however, that the general stated his disagreement to Bush *after* the president's decision was made (this was denied), which is an important point, as early disagreement is a normal part of the decision-making process when senior policymakers are being consulted. Schwarzkopf's gaff was in letting that piece of information loose into the public arena at a terribly poor moment for the policymakers.

The second question that was equally damaging was about the helicopters and whether Schwarzkopf thought they should be shot down. "I think I was suckered [at the ceasefire discussion at Safwan]," he told Frost. "I think they intended right then . . . to use those helicopters against the insurrections that were going on." The mistakes exposed, the logic of inaction revealed by the general himself, and the continuous, daily death count mounting as a result of having been "suckered" was all the media needed to know. They now wanted accountability from the president. As Brit Hume explained, "The problem for the administration is that the President himself has suggested the US will insist Iraq ground its helicopters."[34]

From that day, the civil war and the refugee crisis to follow dominated all the major networks. For the next three weeks, out of a possible 28 evenings, ABC would lead 23 times with Iraq, CBS 17 times, and NBC 22 times. Since the civil war began in early March, the story had only made the lead 7, 6, and 6 times out of a possible 24 days respectively. Newspaper attention in the United States would in both cases more than double in the period 25 March to the second week of April, and on the networks, more than triple. The *New York Times*, during the four-week period from 18 March to 21 April, expanded their coverage of the civil war from 326 paragraphs to 411, to 557, to 583, to a saturated 704 paragraphs. The *Washington Post* in the same period saw a pattern similar to that of the *Independent*, going from 328 to 543 during 25–31 March, to 600, down to 529, then up again to 633, before beginning its steady decline until the beginning of June.

In Britain, the pattern of coverage was virtually identical. The *Guardian*—which only comes out five days a week, unlike the other papers—would increase coverage from 207 paragraphs during 18–25 March, to 309 the next week, 487 the first week of April, and a staggering 592 during 8–15 April. The *Independent* was the same. Coverage went from 146 paragraphs during 18–25 March, to 259 the week the controversies began, to 532 paragraphs the first week of April, and then took a dip to 524 the second week of April; but it would then shoot up to 586 before dropping precipitously at the end of the month.[35] In looking at these numbers, we find that all newspapers and televisions actually increased coverage *after* Britain and the United States announced the 5 April relief effort and the initiation of Operation Provide Comfort.

Though it may have seemed like Desert Calm for the soldiers in southern Iraq, Washington was under media bombardment. ABC and NBC were leading with the refugee crisis every night of the week; CBS skipped only one day. The *Washington Post* was running double the number of photos from its previous high, and most were about suffering and death. The *New York Times* ran nine opinion pieces that week alone, and CBS coverage would hit not only its highest level of attention throughout the March–May period, but over 90 percent of it would position the president and his policies on the defensive (see chapter 6).

The *Guardian* explained the situation that faced John Major:[36]

> [I]f tension drove [Major] into a thoughtless petulance, it was easy to understand why. Unlike Mrs. Thatcher, who hardly read the newspapers, John Major follows them closely and takes some of the things they

say very hard. He knows that, in some quarters, the recently dispossessed have been doing their best to suggest that he just isn't up to the job . . . Under the strapline "It takes Maggie to speak out for the Kurds," a report with the headline "The Voice of Conscience" began: "As President Bush played golf and Prime Minister John Major went to watch football, it took former Premier Margaret Thatcher to stir the world's conscience last night over the genocide looming in Iraq."

On April 4, the press announced that the story was no longer about the Iraqi civil war. That was over, and the rebels lost. Peter Jennings described the storyline shift in his introduction to the evening news: "Tonight for perhaps as many as two million Kurds it is no longer a question of fighting to overthrow Saddam Hussein, it is a matter of survival." One day before the UN ceasefire agreement and the U.S. decision to launch Operation Provide Comfort, the U.S. media had already started to shift the focus of the story from rebellion to refugees.

One of the consequences of the media failure to explain U.S. policy properly was a shift in media attention away from White House pronouncements and the media's own domination of the storyline. The new storyline, as Andrew Wyatt described the coverage from 5 to 12 April, "is not what [Bush] is doing to relieve this suffering, but why he didn't do more to prevent it." With television and journalist access to Iraqi territory restored at just the moment of the refugee crisis itself, questions that had been bottled up for weeks were now asked in the spotlight of dying humanity.

As will be seen more closely in the next chapter on media pressure, the new storyline shift accompanied a new moralizing that was targeted specifically at the White House, and more peripherally at Whitehall. The *Guardian*, in a line as memorable for its prose as its criticism called Bush's handling of the civil war, "as morally anaemic a display of switched off executive apathy as one wants to see."[37]

This was not exclusively the media position. The *New York Times*, in one notable article by Clyde Haberman, did in fact place the causality beyond the idea of media or public pressure, writing "that US airlifts began after the Bush administration was criticized by some of its European allies in the gulf war for not relieving the increasingly desperate situation of Iraqi opposition groups. Britain had announced plans for its own airlift before Washington acted."[38]

This, however, was a rare exception. Instead, motivations were most often found domestically. The question is: where did they get this idea? With the greatest of irony, it appears the source was the

White House itself. The White House clearly noted that the press and what seemed to be the general public held the executive in some disregard for its handling of the Iraqi Civil War, although no consensus existed about how it should have been handled. The White House had insisted that its actions were consistent with UN policy, and all seeming episodes of U.S. support for the rebels were actually U.S. defensive actions to ensure the safety of coalition forces. Once France, Britain, and Turkey pressured the United States into providing aid and support under the guidelines that the UN proscribed, the United States then cynically chose to present the aid efforts as a moral outreach that was responsive to the needs of the American public. This was a bad idea.

Teleology came into play now, with the press, who believed they had just received confirmation that they and public pressure had prompted the policy shift. The idea came directly from the White House who admitted to feelings of guilt and a need to help. If the White House had maintained its reasons, and had admitted to the desire to help based on geopolitical concerns rather than humanitarian ones—paradoxical though it seems—it may have later silenced the conventional wisdom that was building around this topic. By putting a moral spin on it, however, the White House instead cemented the storyline that the press had incorrectly been supposing for weeks and thereby sealed its own fate in the annals of the CNN Effect watchers.

Of course, this is not the way it was being reported. As far as television in particular was concerned, everything Bush did and did not do was based on his own efforts to save his political career. Peter Jennings explained the move to step up aid efforts on 11 April:

> We begin tonight with some basic military wisdom: the best defense is a good offense. For more than a week now, President Bush has been hearing mounting criticism that he abandoned millions of Iraqi Kurds and allowed Saddam Hussein to crush their rebellion and even then was slow to come to their aid when they fled into the mountains. Today here in Washington the Bush Administration has gone very publicly on the record about the relief effort finally under way. It also says it had warned the Iraqis not to do something they hadn't done anyway. Here's ABC's Brit Hume.

The idea that the camera's were attracting the aid, rather than Bush's plans to get the Kurds out of Turkey as the only stable solution for the region, was staring to come from the refugee agencies as well. As ABC news' Jeanne Meserve explained, "Relief organizations credit the turnaround to the powerful pictures coming in from the Turkish and Iranian borders. Pictures of suffering, starvation and death. Pictures so overwhelming that they open pocketbooks."

The day the Americans decided to deploy ground troops, 16 April, was the day of peak American coverage. From this point forward, it would all be downhill. The central storyline of the West's role in a postwar Iraq now seemed answered. They were there to resettle the refugees, and once they were done they would leave. John Major was the hero of the moment, and was widely reported as the prime mover of the safe havens idea. The *Guardian*, generally not a supporter of Tory policies, acquiesced and stated magnanimously, "Mr Major's cautious plea for time while he took 'legal advice' now seems vindicated at a time when domestic pressure as well as humanitarian compassion makes a success doubly welcome to his party."[39]

That the plan originated in Europe and Turkey was often forgotten by the U.S. media, and Bush did little to share the credit for the successes of the operation. The American reporting of the events, however, was rather off in other ways as well, as though the people who had been covering the events for the past month-and-a-half suddenly forgot what they had been reporting. In the *Washington Post*, Mary McGrory wrote that "George Bush has finally done what he should have done a month ago. He is sending US troops to the Turkish mountains to rescue the starving, freezing Kurds." But of course, a month before there *were* no Kurdish refugees in the Turkish mountains and the Kurds were launching their most successful offensives against the Iraqi military in the north of the country. It was just this sort of reporting, however, that confused later analysts of the Kurdish crisis into thinking that the Bush administration had changed its policies when in fact it was initiating wholly new policies in the face of new events, and maintaining its old policies with regard to older events.

The *Washington Post* itself was not immune to the curiosity of not reading its own coverage. An 18 April editorial exhorted:

> President Bush has done one of the hardest things a politician is called on to do—recognize that a policy was wrong or at least failing, and change course. This accounts for his decision to join Britain and France in dispatching troops to northern Iraq to set up havens for a half-million or more displaced Kurds fleeing toward Turkey. A great protest had arisen not simply at his seeming unconcern for the Kurds but at his reluctance to acknowledge greater responsibility for people who had fallen into a terrible predicament partly by reason of his urging them to rise up against Saddam Hussein. Now Mr. Bush has responded.

Jim Hoagland made the same argument:[40] "Like Gregor Samsa, the Bush administration awoke from the Persian Gulf War to find it had been turned into a cockroach, or the moral equivalent thereof. A change as mysterious and hideous as the opening scene in Kafka's 'The Metamorphosis' had come over the gang that shot so straight and fast in getting Saddam Hussein out of Kuwait."

Charles Krauthammer was among very few who noted that the civil war was over and that aid to the refugees was not the same as aid for the rebels: "'Vietnam' is [Bush's] preferred retort to those who fault him for not having used American air power to tilt the balance of the Iraqi civil war, when there was a balance to tilt. (The argument is now, sadly, historical.)."

Nevertheless, the language of public opinion was now fully deployed, a sea-change in American policy was cited, but the facts remained starkly otherwise. The Bush administration had not deployed a single U.S. serviceman into Iraq to fight soldiers, to support Kurdish resistance efforts, or to shoot down helicopters. There was no let-up in the rate of troop withdrawal in the south, no new pressures were put on Saddam Hussein, and no change in the UN resolutions was called for.

Conventional wisdom thought otherwise. The *Washington Post* regularly offered sentences combing public sentiment and geopolitics as co-causes to events they clearly could not explain, such as: "Public outrage over the plight of the Kurds has emboldened governments to take tougher positions against Saddam and more active roles in efforts to prevent a long-term refugee problem that could further destabilize the region." Whether this means that the public was galvanized, or the reporters were, is uncertain and considering that the public polling data was not strongly on the side of intervention, it is interesting to ask where this implicit measurement came from.[41]

But again, the answer may be the White House, which wasn't helping its own cause by wrapping itself in the moral blanket of redemption. After all, when the White House said, "[w]hat's driving this is if we don't use the military to get this done, a lot of refugees will simply die," the journalists are absolved from searching for alternative explanations.

Media coverage had reached it peak. From this point forward, as in Britain, the story would shift dramatically, and in this case, to the opposite side of the American psyche. Now that the Kurds were being fed, the panic (from an embattled Democratic party and from a media with far less to report than during the war) would suddenly become, "how will we get *out* of Iraq; is this intervention the beginning of a new Vietnam?" As the data in the next section makes clear, media pressure is effectively over from this week forward—the actions have been taken, the questions asked, and the monotony of endless repetition has taken the unwelcome role of story's end.

BBC Television, ITN, ABC, CBS, NBC, and CNN were all reporting regularly now from the mountains, and the devastation and sheer human misery bombarded viewers. The U.S. military, far from considering the possible consequences of a "quagmire" were now starting to send information up the chain of command, saying in effect, "if you want this done, then do it right." "In the US, fears are mounting that American troops protecting Kurdish refugees are being sucked into a prolonged new commitment in northern Iraq," reported one paper.[42] The change in tone was notable, but it wasn't the military that was complaining. In fact, many U.S. service personnel in particular who were forced to stand by and watch as villages were razed within sight of U.S. encampments were only too glad to aid in the relief effort.

While the glare of the spotlight was real, and twenty-four-hour coverage was a new phenomenon, it was still a nascent one and the lines of communication between the field and the bureaus were still primitive. In April 1991, all news networks reporting from Cukurca in Turkey were using the same three telephone lines out of a post office and satellite telephones remained a dream. Transportation was also an issue. As David Hearst reported, "ABC television went to join the latest Medecins Sans Frontieres relief flight from Paris. ITN crews are trampling over the mountains, allegedly carrying medicines, but I assume a few videotapes as well. It could well be that the first any refugee sees of Western 'aid' is a well dressed camera crew."[43]

Phase 5, the expansion of Kurdish safe havens on 26 April, was accompanied by low-key coverage about the event. The aforementioned failure of the NSC to sufficiently understand the operational environment, which may have led to a full military invasion of Dohuk, received no important press coverage in the United States. What British coverage existed was casual, though, as seen in chapter 4, the Dohuk situation was anything but. The *Guardian incorrectly* reported as follows:

> The taking of the city is largely symbolic. No opposition is expected and units of all the allied forces will be involved, with American, British, French, Dutch, Italian, Spanish, and even Luxembourg troops moving in. Occupying Dohuk will be the easy part of the allied operation: harder will be helping the jaded refugees re-create a civic structure and

normal services in a town shattered by war. Harder still will be finding a way of leaving it, given Kurdish anxieties about the intentions of the Iraqi government.[44]

In the end, however, due to smart operational work and on-the-ground diplomacy, Dohuk was taken without force, the refugees were resettled, and Operation Provide Comfort began to end. The UN, though generally unprepared for the task, was forced into taking it over with its limited staff based out of Geneva at the UNHCR, and the troubles in northern Iraq began to fade.

If a single episode marks the end of media pressure on behalf of the Kurds and the switch in the national discussions about aid to refugees and the Kurds, it may be the controversy that surrounded a rock concert in London set up to collect aid for the Kurdish refugees. Like Concert for Bangladesh in 1971 and Live Aid in 1985 for the Ethiopian famine, the concern brought together twenty rock performers from Rod Stewart to Tom Jones broadcasting from three continents to raise funds for the Kurds. The initiative came from Jeffery Archer, the author and former deputy chairman of Britain's Conservative Party, who, in April, organized the initiative and persuaded the British government to contribute $17 million to the project. But soon after the initiative began, certain performers, notably Sinead O'Conner, Sting, and Peter Gabriel, raised the question of why the aid wasn't being shared with the Bangladeshi victims of the cyclone, which claimed some 138,000 lives, or else African refugees. This broadening of the discourse about aid to refugees from the Kurds to those simply in need signaled a closure to the prior public focus on Western responsibility for the Kurds in particular. As the data in chapter 6 makes evident, pressure of any kind was now effectively dead.[45]

CHAPTER 6

Measuring Pressure, Testing for Influence

In this chapter we finally bring all the theory and data together and disaggregate pressure from coverage. It's the first chance to put the theory to practice. We begin with the creation of data sets from U.S. press conferences and then discover how to move from the press conferences to measuring pressure in another media venue through the use of "objectionables." The measures are then provided. And as in the previous chapter, we again took at trends in the media by cross-checking the measures created with the claims of the media actors in both countries during the case study period. It will be shown that the explicit measurement techniques are well in line with the implicit readings of media actors in terms of intensity of pressure but are also better because they can empirically undermine false claims.

CREATING DATA SETS

When discussing U.S. press conferences, it was explained how press conference transcripts can be coded for measuring media attention. The first pass was to count all questions fielded that day. The second pass was to then code questions as being on-topic or off-topic, using the central storyline criteria discussed earlier. Coverage was then measured as the percentage of topical questions asked that day from the total that could have been asked on-topic. In this section, a third pass of coding takes place to separate pressure questions from non-pressure questions. To make the determination of whether the executive experienced the force of the journalist's question as pressure, we look for evidence of either *repositioning* or *rhetorical redescription* in the response.

Repositioning will take place along an authoritative axis, whereby either moral authority or agentive authority are being threatened by the question as it was posed by the journalist and understood by the executive. In the case of moral authority, responses that cast the executive in a morally upright manner (as locally defined and experienced) are notable, where its actions are justifiable and demonstrate "goodness." In matters of agentive authority, we'll expect two possible moves. The first positions the executive as strong and capable of acting, as opposed to weak and impotent. The second type of positioning deliberately places the executive *beyond* the realm of accountability for an action or event by positioning the executive as lacking either knowledge that enabled action, or else the physical capacity to act. These moves may be used to distance the executive from actions or events that clearly took place and are admitted by the White House as lacking moral standing as well.

Redescription is a similar but broader act to repositioning. It may be thought of as a superordinate move in a conversational game, much like rephrasing someone's question rather than answering it. The executive will often redescribe events in such a manner as to defend or create increased authority for an action or non-action. Such descriptions are commonly called "characterizations" in the lingo of the press rooms as in the phrase, "I wouldn't characterize it quite like that," or "How would you characterize the U.S. relationship with Turkey?" There should be no doubt that the descriptive words selected are extremely deliberate, and very often are decided in top-level meetings when a list of authorized adjectives describing an event will be produced.

Each time a response repositions the executive, or rhetorically describes events, the question is coded as pressure. *It is argued that repositioning and redescription of acts occur because the White House speaker finds something in the question objectionable to its reputation or standing that needs to be changed immediately.* The number of questions that evokes a repositioning or redescription act, as a subset of the total questions asked on-topic, is coded as pressure questions.

The next step is to transform the raw numbers of pressure questions into more meaningful percentages, as was done with coverage. The number of questions so identified as pressure are used to form a percentage from the total number of questions asked on-topic that day. So if 100 questions were asked, and 50 questions were on-topic (i.e., measure of coverage) and 30 were pressure questions, then pressure was measured as 30 percent on that day. These percentage measures are comparable across time, unlike the raw question counts.

The final stage is to take the daily totals and produce weekly totals. Press conferences are not held every day, and the number of questions asked on any given day varies, so weekly tallies are better for aggregate measures over longer periods to better average the percentages. A week was defined as Monday–Sunday. In some cases, such as 25–31 March 1991, there were a total of 379 questions asked that week. The next week, probably due to a White House communication strategy in response to the massive media pressure that existed during the prior week, only 15 questions were able to be fielded by reporters.[1] In these cases, percentages were still created and treated as comparable on the logic that if one's chances of speaking to the White House are either generous or restricted, one will still ask what is thought is most important in any case. The reason the data will be slightly skewed is that so few opportunities for posing questions surely produce different questions, as journalists can make do without White House quotes for some stories, but not others. Limiting journalists' questions, therefore, probably has a qualitative effect on press conferences. This remains speculative, however and was not tested in this study.

Once pressure has been measured at the press conferences through face-to-face conversational episodes that provide strong coding confidence, it is necessary to expand the scope of measure beyond the press conference and into newspapers and television. In order to ensure that the evidence learned from executive responses is used to inform the coding of news sources such as newspapers and television (or radio, the Internet, etc.), it is necessary to take the information outside into the press conference.

Coding "Objectionables"

How do we know whether or not a media report should be labeled as pressure? The answer is to code the *responses* of the executive to the statements of the media. On the basis of the response, we know for certain that the media said something objectionable. So for simplicity, the list of things that are objectionable are called objectionables. It works like this:

1. Each day, produce a list of questions or characterizations by the journalists at the press conferences that were treated as pressure by the executive.

2. On the basis of these "pressure questions" use a grounded approach to abducing a short list of categories, themes, topics, or key words (like descriptions) that were evidently objectionable to the executive. This list now forms a cluster of "objectionables," that is, those characterizations or claims made by the media found

objectionable by the White House and evidently responded to with repositioning or redescription.

3. Examine the first published or broadcast media reports that come out after we know, for certain, that something is "objectionable" and look for evidence of those objectionables

4. Label that broadcast or article as "pressure" or "not pressure" if those objectionables are found or not found.

5. Disaggregate the media coverage that day from media pressure and enter it as time series data.

6. Display graphically the difference between media attention and media pressure.

This seems a bit complicated at first but can be learned quickly. We are looking at the press conferences, seeing what the government evidently found objectionable because of their acts of repositioning, making a list of things, and then, when the reports actually come out into the world, we know for a fact that the government will view this as bad press because they effectively said so already.

There are a series of assumptions here. First, I assume the White House will find the same acts of positioning or rhetorical description objectionable whether they are spoken, in print, or broadcast. Second, it is also assumed that any publication or broadcast with the listed objectionables from that day will be relevant at the time of dissemination based on the criteria that were observed at the press conferences. As technology increases and the media–government dialogue becomes even faster, this may prove outdated. The method can be updated by using any face-to-face event between the media and government that allows us to spot objectionables, and then looking for the first media broadcasts (or whatever they come to be called!) after the fact. The approach and theory should hopefully withstand the test of time.

Third, in the measures to follow, it is assumed that a few hours on either side of a question will not change what the White House considers objectionable, because policies are seldom made hourly, and when changes are made or events overtake policies, there remain positioning imperatives that provide cohesion to policy statements and objectives. Again, this may change as technology makes the conversation faster, but I suspect the reality will remain rather stable. Likewise, were such rare circumstances to occur, the coding error would be corrected in the next day's measures and, since material is gathered and compared on a *weekly* basis, such variations should not be viewed as problematic. (See figure 6.1.)

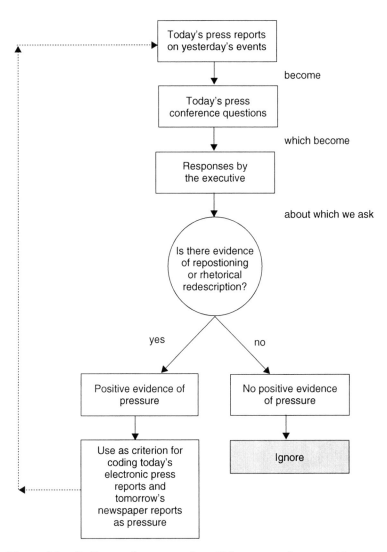

Figure 6.1   Coding media pressure from U.S. press conference evidence

INDEPENDENT MEASURES OF
MEDIA PRESSURE

Press Conference Findings

Fifty news conferences were held between 1 March and 2 June 1991, during which 2,719 questions were asked of the president or the White House spokesman; 636 were asked on the subject of Iraq and U.S. activities toward it, of which 218 were pressure on the White House. This means that 23 percent of all questions of all possible subjects that might have been asked by the media for three months was about this one aspect of U.S. foreign policy. Further, 8 percent of all questions posed to the White House on any subject for a three-month period were objectionable questions about Iraq. Considering that questions to the White House ran a gambit from the president's taxes, to "Travelgate," to farming matters in the Midwest, this figure would seem to belie arguments (at least for this time period) that the U.S. media is uninterested or unconcerned with U.S. foreign policy broadly defined.

Figure 6.2 provides an overview of the press conference findings. Further details on media behavior is found in the section titled "Understanding Trends in Media Pressure, March–June," in this chapter.

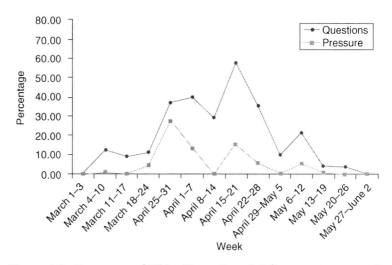

Figure 6.2 Percentage of White House Press Briefing questions on-topic versus pressure questions

The themes of press conference questions on Iraq, as one can expect, changed over time, due partly to the realities on the ground in Iraq, and partly based on the changing political characteristics of U.S. reaction to them. The first event that was covered was the uprisings. Questions were fielded about U.S. actions with regard to them, and also for matters of clarification about events on the ground, especially after 8 March when Saddam expelled all foreign journalists. What was notable here was the reliance the media placed on using the White House for *intelligence* information about the events in Iraq—not only for U.S. policy positions, planning, or other matters relating to the United States as an actor. The more complicated the events in Iraq became, the more the media relied on the White House to provide coherence and meaning to the events. This was more than a simple probing for the White House's "read," but an actual dependence on the institution as a source of intelligence and analysis.

The second main group of questions in early March involved the massacres of Shiites, Marsh Arabs, Kurds, and other groups outside of the Sunni heartland. These questions were asked both for their intelligence value as well as a general query for a moral structure to the events. The media were probing the story, not knowing what to make of the events. Were the revolts sponsored by Iran or another foreign power? Was the coalition backing the uprisings? Were they organized and deliberate, or spontaneous and chaotic? Of central importance was whether or not Saddam Hussein was going to stay in power.

As the uprisings appeared to gain momentum and Saddam's regime was teetering in an unorchestrated pincer movement from the north and the south, questions about a U.S. response increased. There was great equivocation on whether the United States should back the resistance. The general probing for information can be seen in the figures. Until the third week of March (when the tide was turning on behalf of Saddam's regime), press questions on the matter only hovered at some 10 percent. Less than half of these, even into the fourth week, were found to be pressure on the executive. While coverage was increasing in the newspapers and television, there was no "story" in the form of a central tension that split the nation and could be reported from home. With no access to Iraq, and no strong lobby to engage American troops in the region during an Arab civil war, press conference coverage did not shoot up until Schwarzkopf made confessions to David Frost that were not appreciated by his superiors.

When pressure did gather in the week of 18–24 March, it was not of the lobbyist or advocacy variety. David Mindich has argued that objectivity is the deity of American journalism, and press questions were probing for an explicit U.S. policy that was *internally consistent*. What that meant, in effect, was an explanation of U.S. policy actions that was internally sound, whether or not that policy was agreeable to a wider American audience. When the White House was thought to be divided on policy—unable to explain its actions in the light of what was known to the general population; unable to rhetorically reconcile its calls for the helicopters to be grounded and its failures to ground them; and generally thought to be conducting a policy that was not only "murky" but totally undirected and with dire consequences for civilians in Iraq at the same time—then pressure, as in the last week of March, shot through the roof.

The period of early April was not as benign as the statistical data may lead one to believe. Though pressure levels never reached higher than a modest 15.52 percent in the third week in the press conferences, the period was highly acrimonious with journalists pressing the White House for explanations, not only about their current or planned policies, but for explanations on their past behavior. Part of the statistical variance is that fewer on-topic press questions were fielded in April compared to March (793 versus 1,048, or a 25 percent reduction); this was due to a massive reduction of press access to the president in early April and then the beginning of the humanitarian aid relief and the deployment of troops in the middle of the month. The White House effectively shut down all press conferences *the day after the highest recorded pressure during the three-month period*. That day was 29 March, when fully 89 percent of all questions asked on the topic of Iraq were pressure on the government.

This was a period of democratic and moral accountability where the press pool wanted responses from the White House about a matter that now seemed clear: If those suffering in Iraq needed U.S. support now, didn't they need it earlier? And if they did, why didn't the White House provide it, seeing as the government was now evidently willing to deploy thousands of U.S. forces into northern Iraq?

By the end of March, answers provided by the White House were regularly treated as either insufficient or else insufficiently credible. Efforts to get the White House to explain its policies were intense, and the more the White House failed to offer an internally consistent explanation for its actions—as opposed to a political acceptable one—the greater the intensification became. If one lesson from this experience was brought to the communication strategists at the White House, it would be this: "Be clear, be consistent, and be logical. The media will put pressure on the White House if they do not understand the policy. This isn't because they care. It is because they need to file a report with a coherent narrative. If you are unable to provide one, they will make one up themselves." If the White House prevents the media from writing coherent articles and reports by failing to explain its policy in a coherent manner, the journalists' search for coherence *becomes* their job. The longer the White House is unable to provide internally consistent answers to its actions, the harder and the longer the media will push.

There is an overwhelmingly strong tendency on the part of journalists in the United States to assume that U.S. foreign policy is a patterned, logical, deliberate, and sound endeavor. If they are denied explanations that satisfy those assumptions, they will seek or even concoct solutions—no matter how distant from evidence those explanations may sometimes seem. If the policies are internally inconsistent, they will expect opposition leaders to exploit those failings, and the story then becomes a domestic, partisan event. In the absence of a logical foreign policy, coupled with a silent political opposition—as was the case at the end of March 1991—the press will attack.

Newspaper Pressure Measures

Now that the U.S. press conferences have been examined, a list of daily "objectionables" was created to move the matter of media pressure out of the conferences and into the broader world. This section provides the independent measure of pressure as distinct from, and compared to, media coverage in the U.S. and British papers (see figures 6.3–6.6). An explanation is provided on how the White House press conferences, used in conjunction with parliamentary records, allowed for coding of U.K. periodicals.

Newspaper pressure in the United States began mounting the third week in March and climbed steadily until the end of the month that coincided with the crushing of the rebellions and the refugee crisis. It plateaued until the first week in April, and then began a gradual but continual decline until the end of April, at which point pressure vanished whereas coverage dropped further.

Although raw paragraphs are incomparable across papers because the news holes are different, the ratio of pressure to coverage was notably higher in the *Washington Post* than the *New York Times*, though both demonstrated similar patterns of behavior. Recalling Daniel Schorr's argument that intense pressure during 2–12 April forced the hand of the U.S. executive, it is now possible to see that pressure was in *rapid decline* during the second week of April in both papers. Based on the logic of the Positioning Hypothesis (part B), this

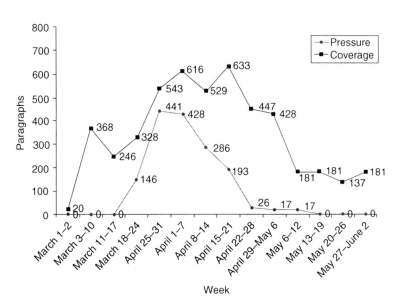

Figure 6.3 *Washington Post*: coverage versus pressure

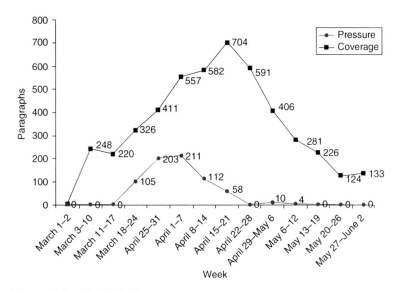

Figure 6.4 *New York Times*: coverage versus pressure

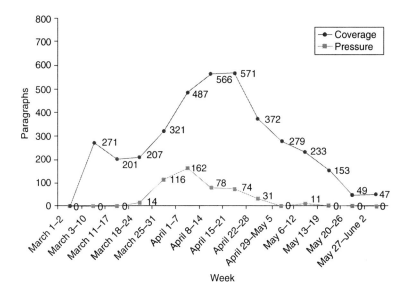

Figure 6.5   *Guardian*: coverage versus pressure

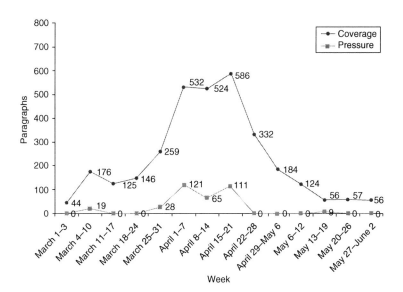

Figure 6.6   *Independent*: coverage versus pressure

was because the 5 April decision to drop aid to the refugees effectively functioned to bring moral condemnation to resolution. What remained after this was: (1) a continual probing for moral accountability of *past* inaction, (2) the continual recitation of the idea that the United States should have acted before it did, and (3) a continued concern for the well-being of the refugees, who were still suffering terribly and not being well-aided by the "international community."[2]

Coding newspaper pressure in Britain during the March–June period presented certain methodological problems because the House of Commons was not in session for the majority of the time that coverage was escalating, during which time pressure was mounting in the United States—leading to the hypothesis that it would be the case in Britain as well (U.S. data was produced first). Furthermore, a day-by-day examination of HANSARD revealed that no substantive debate or objection to governmental policy followed the unilateral ceasefire of 28 February until 28 March, when the Iraqi civil war was nearing termination and the refugee crisis began. This absence of questions to government in parliament during the March period, and then the recess of parliament during the Easter recess (29 March–14 April) makes the strong coding of face-to-face conversation unavailable, as it was for the United States. For this reason, an alternative means of coding had to be found to accommodate this history of events.

It was concluded that the best alternative means of coding the material was to use the list of daily objectionables created from the White House press conferences by the media, the difference being that the objectionables—where they were reflected in the British press, as they very often were—had to somehow pertain *directly* to British policy itself. When coding these articles as pressure, only articles that made reference to British policy *specifically* or else policy that included Britain as an actor more generally (as with collective terms such as "the Coalition," or "the allies" or "the European Community") were coded as pressure.

Pressure began to mount in Britain in the final week of March, a full week after it began to appear in the United States. While U.S. papers and television were concerned about the inconsistency of Bush's policies, and particularly the helicopter issue, in Britain, moral condemnation followed the UN report, released on 22 March, that described the conditions in Iraq as "near apocalyptic."[3] One of the most notable aspects of the coverage, however, was that the British government was not the general or concerted focus of news reports about coalition policy in the post–Gulf War period. In fact, the U.S. government was overwhelming the focus of newspaper reports, and U.S. officials were the main sources of information and quotation about events in Iraq. Though this conclusion may be suspect because the list of objectionables was generated in the United States, this concern is unwarranted because U.K. newspaper reports (and lead articles and opinion pieces), *clearly* indexed the United States as the primary source of condemnation. The list of objectionables was relevant only in determining when criticism of *British* policy could be proved to be pressure on the British government.

The one major exception was the adjournment debate at the House of Commons on 29 March before the Easter break—coming, again coincidently, at almost the exact moment the civil war ended and the refugee crisis began. In one report in the *Guardian*, Dale Campbell-Savours (Lab. Workington) was the subject of a seven-paragraph article that detailed his opposition to British complicity in the civil war by virtue of its non-action. However, neither the Tories as a party nor the government itself were generally targets of criticism or even the subject of news reports.

Throughout the entire month of March and into the first week of April, there was no particular pressure placed on the government other than the indexed stories to parliamentary debate, which only commenced, and then ceased, on 29 March, and then the reporting of an all-party group of MPs who wanted British intervention of some sort (discussed in the next section). Reporting on U.S. actions, however, continued regularly, and as some of that coverage positioned the United States on defensive moral grounds, or else redescribed White House policy in ways that did not comply with the communication strategy of the administration, the United States was actually more the target of British media pressure than their own government.

The first links between the events in Iraq and British policy—other than a few lead articles in late March—came after the 29 March adjournment session in the House of Commons, and the statements of Lady Thatcher and several members of the Tory party calling for British aid to the refugees. At this point, in the public discourse, Britain's non-action was treated as somehow complicit in the suffering of the Kurds and other minorities. However, Britain was still not treated as an actor capable of unilateral action in the media reports, and therefore was not treated as uniquely responsible. Pressure on the British government from the media collectively (using these two papers as reasonable proxy measures) was generally low.

U.S. Television Pressure Measures

Transcripts of *ABC Evening News* and *CBS Evening News* were collected from the Lexis/Nexis service (NBC was unavailable), and CNN transcripts, though not coded, were also reviewed to check discrepancies, if they existed (see figures 6.7 and 6.8).

ABC News transcripts and CBS News transcripts were read and evaluated on a day-by-day basis, using the same criteria as for the newspapers and the same list of objectionables created with the press conferences. Due to the unavailability of NBC transcripts, this broadcaster was not coded for pressure. Vanderbilt news summaries, though extremely helpful for coding coverage, were found insufficient for coding pressure. The reason is that, noticeably often, those who summarized the evening stories did so in such a manner as to make them "less offensive," even at the evident risk of getting the summaries wrong. Daily transcripts therefore needed to be reviewed. However, transcripts did not provide the duration of the segments, and so the Vanderbilt archives were an essential companion to this data set. A typical description of a Vanderbilt entry is provided here for reference:

1991.03.27 **IRAQ / UNREST / BUSH / SCHWARZKOPF**

5:30:20–5:34:50 . . . Wednesday . . . CBS

(Studio: Dan Rather) Report introduced.

(White House: Wyatt Andrews) President Bush reported predicting President Saddam Hussein will fall, which explains non-intervention policy; General H. Norman Schwarzkopf noted having opposed Bush's decision to stop war. [BUSH—talks about Iraqi unrest.] [In David Frost TV interview, SCHWARZKOPF—comments.] [BUSH—refutes Schwarzkopf's statements.]

(Studio: Dan Rather) British commander reported saying Iraq is violating ceasefire by using helicopters against rebels. Report introduced.

(Pentagon: David Martin) Iraq unrest examined; details given of northern Kurdish victories under leader Massoud Barzani; scenes shown. [BARZANI—comments on rebellion.] [State Department spokeswoman Margaret TUTWILER—talks about Saddam's planning to retake Kirkuk, Iraq.] Administration's decisions to allow Iraqi army to keep armaments and use them against rebels examined; Pentagon analyst quoted.

[SCHWARZKOPF—comments.] Certainty of U.S. intervention if Saddam uses chemical weapons noted.

Nowhere has the value of independent measures of coverage and pressure been more obviously apparent than for ABC News coverage. The divergence between the two—and therefore the vital importance of not mistaking one for another—is striking in the third week of

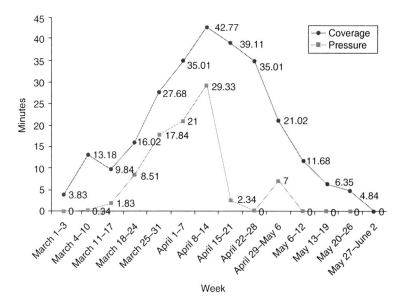

Figure 6.7 ABC News: coverage versus pressure, 1991

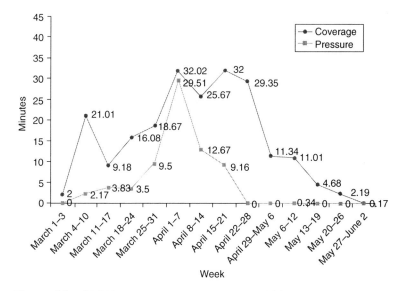

Figure 6.8 CBS News: coverage versus pressure, 1991

April. Pressure began to mount in the week of 18–24 March, when pressure measures jumped from 18.6 percent the preceding week to 53.12 percent. This week, and the first few days of the next, saw the first pictures from northern Iraq, firsthand reporting of events there, the beginning of the refugee crisis, the end of the revolt in the south, and the Schwarzkopf controversy over when the war should have ended. By the week of 25–31 March, pressure on the U.S. executive from television coverage was at a high of 64.45 percent of all coverage and still rising.

As with newspapers, this period marked the end of optimism about the potential for Saddam Hussein to be overthrown and a turn on the U.S. policymakers to find out "what went wrong." The UN report about conditions in Iraq was also regularly cited. What is so remarkable is how pressure would keep climbing to a peak of 68.58 percent the week of 8–14 April and then plummet—as though nothing had happened—to 5.98 percent as soon as the United States and the United Kingdom made the announcement they would deploy ground forces on 15 April.

The data from television produced here makes certain lessons plain to both the White House and 10 Downing Street. By identifying the primary storyline (i.e., the central tension and its incumbent actors), the executive should be able to rapidly and soundly reduce television pressure by providing a storyline resolution in the form of a plausible policy or statement that addresses *exactly* the story the television is covering. This cannot be done with newspapers, if the data produced here is representative of a wider phenomenon. Other cases will need to be studied to see whether the pattern is replicated.

The first weeks of April were concentrated on the controversy surrounding the U.S. decision to end the war when it did, to not assist the rebellions—or more specifically, not shoot down the helicopters—and then to not aid the refugees. The sudden and dramatic decline in ABC pressure was because the primary storyline tension of "why isn't the United States aiding the Kurds" was resolved when the airdrops began, and then silenced as soon as the U.S. troops were actually deployed on the ground. Television seemed only able to present and follow a single storyline that, in turn, brought rhetorical closure by the single act of the airdrops. Newspapers, on the other hand, showed the ability to maintain numerous, simultaneous storylines that in turn required far more actions or statements by the executive to end the numerous controversies. This explains the slow decline in newspaper pressure compared to television.

It can be seen from the slow rise in pressure as compared to coverage, and then the precipitous drop in pressure compared to the lingering coverage, that not only can coverage not be used as proxy measure for pressure in U.S. television coverage, but that the pressure from television is highly correlated to the changes in U.S. policymaking, adding further support to the metaphor of a "conversation" between the media and government, and demonstrating how positioning acts by the government can work effectively to silence media opposition. Who is leading whom is being seen as the wrong metaphor. Instead, the government's statements and actions are providing the content for the media organizations. When the content provided by the government's statements and deeds no longer supports central storylines the media has constructed, the storyline is brought to a close. If that close was morally satisfying, the story is dropped. If it is not satisfying, the story will linger for as long as the media have a conversational partner. Once the government and the opposition fall silent, there is no one else to talk to.

NET FIGURES ON PRESSURE

Figure 6.9 provides the weekly totals of newspaper coverage versus pressure. For the United States, the *Washington Post* yielded 4,822 paragraphs of coverage, of which 1,554, or 32 percent, were pressure. The *New York Times* provided 4,813 paragraphs of coverage, of which 703 paragraphs, or 15 percent, were pressure.

In Britain, the *Independent* provided 3,201 paragraphs of coverage, of which 353, or 11 percent, were pressure. The *Guardian* provided 3,771 paragraphs of coverage and 486 paragraphs of pressure, or 13 percent of the total published for the period. Though these total figures are of limited utility in understanding the relations between the media and government over the case study period, they are interesting in terms of media behavior in the two countries. Knowing the American predilection toward "objectivity" and the generally partisan nature of British reporting by comparison, it would not have been expected that both U.S. broadsheets put more pressure on their government than did

	Paragraphs as coverage	Paragraphs as pressure	Aqqreqate pressure over period (%)
Washington Post	4822	1554	32
New York Times	4813	703	15
Guardian	3771	486	13
Independent	3201	353	11

Figure 6.9 Weekly totals of newspaper coverage versus pressure, 1 March–2 June 1991

the broadsheets aligned with the British opposition. The comparison cannot be pushed too far because Britain was not able to act independently in the Civil War as could have the Americans. However, calls for action were not the only form of pressure the government was under. Claims of cynicism, immorality, and impotence were dogging John Major throughout the period, and pressure to act could well have been higher—if only that action were supported via the United Nations, the European Community, or some other body that could have supported the British need for a land force to carry out an independent operation.

Measures of coverage and pressure alike vary widely. During the week of 25–31 March, when coverage shot up, intensive media pressure accompanied the increased coverage, as seen in figure 6.10. During this week, 379 questions were asked at press conferences, and 142 were about the U.S. role in a postwar Iraq. Of these, fully 75 percent were pressure questions. During the week of 15–21 April, when the United States and the United Kingdom announced the deployment of ground troops in support of the relief efforts, a similar number of questions were fielded to the White House (393) with almost 20 percent more questions on the matter of Iraq. Despite the similar number of total questions and the notable increase in coverage, only 27 percent of the questions were objectionable to the White House and could be coded as pressure.

This demonstrates that media attention (questions on topic) is not a sufficient proxy measure for media pressure. What is important about these comparative measures is that independent measures of pressure produce an entirely different result from the measures of media coverage—results so different they produce a new history of events. Note that from a similar number of questions asked (393 versus 379), the April period showed a marked increase in media coverage (questions on-topic) compared to only two weeks earlier, but media pressure had decreased during the same period. The reason, in this case, was that at the end of March, an estimated 1,000 people a day were dying in the Turkish and Iraqi mountains and the United States had made no

	Total questions asked	Questions on topic	On topic as a percentage	Pressure questions	Pressure questions as percentage of total questions	Pressure questions as percentage of on total questions
March 25–31	379	142	34.47	107	28.23	75.35
April 15–21	393	228	58.02	61	15.52	26.75

Figure 6.10   The value of disaggregation

effort to help them, though it was being blamed for their plight. By 15 April, the United States (with the support of Belgium, Canada, France, Germany, Italy, the Netherlands, New Zealand, Turkey [the host country for the refugees], and the United Kingdom) had committed massive aid and military support to ameliorate their suffering and return them to their homes in northern Iraq.

Interest increased because of the deployment of troops, the sudden availability of both visuals and access, the feed-in to the post–Gulf War storylines and other reasons. But pressure had dropped because the executive had resolved the storyline that took as its central conflict American inaction and amoral policy in the face of a humanitarian disaster for which it was deemed partly responsible. In this single example, we can see how inadequate it would have been to equate attention with pressure, the utility of providing such measures, and how the logic of events provides the explanation for the observed differences in the context of that society's moral discourse.

These problems would be cause for concern if there were not an independent, external measurement available against which to cross-check whether our empirically generated one is on the mark. Luckily, there is in the conventional wisdom and experience of the press itself. There are excellent indicators by journalists and editorial writers that suggest the explicit measure of pressure conducted here is quite similar to their own intuitive measures of it, perhaps the most explicit in this study being that of March 29. The press conference that day demonstrated, by far, the highest percentage of questions asked on the topic (at a regular press conference) at 64 percent—up from a previous high of 35 percent—of which fully 88.89 percent—also the highest recorded—were coded as pressure. It was, not coincidentally, the day that one exasperated journalist would finally shout out, "have we beaten this to death yet and I'm free to change the topic?" It was also the last press conference the White House would give for the next sixteen days—by far the longest period of silence since the crisis began. Regular briefings would begin only after the United States had started to aid the refugees and the press had started to calm down. Completing this quantitative analysis with a traditional history of the communication strategies of the White house would provide for a much more complete record of the policymaking history from the period.

Other evidence of journalist's own intuitive measures of pressure can be found in Britain. On 4 April, the *Guardian* ran an article detailing the abuse the U.S. administration was under from newspaper columnists and journalists alike. According to the measures here, the last week of March was the most intense period of pressure questions on the executive at White House press conferences. The following week, when the press conferences were largely cancelled at the White House, the few questions that were raised were intense. The *Guardian* observed of this same period: "While Mr Bush and his top officials have been on holiday [in early April], the thankless task of sustaining a broad defense of U.S. policy has fallen on the spokesmen at the White House and State Department, who have had to endure some of the most intensive grillings in their careers." Again, the insight of professional journalists and their implicit sense of pressure levels are helpful means of cross-checking our own findings. They are not, however, sufficient for producing accurate history, as seen in Daniel Schorr's understandable miscalculation about impact.

Understanding Trends in Media Pressure, March–June

The White House built a very public argument that eventually trapped them in their own rhetoric because they were unwilling to accept the imperatives their own argument dictated. The argument was built on three steps. First, Bush describes the situation as one that merits concern. Second, he states that the concern is at such a level of significance to the United States that it "has got to be resolved." Third, the resolution of the problem must be accomplished before there can be any permanence to the unilateral coalition ceasefire. And implicit in the answer, based on pervious statements, is that American forces will not come home until that permanent ceasefire is in effect. This means that *the primary obstacle keeping U.S. forces from returning home was the Iraqi use of helicopters* that violated Bush's understanding of the pervious ceasefire arrangement negotiated by Schwarzkopf at Safwan. By no stretch of the imagination could such a statement be taken as a casual concern over the plight of terrorized civilians.

Professor Eliot Cohen described the problem well as he looked back on what transpired during this turbulent period:[4]

> "I was somebody who thought and still thinks we shouldn't go to Baghdad," said Eliot A. Cohen, professor of strategic studies at the Johns Hopkins School of Advanced International Studies, who supported Bush's war policies. "But by saying the things the president said, we did incur some moral obligations," Cohen went on. "When you compare Saddam to Hitler and you call on the people to overthrow him, you simply can't stand aside when Saddam brutalizes them."
>
> "The most troubling thing about the moral debate is that one doesn't have the sense that the administration feels at all responsible, that

their actions led us to these events," Cohen concluded. "Of course they're not responsible, Saddam Hussein is responsible . . . But did we say things that led to these ghastly events?"

April 26 was a very bad day for the U.S. administration. It was the first day that the American newspaper journalists visited rebel-held territory, and those around Safwan published reports of atrocities being carried out by the Iraqis against the Shiites in the south, as the latter were now spilling over in the American-held zone and being treated by doctors and interviewed by reporters. It was the first day that Massoud Barzani held a press conference with Western journalists that would fuel the rise in atrocity stories coming from the north.[5] It was the first day of serious media pressure on the U.S. executive, when almost 36 percent of all questions asked at that day's press conference were on the events in Iraq, and of those, over 80 percent were objectionable to the White House position. It was the day that the Schwarzkopf story broke and the unity of the postwar period marked its end. It was also the day the White House announced explicitly it would not shoot down Iraqi helicopters ending any "constructive ambiguity."

The *Independent*'s headline on page 9 read, "President Bush hoped the Iraqi army would topple Saddam Hussein. Now the administration is not sure what to do." The *Washington Post* called their front-page article, "Border Town Becomes Wasteland of Refugees" and another, "A Trail of Death in Iraq; Shiite Refugees Tell of Atrocities by Republican Guard." The first sentence in this otherwise conservative and non-sensationalist paper read: "Iraqi President Saddam Hussein's shock Republican Guard has carved a trail of death through rebellious central and southern Iraq, shelling families on the streets, gunning them down in fields and summarily executing young Shiite Muslim males, according to haggard, grief-stricken refugees reaching this U.S.-held area today." Though the language was strong, this is exactly what had been happening for weeks.

The articles had been written and submitted the day before, and were now on the front page the very day that Schwarzkopf made his admissions about disagreement with Bush and about being suckered.

Media attention not only skyrocketed from now until the first week of April, but pressure mounted in the newspapers, television, and at the White House press conferences to such an extent that on April 29, 72 percent of all questions posed that day were about the insurrections in Iraq, and 89 percent of those were in turn "pressure questions" as defined in chapter 3.

To say there was strong pressure on the White House in the form of reporting that was objectionable to U.S. policymakers, however, is not to say that there was a unified media voice calling for American intervention. The reality, in fact, was surprisingly different. On 20 March, for example, the *New York Times* published its first editorial about American involvement in the Iraqi Civil War. Even as pressure was beginning to mount against the White House to explain the evident inconsistency of its policy and the absence of a discernible rational behind it, the "newspaper of record" came out squarely *against* coalition involvement in the Iraqi Civil War. That day, they also published an opinion by Leslie Gelb against intervention in which he suggests that Bush pull forces out of Iraq and into Kuwait to avoid possible casualties.[6] The *Post* was singing a similar tune, though its editorial was as indecisive as the policies they referred to. Rather than prompting the United States for action and intervention, or else to stay out of the fighting for the sake of regional stability, they concluded obliquely that "the way the United States handles the shorter-term task of seeing out Saddam Hussein will bear crucially on its longer-term policy." It was hardly an opinion, let alone a call to arms, in favor of the insurgents. Furthermore, even as the rebellion degraded and the first hints of a refugee crisis appeared near the end of the month, the *Post* remained uncertain but generally against intervention: "the inclination not to intervene heavily and directly in the internal fighting in Iraq seems to us right."[7]

And yet, even in the *Independent*, moral outrage was not turning to cries for intervention. In the entire month of March—when events were unfolding and could have been affected, as opposed to April when the civil war was effectively over—only eight opinion pieces would be published about the events in Iraq. In April, once the humanitarian relief efforts had been launched and the firing had stopped, a wave of post-hoc moral anxiety swept the country and forty-nine opinion pieces would be published about what had just happened and who was responsible. This was not an isolated case. The *Guardian* only published five opinion pieces from 1 March through 30 June, and all were in the first two weeks of April. Likewise, in the first week of April they would publish five editorials—one each day—which was as many as they published in the entire month of March. In the United States, the situation was the same. The *Washington Post* published six op/ed pieces from outside authors (not all calling for intervention) during the month of March, and twenty-eight during April. The *New York Times* published seven opinion pieces in March, and fifteen in the first two weeks of April. Two editorials, neither of which called for intervention, were published in March, and five were published in the first two weeks of April alone. This simple measure of media attention (supported by other measures in the next section) illustrates clearly how all possible media pressure to act (the few late pieces in the *Independent* notwithstanding) came *after the civil war was over and the refugee crisis began*. It wasn't until it was all over and the refugees were streaming out of the country that media coverage, media pressure, and government policy in the United States and Great Britain would change.

But even as attention increased, pressure dropped. This new finding undermines Schorr's claim that it was the media that pressured the governments into the commitment of ground forces on 15 April. We will return to this. Schorr claimed that during the period 2–12 April, "[c]overage of the massacre and exodus of the Kurds generated public pressures that were instrumental in slowing the hasty American military withdrawal from Iraq and forcing a return to help guard and care for the victims of Saddam Hussein's vengeance." Comparative polling data from the two ends of the time period is unavailable, but media pressure data is. CBS during the first week of April (1–7), presented 32.02 minutes of coverage. A total of 92.16 percent of it was pressure on the government in the form of objectionable reporting about U.S. policy. The second week, coverage dropped a bit to 25.67 minutes, but pressure dropped to 49.36 percent. If we examine the daily data, we find that pressure dropped exactly where we might expect it: on 6 April, CBS pressure dropped as attention shifted to helping the Kurds, and on 16 April—rated at 58.59 percent of coverage—it would be the last day over 30 percent and the beginning of the complete closure of the story of U.S. prior inaction or moral responsibility. In the *New York Times*, pressure dropped from 37.88 percent in the first week of April to 19.24 percent the second week. In the *Washington Post*, pressure dropped from 69.48 percent the fist week to 54.06 percent. In both cases, pressure would continue to decline from this point forward. ABC News was the only exception, but the pattern was not very contradictory to the other findings. Pressure went from 65.26 percent the first week to 68.58 percent, but would then drop dramatically to 5.98 percent in the third week of April, when the troops were being deployed and the recovery effort was rapidly improving the conditions of the refugees.

Newspaper pressure peaked during 25–31 March when the *Washington Post* demonstrated a pressure level of 81.22 percent; the *New York Times* peaked at 49.39 percent and then dropped over the next three weeks. Television pressure, however, increased during the first week of April. Pressure from ABC would hold steady, averaging about 65 percent of coverage from 25 March to 14 April, dropping quickly with the introduction of ground forces after April 16. CBS pressure shot up during the first week of April but then dropped drastically once the airdrops were under way. As media pressure was at its height *before* Bush instructed the military to prepare for a relief operation, we are left with the conclusion that something else changed his mind about what to do about the Kurds. That something else was allied pressure from Britain, France, and Turkey.

Following Bush's announcement of the new policy to airdrop aid to the refugees around the Turkish border and couching the actions as a moral imperative, media pressure in both U.S. papers and on CBS News immediately tapered and then declined from this point forward. Pressure from ABC News increased until the following week and the initiation of ground troops, but then dropped precipitously. The objectionable coverage coming from the media, furthermore, was not suggestive of new American policies, but rather picked up the new political communication strategy of the White House and used it to blame and castigate *prior* U.S. non-action on behalf of the Kurds. Likewise, as discussed earlier, political opposition voices from the Democratic camp now became more vocal on behalf of the Kurds and the media clearly indexed their coverage to these political voices.

The entire problem of episodic ambiguity about Bush's initial calls for Iraqis to take matters into their own hands, the subsequent— which is not to say consequent—uprisings themselves, and then the decision not to intervene on their behalf was well summed up by Allen Pizzey on CBS News. "The failure of the U.S. and its allies to do anything to stop Saddam Hussein's troops from ravaging the rebellion they encouraged has left a bitter taste here."[8]

Conventional wisdom that the United States had changed its policies because of media pressure began to take shape during the period 5–15 April. The reason the conventional wisdom developed as it did was because the episodes the media was analyzing—such as troop movements and shooting down planes—and the explanations from the White House—namely that none of this was intended to aid the insurgents—didn't make sense. In fact, the two were at times outlandishly incompatible because the policymaking that undergirded American action was inconsistent and unplanned. Journalists had a tendency—perhaps a necessary tendency—to assume consistency in policymaking, even if that is a chimera. So when in doubt, they force the episodes together in such a manner that things make sense to themselves and their readers. In this case, not seeing the back channel diplomacy, seeing only the pressure, conflict, and confusion, they assumed that they *themselves* were the catalyst for U.S. policy changes. With the 5 April policy announcement, they next found senior policymakers *confirming* that Bush was "stung and defensive" about criticisms of his non-actions in the Iraq. This "CNN Effect" was not the result of bad journalism, but rather an attempt to forge a storyline when no other was offered by the White House.

Phase 4, which lasted until the 10 May decision to expand the Kurdish safe havens, moved quickly and for the media the show was ending. In the United States, the last week of April was the last week of intense media coverage, and the first week where pressure dropped to negligible levels. The *New York Times* carried 591 paragraphs of news coverage on the Kurdish relief efforts, the second highest week of coverage for the period March–June (second only to the previous week of 704 paragraphs). However, for the first time since the beginning of March, none of it was pressure on the government.

The *Washington Post* was quite similar: 22–28 April saw strong media coverage (i.e., 401–600 paragraphs per week) at 447 paragraphs, but of this only 26 paragraphs, or 5.82 percent was pressure. On television, the change was equally apparent and equally abrupt. ABC News from 22 to 28 April provided fully 35.01 minutes of coverage to the relief efforts—in the "feeding frenzy" range—but pressure had dropped from 68.58 percent two weeks earlier to a stunning zero percent.[9] CBS News ran 29.35 minutes of coverage that week and none of it was pressure either. Apparently, the concern over a "quagmire" did not captivate the media, which were still reporting the events as a needed success rather than a potential pitfall, although such questions did appear in the White House press conferences, where pressure stood at 5.72 percent mainly over this subject.

In Great Britain, pressure was effectively gone, and coverage was petering out. Coverage in the *Independent* for the same week of 22 to 28 April dropped from 586 paragraphs the previous week to 332 this week, only to drop to 186 at the beginning of May. This was little different from the *Guardian*, with coverage dropping from 571 paragraphs of coverage at 12.96 percent pressure for the week 15–21 April, to 372 paragraphs of coverage at 8.33 percent pressure the last week of April, and then down to 279 paragraphs of coverage at 0 percent pressure at the beginning of May.

Pressure in the *Independent* was slightly different from the other papers examined because interest and pressure bobbed up during the week of 15–21 April after a small dip the week before, but the overall pattern was similar. Coverage and pressure dropped from 586 paragraphs of coverage at 18.94 percent pressure during the week 15–21 April, to 524 paragraphs at 12.40 percent pressure, and then peaking for a last time at 586 paragraphs of coverage at 18.94 percent before dropping to 332 paragraphs at 0 percent pressure during the week 22–28 April. After the troops were deployed, the crisis was over and blame had been allocated, there was no longer a central tension to keep the story going, nor an opposition voicing criticism at the elite level for the papers to index or peg their coverage. At the beginning of May, it was all over.

Media Influence

If an actor yields to pressure, then that actor has been influenced. It is speculative, but not unreasonable, to assume that the more pressure is exerted, the more likely it is for influence to result. The Positioning Hypothesis says that influence is discernible by deliberate changes in executive policy intended to recover the authority lost by media pressure (see figure 6.11). In this section, we try and determine whether the policy changes apropos U.S. and U.K. involvement in the insurrection and refugee crisis were actually attributable to the media pressure just measured.

Percentage of newspaper pressure per week	Percentage of television pressure per week	Level of pressure	Definition
0–15	0–30	Low	Oppositional voices and opinions are receiving minimal coverage
16–30	31–50	Moderate	Challenges to the executive or its policies appear regularly requiring constant vigilance by the executive to craft a communication strategy that will be conducive to maintaining coalition cohesion
31+	51+	Strong	Story is challenging the reputation and authority of the executive, thereby threatening coalition cohesion

Figure 6.11 Levels of media pressure on the executive as a percentage of coverage

Five possible conclusions can be reached at any given time:

A. Media *was not* a determinant of a policy change.
B. Media *was not* a likely determinant of a policy change.
C. The likelihood of influence cannot be assessed.
D. Media pressure *was* a likely determinant of the policy change.
E. Media pressure *was* a determinant of the policy change.

Phase 1: Non-Engagement, 6 March 1991
No pressure was discernible from any news organization during the first week of March, when the uprisings just began, and the policy change itself did not bring media pressure to a close, hence: (A) *Media was not a determinant of policy change.* A certain euphoria at the recently won war—concluded only a week early—left media criticism of any kind completely silent in both countries. On 6 March, Bush addressed a Joint Session of Congress where he laid out the four-point plan for Iraq, none of which discussed aid to the rebellion or taking troops to Baghdad to conquer the city. This policy announcement did not curb the very low levels of media concern about the events in the city, thereby undermining any possibility that the actions were taken to reduce media pressure. Though the factors leading to this decision certainly lay in the broadly defined "exogenous factors" that lay outside the media–government relationship, they are not relevant to the question of whether the policy change was attributable to the pressure from the media.

Phase 2: Explicit banning of helicopters and chemical weapons,
13 March 1991
There were very low levels of media pressure across the news organizations in both countries in the week prior to the 13 March decision. The *Independent* was the only paper that provided any pressure, rated at 10.8 percent for the week 4–10 March. The three other newspapers remained at 0 percent. In U.S. television, ABC News provided a low 18.6 percent, whereas CBS News was rated a moderate 41.72 percent. The banning of helicopters and chemical weapons was a policy move that did address the first concerns about the fate of the rebellion. But helicopters and chemical weapons were not issues that were at the forefront of media concern, and, in fact, optimism remained about the potential for the rebellions to succeed. Pressure itself differed from one organization to the next. Overall levels of coverage themselves— while not strictly relevant—were nevertheless all in the "low coverage" zone. The low levels of pressure, combined with the indirect relevance

of the policy change to the challenges being posed to the White House, makes the best conclusion: (A) *Media was not a determinant of a policy change.*

As the questions from the media that day make clear, the president was under no particular pressure from the media, and certainly none to account for the use of the helicopters by the Iraqi forces. According to the graphs produced for the four U.S. news sources, pressure of any notable kind would not begin until a full week later. This "warning," followed by inaction, instead opened the floodgates of opposition and the media pressure that did follow. As Brit Hume explained, "[t]he problem for the Administration is that the President himself has suggested the U.S. will insist Iraq ground its helicopters."

Phase 3: Airdrops and Aid, 5 April 1991
Intense media pressure was noted from all news organizations, and coverage was at the level of a feeding frenzy everywhere in the period just before this policy change was announced. In all cases, the intervention policy successfully functioned as a repositioning act and pressure subsequently dropped and continued to drop following this policy shift. This leaves open all possibilities except A. The conclusion depends on establishing whether better explanations exist to understand the policy changes from factors exogenous to the media–government dialogue. The United States and Britain are examined separately for answers.

The U.S. Decision

As mentioned in chapter 4, on April 5, the day of the decision to begin Operation Provide Comfort, Bush, Colin Powell, Dick Cheney (secretary of defense), and Brendt Scowcroft (national security adviser) were all at a hotel in California attending the fiftieth anniversary of the USO with Bob Hope.[10] They were informed that the pathbreaking resolution 688 was passed by the UN Security Council. For the first time, the Kurds were specifically mentioned in a UN document, and also for the first time, the internal repression of a people within state borders was identified as a threat to international peace and security. Without explicit regard for Iraq's sovereignty, the UN Security Council, in paragraph 3 of the resolution, "insisted" that Iraq allow immediate access to those in need within the country.

Reviews of Rudd's operational history for the U.S. military shows clearly that the Pentagon was completely unprepared for the tasks they were assigned on 5 April and had to develop operational plans *after* that date. After consultation with his advisers, Bush addressed the nation and stated that the United States was now undertaking a new operation and a new policy.

> I have directed a major new effort be undertaken to assist Iraqi refugees. Beginning this Sunday, U.S. Air Force transport planes will fly over northern Iraq and drop supplies of food, blankets, clothing, tents, and other relief-related items for refugees and other Iraqi civilians suffering as a result of the situation there. I want to emphasize that this effort is prompted only by humanitarian concerns. We expect the Government of Iraq to permit this effort to be carried out without any interference.[12]

Numerous writers, as indicated earlier, have suggested this constituted a reversal of prior U.S. policy. That is not the finding here. Instead, the 5 April decision was a new policy that did not change the U.S. policy of non-engagement in the civil war, precipitate action on behalf of the rebels, or commit itself to overthrowing Saddam Hussein. Rather, the civil war had ended, Iraq's territorial integrity was maintained (under Saddam's leadership), and the UN resolution creating a permanent ceasefire had been obtained. The consequence of the failed uprisings, however, was the refugee crisis of some two million people pouring into neighboring Turkey, which was keeping its borders closed, or else keeping the refugees on a thin strip of Turkish land high in the mountains along the Iraqi border. With the backing of France and Great Britain, Turkey was pleading with the Americans to resolve the crisis, and it was becoming clear that only the Americans had the airlift capability and ready ground forces to provide relief and return the refugees.

The result of this analysis is therefore: (B) Media *was not* a likely determinant of a policy change. Though it cannot be entirely ruled out given high media pressure and a change in policy, the historical record speaks better than the social science. Pressure was very high on the government to act, and the policy change did reposition the executive. However, very persuasive alternative explanations exist that may have alone, or in conjunction with media pressure, been instrumental in encouraging a policy shift by the administration. The Bush administration had an evident capacity to resist media pressure at other times. However, it also had a remarkable willingness to enlist images of suffering people as the motives for U.S. action. Given that media pressure was highest when European pressure to act was also high, as was a desire to extricate U.S. troops from the region, Turkish appeals for aid, the prospect of further instability at the Turkish border, extremely high polling figures for Bush, and a general contempt by his administration for interfering columnists and other "sandal clad minions," it seems that Bush's decision was *not* strongly affected by high levels of media pressure.

The British Decision

Prime Minister John Major was under very little pressure to act on behalf of the Iraqi civilian population until April. As previously described in the Historical Overview of Events in chapter 4, despite some later queries, the questioning of government by the opposition was extremely timid largely because Labour had opposed the use of force to liberate Kuwait, and would have a rather difficult time suggesting that the use of force was legitimate and necessary now. Early in the month of March, concerns or simple inquiries made to the prime minister during House of Commons question periods were about returning troops, support groups for veterans, war costs, POWs, and the Kuwaiti oil fires. No questions were asked about the uprisings until 12 March.

When parliament did engage the issue, condemnation was vociferous, but actual policy suggestions were muted. The opposition voices, though needling the government into blunt statements about amoral policy, were otherwise consistent in their inconsistency. A daily reading of HANSARD found that some MPs raised the historical injustices done to the Kurds, others the suffering of innocents in Iraq. Others suggested that more immediate humanitarian aid should be sent almost everywhere. The problems the opposition raised were real and valid, but there was no concerted call for a specific change in British policy. It therefore cannot be argued that parliament in any way was a strong pressure on John Major's government to intervene in the civil war before the 5 April decision. Likewise, because parliament would be in recess until Operation Safe Haven (the British name for Provide Comfort) was well under way, parliament as an institution was not an actor pressuring the government for the relief effort, although individual members of parliament would make public statements during the recess period.

The day before UN resolution 688 formally ended Operation Desert Storm and saw Iraqi acceptance of—if not actual compliance— with UN demands, the rift between Turkey and the United States began to widen, and Britain's internal coalition began to crack. Robert Kimmitt, U.S. undersecretary of state for Political Affairs was tasked with pressing Ozal to open Turkey's borders to some 500,000 Kurdish refugees, though having rejected, thus far, Ozal's request for support of a resolution that would aid the Kurds in their own country of Iraq. Morton Abramowitz was the U.S. ambassador in Ankara and was therefore well placed as a lynch-pin in this final stage of U.S. policymaking toward the new refugees, and it was his opinion that the United States should aid the Kurdish refugees, thereby reviving Major's safe haven plan.

After the resolution was signed, Western support for the refugees, but not the rebels, quickly materialized. For John Major it came from domestic forces, particularly those from his own political party with the backing of a still-popular and powerful Lady Thatcher. For George Bush the pressure came internationally, from his key military allies of Britain, France, and Turkey. Minority voices in Britain—backed by wide media coverage of the refugee crisis and the human costs of non-action—changed not only British policy, but strongly influenced the Bush decision to act on a humanitarian basis for the Kurds. In each case, the chief executive undertook actions that were *supported* by key members of their policy coalitions.

For the United States we concluded that the best answer was (B), but for Britain it may appear that the best answer is: (C) *Effects of media pressure are uncertain.* More than Bush and company, Major may well have been influenced in his decisions by political pressure from numerous sides, *including* harsh media criticism (often mistakenly considered the same as public opinion by policymakers) as well as opposition from his own party. Surrounded, as it were, his actions were more likely to be impressed by the general support that suddenly appeared for British action. With the support of the United States, EU, France, Turkey, his own party, and media, Major risked little by encouraging the airlifts and indeed demonstrated an unexpected level of moral courage. It is crucial to remember that the United States was far more implicated in ground operations at this point than Britain, and so the cost of Major advocating for more Western engagement came at *less cost* in terms of blood and treasure than did such a move for the United States. In a word, swaying to media pressure was more tenable for Major than Bush because the upside strongly outweighed the downside.

Phase 4: Introduction of ground troops, 16 April 2001
Despite the wide acceptance that pressure peaked during the week 8–14 April, the first full week before the policy change, this study shows that in all news organizations studied but one, pressure dropped this week from its high during the week 1–7 April. ABC News, the one exception, showed only a small increase of 3.5 percent.

On April 12, ABC showed a nearly five-minute program featuring what Vanderbilt described as "[t]he bureaucratic & political nightmare that is trapping these people." However from this day forward, the story shifted to become upbeat. America, it seemed, was resolute to help, and the focus on media attention became the logistics of doing so. Pressure to account for past actions and pressure to undertake future action *declined* at least four days before the decision to send in ground troops was announced (see figure 6.12).

When the pressure on the executives is looked at more closely for what it was, rather than how much of it existed, the difference between accountability pressure and policy pressure becomes vividly apparent in Phase 4.

After 5 April, media reports and political discussion in the two countries shows that hostility toward the two governments and their policies *was mostly retrospective*. The civil war was over, and relief efforts had begun. Considering the massive scale of the operation, strong political statements about dedicated support, and the absence of any obvious way to do things better or faster other then send more troops, there were no voices calling for future policy to change direction, only an increase in intensity of efforts. Scholars and observers listed earlier—including Strobel, Seib, Amos, Shaw, Carruthers, Bloomfield, and Schorr—were quite right about there being high levels of pressure on the U.S. and British governments in the first two weeks of April, despite its clear decline after the airdrops began. They were wrong, however, about the nature of the pressure itself and its significance in a wider context.

What was being sought was accountability and explanations for past inaction. Pressure was internally focused on the functioning of the state in both countries, not externally focused on the need for state action. What happened? Why didn't we act earlier? How could

	1–7 April (%)	8–14 April (%)
New York Times	37.88	19.24
Washington Post	69.48	54.06
Independent	22.74	12.40
Guardian	33.26	13.78
ABC News	65.26	68.58
CBS News	92.16	40.36

Figure 6.12   Dropping media pressure before ground troops were deployed

we let such a thing happen? Didn't you see this coming? Could we have stopped this had we acted differently? Are we morally accountable for this, and if so, how can we (as societies) shift that responsibility from our collective shoulders to that of the decision makers? Who is to blame?

"'We nudged and nudged the Americans, and suddenly, on Tuesday, they came like a rocket," is how a British diplomat described it.[19] What was driving U.S. policy at this late date was a fear that the refugees would permanently reside in Turkey, create massive political upheaval within Turkish politics, and would eventually become a politicized entity possibly seeking statehood in parts of NATO-member Turkey. Thousands of lives were being saved, and the United States deserves recognition for doing what no one else could have done. However, this still does not make Operation Provide Comfort a morally driven policy initiative. Had moral action by the Bush administration been *contradictory* to other coalition interests; had no other explanations for U.S. policymaking been available; and had the administration *changed* its policies rather than adapt them to new realities, we may have been able to argue for a clear CNN Effect. However, this was not the case.

The CNN Effect was an illusion because there was *no evidence of direct influence*, and very compelling reasons to suspect that media pressure—though perhaps a factor—was not a prime mover of U.S. or U.K. security policy. At best, the media may have been a contributing factor, hence: (B) Media *was not* a likely determinant of a policy change.

The reasons for the error are due to (1) mistaking coverage for pressure, especially at the early stages and also after 5 April when coverage increased before the deployment of ground troops *but pressure went down*; (2) the unquestioned problems of episodic ambiguity in the media–government conversation; (3) failure to look for other compelling explanations; and, most curiously (4) the cynical adoption of a White House communication strategy that claimed U.S. aid to the Kurds was forthcoming as a result of the spectacle—on television—of their suffering. Indeed, the Bush team explained the U.S. relief effort in emotive terms, as Strobel stated, thereby confirming to journalists that their work had forced the hand of the government. But it was a sleight of hand all the same.

Phase 5: Expansion of Safe Havens, 10 May 1991
Coverage was now at the level of moderate interest (100–200 paragraphs per week), and pressure had trailed off to nearly nothing. The *New*

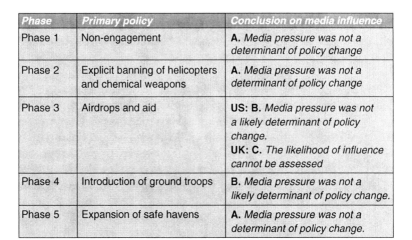

Phase	Primary policy	Conclusion on media influence
Phase 1	Non-engagement	**A.** *Media pressure was not a determinant of policy change*
Phase 2	Explicit banning of helicopters and chemical weapons	**A.** *Media pressure was not a determinant of policy change*
Phase 3	Airdrops and aid	**US: B.** *Media pressure was not a likely determinant of policy change.* **UK: C.** *The likelihood of influence cannot be assessed*
Phase 4	Introduction of ground troops	**B.** *Media pressure was not a likely determinant of policy change.*
Phase 5	Expansion of safe havens	**A.** *Media pressure was not a determinant of policy change.*

Figure 6.13   Media influence on the five policymaking phases

York Times and *Washington Post* were rated at only 2.46 percent and 3.97 percent respectively during the week 29 April to 6 May, and both British papers were now at 0 percent. ABC News was excited with an aberrant peak from zero to 33 percent that week, only to drop to zero again the week of the decision itself (6–12 May). CBS had lost interest as well with a 0 percent pressure rating. Consequently: (A) Media pressure was not a determinant of policy change. (Figure 6.13 shows the media influence on the five policymaking phases.)

CHAPTER 7

Summing Up and Pressing On

OVERVIEW

On 8 September 2000, former White House press secretary Marlin Fitzwater granted a friendly interview to U.S. Public Broadcasting Service about a hot new television show called *West Wing*. The show was a drama of life in a fictional White House. *News Hour* with Jim Lehrer wanted to know how realistic the show was.

Asking about the scenes between the White House and press, Fitzwater confirmed that media positioning of the executive and its policies is a matter than goes right to the Oval Office.[1]

> **Terence Smith**: For ten years you dealt with news organizations who were covering the White House and the president in a conventional news way, trying to report what happened.
> **Fitzwater**: Right.
> **Terence Smith**: Who gets closer to the truth?
> **Fitzwater**: Well, I think the show shows the kind of frustrations that exist between a press secretary and the press corps, and there's always truth on both sides. I think C. J. [press secretary portrayed by actress Allison Janney] does a great job. She suffers the same pain and anguish that I suffered. I can see it in her face. I think, "That's me 10 years ago", you know? And I think it's very healthy.
> **Terence Smith**: So it really rings true to you?
> **Fitzwater**: It rings true to me in so many different ways, certainly in a press way. It also shows how the press guides issues. It shows how they influence the agenda. You see her running in to the president and saying, "Mr. President, the press corps thinks this is all wet." And he says, "Why?" And they start worrying about it, and thinking, "How are we going to deal with this?" Those things really happen.

The Positioning Hypothesis, though not as memorable or punchy as Aaron Sorkin's dialogue for *West Wing*, nevertheless provides an explanation for what we witness with such drama on the show. It argues that the reason the president cares (and why it is brought to his attention in the first place) is that it can affect his power to get things done. This is because reputation and authority make power possible and bad press can take that away as quickly as a barrel of a gun if the challenge is of a high enough caliber.

Despite being real it is also nothing essentially new. Chapter 2 showed that this concern over political communication has long been a key concern for rulers of all kinds from royal to democrat. What makes the modern iteration of this concern fresh is the sheer speed of modern technology and how it affects the rate at which the conversation between the media and the government takes place. This change can certainly affect the quality of journalism and the quality of good governance. In this sense, it is a new phenomenon, but the fundamentals of social interaction and how conversation affects the participants in a moral world is the same today as it was hundreds of years ago. I also can't see any reason for it to change in the future though the *mechanisms* of conversation may be entirely unfamiliar.

Though the CNN Effect still awaits its biographer, a reasonable birthday is Friday 12 April 1991, approximately one week after the initiation of Operation Provide Comfort. The place of birth was the editorial page of the *Washington Post*. The paper argued as follows:

> International public opinion may be doing what international statecraft earlier failed to do: provide at least some relief for the 2 million or so Kurds being driven out of their homes in Iraq by Saddam Hussein. Fed first by media coverage of their desperate straits and then by the spectacle of their alleged betrayal by the American government and others, a great public outcry has gone up for the Kurds. As a result, official hesitations about interfering in sovereign Iraqi affairs have been swept aside, and a half-billion-dollar international relief effort has begun.

The idea was intoxicating, new, and helped morally vindicate the press corps for having been equivocal during the rebellion itself. The idea spread quickly in both the United States and the United Kingdom. Two weeks later, Richard Cohen wrote for the *Washington Post* that:

> Television exposes the reality of power politics. After World War II, Stalin rearranged the peoples of Eastern Europe like so much furniture— a horrible time of much needless suffering in which the Allies were complicitous. Few outsiders ever saw it . . . . The difference this time is

that television was on hand to record it. Starving Kurds, dead children, an army of desperate refugees winding their way through mountain passes—it all led to a slowly dawning realization: George Bush had ended the war prematurely. The Iraqi army, pronounced lifeless in briefing after briefing, nevertheless inflicted great damage on rebels and noncombatants alike. Bush had miscalculated. [2]

By 26 April, the idea that television prompted the humanitarian operation was on both sides of the Atlantic and was spreading from newspaper to newspaper. While the relief effort was well under way, Victoria Brittain picked up the idea for the *Guardian* and helped carry the CNN Effect to Britain: "International reaction to the two tragedies [of the Kurds and Africans] says much about the relationship between media and Western interests, and how television's priorities set agendas. Many of the Kurds can well articulate their crisis for Western television. Africa's starving are peasants, often in areas unreachable by outsiders, and with a language and culture barrier which precludes a television soundbite."[3]

Fitzwater explained in the interview that the statements and actions of the media are indeed a high concern to the president. The journalists' accounts in both countries testify that the media think they can not only make their voices heard, but can change the actions of the executive itself. Clearly, something very important is happening in the area of foreign policy decision making that needs the attention of international relations scholars.

Media Pressure on Foreign Policy has been a study of how security decision making can be affected by the words and actions of the media in Liberal states. Its goal has been to offer a grounded and testable metatheory of political communication pertinent to the media–government dialogue in Western states—in the United States and the United Kingdom in particular. We asked two questions. First, by what means might the media influence national security decision making? And second, can we find evidence that the media have influenced national security decision making in the manner suspected—in this case, in the United States or the United Kingdom during the Iraqi Civil War and its aftermath?

In the first case, few writers have dared offer explanations of what they are witnessing, leaving the mechanics of this relationship insufficiently explored. In large part this is because the causality problem has stopped many researchers in their tracks. What we need to avoid is giving up entirely, though, as Robinson did saying the phenomenon of influence is unobservable, or to dismiss one's explanatory responsibility by saying "authors are careful to reject any causal conclusions." Though scholastically cautious, we're all left with reports that sound like they were written by accident witnesses. "Well your honor" they appear to say, "I saw this, and then I saw that. Wouldn't want to speculate on what happened though." But if scholars aren't making these arguments, where are they supposed to come from?

The need for this study came from several facts about the world today—and the continued need to explain their relevance—that can reasonably be expected to continue into the foreseeable future. More than simply memories of staffers and claims by journalists, certain realities make these claims salient because they are likely to both extend into the future and either intensify or else be met with some resistance. Either way, international relations will be affected by political communication and the media-government dialogue.

Technological innovations that enable people from disparate locations to learn about things and communicate them to others are improving and proliferating. The gap between the "haves" and the "have-nots" is extraordinarily wide, as some people have access to intercontinental airliners, the Internet, and satellite technology whereas others have no electricity and cannot read. But the edge of innovation presses onward. Travel is faster, easier, and safer. Distant communication with people beyond earshot or the line of sight is cheaper, faster, more reliable, and, importantly, more widely available than ever before. The ability to learn about distant events and communicate them to others—though by no means a new phenomenon—is nevertheless impressing itself upon us as a consideration for how we conduct statecraft. Communication is in every sense a matter for international relations to consider deeply.

Liberal democratic states have protections for a "free press," which is a manner of communication made possible through these technological advancements. The term is a misnomer, because in no Liberal democratic country is the press at complete liberty to say or do whatever it wishes. The very act of communication carries with it locally situated rights and obligations, often of a legal kind, that extend to those who work in the media. Laws against slander and libel constrain or make accountable the acts of the media. Laws protecting the rights of children make certain programs that might exploit them illegal. Concepts of morality, decency, and simple "good taste" can act as social controls on the actions of media organizations whereby they deliberately (try to) alter their own behavior to align themselves with the populations they are trying to serve—or sell to. Though constraints on media behavior exist at many levels, the value and reality of a "free press" is still real compared to both the West's own historical experience (see chapter 2) and the experience of many states around the world today.

As was explained in chapter 2, the need for the sovereign people to communicate among themselves was recognized early on as a foundational necessity for Liberal statecraft. Unless the people could talk to each other at a distance through print, or in person by congregating, they would be unable to govern themselves. And with the overthrow of the seditious libel laws (laws that men and women in power today still covet during times of national uncertainty and threat), the act of communicating the *truth* became a protected act. Although the truth may be a thing in doubt in many cases, the search for that truth and the need to express it was recognized as a paramount concern for the people to govern.

With a greater ability to communicate and a state structure that makes this communication a social obligation for self government—not simply a right provided by the executive—the media's role in informing the public on the one hand and directly challenging the assertions and authority of the executive on the other is set to increase. There is a greater need than any since the Liberal revolutions in the eighteenth and early nineteenth centuries to revisit our study of political communication, the relationships inherent to that communication, the meaning provided by and created through that communication, and the role of technology in facilitating or retarding those processes and meanings.

Indeed, technology's potential impact on political communication is not a one-way street and the genie is hardly out of any bottle. Political communication is only possible when people can talk to each other, and that often requires the use of technology. When those who *control* that technology choose to use that power for the good of communication itself, political communication becomes increasingly possible (all else being equal, such as our desire to engage in this form of talk and our freedom to do so).

The political economy is the environment of control in which political communication takes place. Political communication always takes place in some environment of control, and though the relationship of influential political communication to different political economy environments is still weakly understood, it stands to reason that freer discourse means more influential discourse. What is unclear are the operable conditions for "freedom." Whether in a free market economy or a fascist regime, certain hands of power and their own goals will control the access to the resources that make political communication possible. Simply having the right to communicate in a Liberal democratic state is not enough for people to be able to talk and learn from one another. Barriers that prevent them from doing so need to be challenged so that self-governance remains viable.

Should an environment persist in the United States and Britain and other Liberal democratic states, whereby the elements of control continue to permit an effective media to inform the sovereign public, then it is incumbent on scholars to know how that freedom and capacity to communicate may affect the workings of the state. By understanding the impact of technology on political communication and political communication on decision making, the democratic process is better understood. With that understanding comes new possibilities for strengthening those normative aspects of democracy deemed good and valuable, and correcting those faults seen as bad and undesirable. Without that understanding, the very need to retrench or reconsider can never be known and better statecraft remains in the sphere of caprice or speculation.

To advance through the study, a literature review was undertaken in chapter 1 to assess the state of the art in understanding media–government relations and how they impact on security decision making. Because of the limited attention provided to these concerns in the past thirty-odd years, the range of relevant voices on media–government relations was expanded beyond just security matters to include research into democratic theory, public opinion literature, media agenda-setting and foreign policy analysis. Still, the universe of relevant material was alarmingly limited.

The power of the media was almost universally determined to be the power to mobilize public opinion.[4] In no study examined was a theory advanced that was not dependent on the mobilization of the public to influence government. And yet, the agenda-setting work in political communication was not yet aware of how the media can set the agenda of the public, and the public opinion literature is awkwardly silent on how changes to public opinion actually effectuate a change inside the executive other than through voting retribution—itself a theory under increasing scrutiny.

Evidently pressing was the need for a metatheory of media pressure to unify the observations and correlation studies that have been generally unsuccessful in presenting arguments we can richly engage. Solid observations were not sufficiently explained in terms of how media coverage might *become* pressure, and how that pressure in turn could influence the decision-making process. The public opinion literature and agenda-setting work, though flush with correlation studies dating back decades, were awkwardly silent on how the media influenced the decision-making process other than attributing media influence on the public (still insufficiently explained) as being enough to understand the democratic process.

Several observations that appeared time and again from scholars, journalists, and decision makers formed the parameters within which a metatheory would be produced. Whereas explanations may have been weak, the observational work was solid and formed a platform from which to work. First, this study accepted the claim that media coverage is "indexed" to elite discourse in both the United States and Great Britain. Unfortunately, insufficient attention to comparative studies on this interesting phenomenon means that the growing support for this claim within the United States cannot be automatically extended to other Liberal democratic states—or any states at all, for that matter. It is supported here for Britain as media coverage did carefully track governmental actions and statements, but a measure of indexing was not explicitly made. Likewise, parliament was out of session for much of the period examined, and the opposition was notably silent during most of the decision-making period in Britain. However, when opposition voices did arise in late March and early April in Britain, the media were indeed quick to cover it. It must be noted, though, that the two papers studied here (the *Independent* and the *Guardian*) were selected specifically because they would be more likely to voice the views of Labour. Consequently, the observations are biased toward the Left-leaning press. One cannot make general observations for Britain as a whole on the basis of this sample. We are left to wonder at the extent to which indexing is in evidence in other Liberal democratic states, and the reasons for it.

Indexing as a practice may have been broadly accepted here, but its significance was challenged. It was argued in chapter 1 and then successfully proved in chapters 6 and 7 that media indexing does not preclude the possibility of influence. Every statement made by President Bush was used as a peg for a media story, and oppositional voices from within the administration (such as General Schwarzkopf's) and from the Democratic Party did make headlines constantly. But the daily press briefings showed clearly how the media reports were not simply an echo of the official pronouncements. The very ability to code the conversational episodes was made possible by the objectionable questions posed by the media; and they were objectionable because the executive told us so by its responses to the questions. That the government would generally determine the topics covered by the media in no way suggested they had any control over how that conversation would evolve. A clear example of this was when George Bush brought up the matter of helicopters. Indexing indeed took place, but it was by the act of indexing that pressure was created—not stopped.

Though not covered in detail, the excellent work of Martin Linsky (1986) found that "foreign policy was the area with by far the highest potential for press impact" as senior foreign policy officials (in the case they studied) "spent substantially more time with the press and were much more likely to have sought coverage than their counterparts in the rest of the government."[5] An explanation for this observation was not offered by Linsky. He specifically writes, "the findings suggest that the effect of the press is in general more substantial in foreign policy than in domestic policy. We are not at all sure why this is so, or what are the consequences for both of the specific differences."[6] Though the consequences remain in doubt, the Positioning Hypothesis provides the grounds for an answer to Linsky's observation.

The explanation can be found in the unique status of the executives in both the United States and the United Kingdom regarding their *independent* capacity to speak on behalf of the nations they serve. In the former, only the president—or someone empowered to speak for the president—may address another world actor on behalf of the country as a whole. In the latter, the monarch has that power, but it is a power used to minimal effect in present times. The prime minister therefore assumes much of the same authority as a U.S. president in public speeches and international diplomacy. With this unique opportunity comes a unique challenge. The media become the vehicle through which rhetorical authority is exercised, but at the same time, the executive is alone in shouldering the burden for foreign policy authority.

The exercise of power and authority, and hence the reputation derived from doing so, is grounded on the executive's unique capacity to *speak for the nation*. In domestic affairs, many other actors are responsible for many things. The central bank adjusts the interest rates that affect the economy and the parliament or Congress passes the budgets and sets the taxes. Healthcare, road work, and immigration are all determined by party, and inter-party politics and the process is complex and almost never the sole result of the executive's own agenda. In foreign policy, however, the executive remains far and away more independent than in domestic action—and likely more so in the United States than in the United Kingdom. In the latter, the parliamentary system is more conducive to votes of no-confidence to bring down a government, and one's own party can replace the prime minister, which is how John Major came to power in 1991—with the deposing of Margaret Thatcher. In the former, the impeachment process does make possible the removal of an executive, but it has only been used twice in U.S. history (Jackson and Clinton) and in neither case was the president removed from office. In both cases, the reasons were domestic and not based on the conduct of foreign policy.

If power is concentrated and coalitions are less necessary than in domestic politics (as with healthcare, taxes, etc) than it would seem that the Positioning Hypothesis would predict a *weaker* influence over foreign policy than domestic. After all, if the power of the media is to serve as an instrument of faction, then the more reliant one is on a coalition, the greater threat the media would seem to be. This would be the case were it not for two important realities. First, one's conduct in foreign affairs affects one's reputation and hence authority in *all* aspects of governance. Any government in the United States and the United Kingdom is only run by a small group of people—several hundred at the most. Politicians, unlike civil servants, are concerned with all aspects of state conduct. Since the same politicians are involved in all matters of governance, then the connection between foreign and domestic policy becomes clear. The connection is the people themselves.

The second reason, as mentioned earlier, is that the president and prime minister cannot avoid being the final authority for all foreign policy conduct. "I don't know" or "That's not my responsibility" are simply not available positioning moves. Executives must attend to foreign affairs because it is their responsibility. How it goes will affect their domestic agendas. The media are more influential in foreign affairs because the actors and their roles are very clear, as is the chain of command.

Supporting this argument is the central importance placed on the concept of reputation and its incumbent authority. Reputation has been a consistent theme to all laws in the Anglo-American world involving political communication since at least the thirteenth century. Reputation is not meant here to be an immutable or transcendent quality. Rather, it is a stable cluster of locally determined attributes temporally defined by a given community. In the West, though the cluster of attributes changes it never drifts beyond the parameters of honoring one's contractual obligations. It was argued that this quality of keeping one's promises forms a profound basis for one's reputation, as it applies to both domestic governance and international relations. *Pactus sunt servanda*—that which has been agreed to must be honored—is the nexus around which all ideas of reputation coalesce.

Reputation and moral placement in the world are not popular subjects of political communication today where more interest remains on processing than meaning and on universality rather than difference. Rather than looking even further abroad for theories beyond those examined in chapter 1, the decision was made to go back in time to see whether the experience of media–government relations in our own societies in the West from long ago could shed some light on the experience of today. To know whether technology had changed the rules of the game, it was necessary to know what it looked liked earlier. It was found to be remarkably familiar. What was unfamiliar was the richness of theorizing that existed then but has been forgotten, lost, or ignored today.

Francis Squire's theory from 1741 was examined for several reasons. "The Stability and very Being of any Government" he argued as though it were obvious, "consists in its Credit and Reputation; in the high Esteem and Veneration it retains in the Breast of its Subjects, and the proportionable Respect paid to it by Foreigners." In order to remain viable, its reputation needed to be managed domestically and in foreign affairs. This was not a Liberal argument because the populace was best if it was in awe of the sovereign, and the sovereign's reputation in terms of keeping its word was only relevant among peers, meaning other heads of state. Despite these differences in the pre-Liberal world of eighteenth-century England, the power of political communication was in its ability to bring down the entire house of cards. Whereas good credit might lend itself to a better reputation, it was the reputation that ultimately mattered—not the credit that was a means to an end. When the Liberal divide was crossed, Hallam would confirm the continued viability *and popularity* of this idea in 1826 by showing the importance of reputation in gaining or losing political power vis-à-vis opposition parties.

Reputation and authority, inseparable from the notion of trust as a foundation for all contract and hence all management of the future in Western culture, were found to be the missing link in current theories of media pressure and political communication. The gap was observed in chapter 1 and filled in chapter 2 by offering answers that dove-tailed the observations made by scholars such as Linsky and O'Heffernan, but were unexplained.

Chapter 4 provided a first-pass at the history of events in Iraq from March through June, 1991, which remains a scholastically neglected period of contemporary history. The history of the events was provided, along with the decision-making phases in Britain and the United States, as well the coverage both received in the media. Five decision-making junctures were identified that were used to test the Positioning Hypothesis in chapter 6.

Coverage was measured in chapter 5. Here, using the data from the case study period, we saw how counting news stories—rather than paragraphs—needs to be avoided as a means of measurement because in some cases it can produce entirely opposite results and misdirect our conclusions about coverage. We documented the rise and fall of media coverage around the central storyline identified for this study and drew remarkable observations about the similarity in news coverage across countries and media types.

U.S. press conferences were shown to be an excellent source of "face-to-face conversation" between the media and government whereby "uptake" was clear and conversational episodes could be confidently determined. This makes them a useful data set for coding media pressure later. Measures of attention were provided that, not coincidently, correlated nicely to media coverage in newspapers and television later.

In the second part of the chapter, we looked back at the case study period to understand these trends informed now from explicit measures. This made it possible to understand the movement of coverage as aligned to events in a new way and bring greater clarity to the history.

In chapter 6 we disaggregated media pressure from media coverage using the Positioning Hypothesis to create a coding system. This new method, should it withstand the scrutiny of students and fellow researchers, may prove quite useful. Without a means to measure pressure, it is impossible to provide evidence that it exists. Without such evidence, it is impossible to argue that media pressure was an influence on policy. Furthermore, by measuring media pressure over time, it is possible to generate hypotheses about media influence that can then be tested against the historical records. In the absence of these measures, it is impossible to generate these hypotheses. Finally, without the availability of these measures, it is impossible to disprove claims of media influence where the data supports this conclusion.

Consequently, this study provides a new means of: measuring media pressure; testing historical claims about media pressure; generating hypotheses of media influence; measuring pressure over time; and conducting comparative studies of government–media relations and other activities that require the explicit measure of pressure, as distinct from coverage, in a manner that is empirically grounded and not based on the impressionistic views of the researcher. Though emphasis is placed here on detailed histories in order to know how decisions were made, explicit theorizing and means of testing those theories remain necessary, because only explicit arguments about why historical experience is generalizable can be tested, refined, refuted, or undermined.

This chapter also tested the likely influence of the media on the basis of the level of pressure measure and the actions of the government. Central to this process was the attempt to undermine the hypothesis that media pressure was the most likely consideration for the policy change by either executive. In only one case was media pressure an uncertain factor, whereby pressure may well have been a notable influence on the decision-making process: the 5 April decision to initiate airdrops and aid to the Kurdish refugees in southern Turkey and northern Iraq. The matter of influence is complicated because pressure existed on the United States and Britain from *many sides* to undertake action, especially in the latter, where Major's own political party was in favor of support for them. With key allies calling for action, including Turkey and France, both George Bush and John Major would have had to ignore media pressure as well as the wishes of their main coalition partners, their local constituents, the UN, and major domestic political actors to have avoided taking action.

The conclusions reached here challenge the prevailing wisdom about the causes of the 1991 intervention. It casts serious doubt on the media having been the prime mover of the 5 April decision, and undermines that same idea with regard to the 15 April decision to deploy ground troops. In doing so, it reorients the history of the period back toward politics and diplomacy as the movers of security policy and away from speculation about media-driven democracy.

The Positioning Hypothesis appears to be consistent with—or at least does not contradict—the five observations made by researchers on media–government relations, and as such provides a parsimonious explanatory metatheory for how they take place.

1. First, the Positioning Hypothesis appears to agree with the commonsense observations of those who suggest that decision making "speeds up" as a consequence of media coverage. David Gergen was concerned with this practice, writing: "[i]t is a serious mistake for executive branch officials to make policy hastily in order to meet news broadcast deadlines."[7] Timothy McNulty similarly observes: ". . . the ability to see events in real time speeds up the decision-making process and accelerates diplomatic exchange."[8] The reason such speeding-up takes place, it can now be argued, is due to the imperative of maintaining a moral position for the sake of coalition cohesion, and hence policy continuity. If the media can position the executive and its actions as in some sense immoral or incompetent than the executive and this rhetorical act can challenge coalition cohesion, then authority

can only be regained by making contrary statements or undertaking action.

2. Second, the Positioning Hypothesis is not at odds with the possibility of media indexing—whereby the media pegs its coverage to elite discourse—but rather provides an explanation for how the media might actuate an influence on the government *even if* indexing is taking place. Consequently, the proving or disproving of the indexing hypothesis does not address matters of media influence. As such, Zaller and Chiu's concern that indexing functions as "Government's little helper" may be overstated, because there is no evidence that indexing precludes the possibility of media influence.[9]

3. Third, the oppositional norm is well explained by the Positioning Hypothesis because it would predict that journalists are naturally attuned to the importance of matters of moral authority in the maintenance of power in democratic societies. Though it is no doubt easier to report on what two sides say on a given matter than finding the actual truth of the situation, journalists appear to know full well that the debate *itself* actually *matters*. Positioning theory would suggest that what matters about the debate is how the public conversation affects the social standing of the conversants—which in this case means members of the executive. Further evidence for this claim comes from the fact that the Positioning Hypothesis is measuring exactly what journalists think of as pressure—evidenced by the perfect alignment of journalistic claims to pressure being "high" and the measures taken in chapter 6.

4. The fourth observation is that negative coverage tends to push the decision making up the bureaucracy. If the imperative for maintaining moral and agentive positioning is sufficient and lower-level bureaucrats are unable to silence negative positioning acts by the media, then the matter will have to be addressed by high-level officials because (i) they have greater access to information, (ii) they have greater vested authority in an administration to make public statements on behalf of the executive (e.g., the secretary of defense versus a deputy secretary), and (iii) they stand in for the "ultimate authority" (i.e., the president, prime minister, etc.) so as to provide continued strategic depth for the executive to rhetorically maneuver in its public conversation. This is accomplished by enabling deniability to be used as a positioning device by higher-ups, and also by allowing higher-ups to contradict the statements of lower officials if their statements generate negative reactions (i.e., the practice of "scapegoating").

5. The fifth observation—that press coverage is more influential in foreign than in domestic policy—may be explicable in that only the executive has the vested authority to speak on behalf of the state in its international dealings. In domestic policy, however, the executive shares

moral responsibility with Congress, the executive's own political party, or the opposition in parliament. For this reason, there is far more room for rhetorical maneuvering because other influential members of government, writ large, can be blamed for policy outcomes.

THE POSITIONING HYPOTHESIS IN BROADER CONTEXT: POLITICAL COMMUNICATION AND INTERNATIONAL RELATIONS

At the very beginning of this book I wrote, "This is a study of political communication in the liberal democratic state and how media pressure on the executive may affect state conduct in international relations." I hope this book has provided a convincing argument about the means by which media–government relations can affect the conduct of statecraft. At this point we can elevate the discussion to how the study of communication might enrich the study of international relations itself.

Since political communication became a distinct subject of study in the 1980s it has shared a number of topical interests with international relations. These include, but are no means limited to, public diplomacy, democratic theory, media influence on foreign policy, and propaganda and warfare. What I have yet to see, however, is an effort to articulate the unique contributions political communication will bring to studying international relations writ large. This section argues that certain epistemological problems that now exist in international relations theory can be overcome, worked through, or side-stepped entirely if the value of political communication and its approach to social theory is better appreciated and utilized.

To make this case I start with a brief overview of international relations theory, explain one of its central tensions concerning epistemology, and then I argue how a communication approach will help us overcome this tension. It is my hope that this bridge might open greater cooperation between those studying communication and those seized by concerns over international relations.

*   *   *

The field of International Relations is chiefly concerned with the conduct of states (or the decisions made by state decision makers) in an anarchic system. The metaphor of anarchy has a powerful hold over the Western imagination about international affairs. Thomas Hobbes famously described people's lives as "nasty, brutish and short" thereby requiring some form of governance to bring control and order to the natural state of disorder. Anarchy is a term used commonly in international relations to describe a world in which autonomous states exist in an international system with no higher power capable of holding them in check. In the absence of this hegemony, or Leviathan, they are inevitably concerned with their security vis-à-vis other states, and therefore use different techniques to achieve it such as cooperation, balancing, bandwagoning, and domination of other states or societies.

Though seldom discussed outright, an implied concern in these ongoing theoretical debates is what this all means to the proper conduct of foreign policy and the matter of ethical permissiveness in an unruly world. It is one thing to describe a reality. It is another entirely to determine how one should acts toward it. Realists in this debate are treated as pessimistic but pragmatic, itself an American term coined by William James in 1907, and one he borrowed from a Harvard colleague named Charles Sanders Peirce. These realists presumably submit to the compelling realities that anarchy is alleged to create. Liberals (now including constructivists) are comparably optimistic arguing that anarchy is not so compelling as to determine the fate of international affairs. Rather, they often argue, we need to look elsewhere for explanation, and seek different inspirations for foreign policy decision making. The pursuit of national interest is not the only possible course in an anarchic system. It is noteworthy, in this discussion, that both realists and liberals often argue bitterly about history and theory because there is an unspoken premise that one's reading of international affairs determines how one is to act within it.

If anarchy is the setting for the inquiry, then the unifying inquiry itself is whether there are timeless laws to state behavior. The conversation around anarchy in its current iteration can arguably be traced to Hans Morganthau in 1948 with his now-classic *Politics among Nations: The Struggle for Power and Peace*. He proposed realism as a theory "to bring order and meaning to a mass of phenomena which without it would remain disconnected and unintelligible."[10] This goal set the agenda for international relations scholars and remains dominant today.

Kenneth Waltz, in *Man, the State and War* (1959), revised this argument (but not the goal) to talk of relative power in an international system, rather than absolute power deriving from ideas of human nature. The term "neo-realism" was coined to draw the distinction. In one variety or another, "Realism remains the primary or alternative theory in virtually every major book and article addressing general theories of world politics, particularly in security affairs."[11] If realism serves as the primary theory, then alternative ideas of international relations have generally challenged realist claims on the basis of the theory's internal soundness, its validity as it pertains to certain historical periods (e.g.. the Greek city states, the Chinese kingdoms, etc.), or its capacity to explain seemingly aberrant state behavior such as international cooperation. In all these cases, even those with a constructionist or comparative bend, international relations study remains today centrally concerned with the preternatural law of state conduct in an anarchic system.

If anarchy is the setting and realism remains a core theory, then the prominent approach to analysis (at least in the United States) remains rationalism. As Stephen Walt explained, "Rational choice models have been an accepted part of the academic study of politics since the 1950s, but their popularity has grown significantly in recent years. Elite academic departments are now expected to include game theorists and other formal modelers in order to be regarded as 'up to date,' graduate students increasingly view of formal rational choice models as a prerequisite for professional advancement, and research employing rational choice methods is becoming more widespread throughout the discipline."[12]

Rational choice, formal modeling, and material power—all at work in an anarchic system—are now the key considerations in international relations theory and have come to dominate the field. It is not, however, universally appreciated for its explanatory power, especially if comparative study is valued. Jerome Bruner has put his finger on one key problem in rational choice theory when he explained how both rationalist and irrationalist approaches to "choice" miss the central point. As he explained, the rationalists still hold to the idea that "we express our values in our choices, situation by situation, guided by such rational models as utility theory, optimization rules, minimization of chagrin, or whatever. These choices reveal notable regularities, ones very reminiscent of the kinds of functions one observes in operant conditioning experiments with pigeons." So far so good; but in labeling these choices, "the value assigned is one that makes the result conform to utility theory. And this, of course, gives the game away. If you accept utility theory (or one of its variants) you simply assign values to choices in a manner that makes choice behavior conform to its tenets."[13]

The disservice here is that rational choice models do not approach the investigation of a social system on the basis of its own values and ideas and hence its own motives. Rather, it constructs an alien language to describe a foreign society rather than try to understand that society on its own terms. In the context of international relations and security policy, this approach to analysis effectively masks the uniqueness of foreign societies (and our own) and renders it impossible to take duly informed decisions. As a consequence, the need to create truly valuable strategic intelligence is unappreciated and the capacity is lost. This is no mere academic quibble. During these times of increased communication among disparate societies in the world, we will face ever-deeper perils in our foreign policy if we fail to recognize Bruner's point that "values inhere in commitments to 'ways of life,' and ways of life in their complex interaction constitute a culture." Cultural research, based on an approach that centers on communication and meaning, should be the essence of international relations study that is directed toward policy significance.

There are some cracks in the mantle of realism and rational choice, but the bridge to political communication is not yet built. Bruner's point is still not appreciated, and the name of the game in academics—to get published, to get a job, to get tenure, to be heard—is still defined in the same parameters of inquiry that Morganthau set down, namely the metaphor of anarchy and the concern over universality of explanations.

One proponent of a new approach—if not a new set of questions altogether as I will propose—was Alexander Wendt. He put forward his argument that international institutions can transform state identities and interests and hence overcome what neorealists consider the inevitable causal power of anarchy. He does this by explaining that the problem with realism is that process and institutions are always subordinated to structure, making matters of identities and interests uninteresting to realists and rationalists alike. This article and argument has had a strong ripple effect in international relations theory in the last decade or so and contributed to some reconsideration in the field.

Alexander Wendt is credited with introducing the notion of social constructivism in the field of international relations with his memorably titled *Anarchy Is What States Make of It*. As with other international relations theorists, he is chiefly concerned with explicating the laws of state behavior. His attack on, or contribution toward, international relations theory is not over the metaphor of anarchy but rather the *overemphasis* on structure and the subordination of social interaction as an explanatory approach to state response and behavior. For him, a constructivist turn offers an explanation for what appears to be the anomalies in state conduct, especially acts of cooperation. For Wendt, conflict is not the inevitable response to chaos or anarchy in that states can decide to cooperate as a reasonable and rational solution to the structural reality. In short, anarchy is what states make of it.

In *Anarchy and Culture: Insights from the Anthropology of War*, Jack Snyder exploits the now-brewing dichotomy between structural (i.e., realist) and cultural (i.e., constructivist) arguments to take issue with Wendt's alleged optimism. Comparative cultural research is essentially under attack before it has even begun. He writes, "Those who foresee substantial opportunities to transform the war-prone international system into a realm governed by benign norms contend that 'anarchy is what states make of it.' In their view, culture, defined as shared knowledge of symbols that create meaning within a social group, determines whether behavior in the absence of a common governing authority is bloody or benign. If more benign ideas and identities are effectively spread across the globe through cultural change and normative persuasion, then 'ought' can be transformed into 'is': support for warlike dictators can be undermined, perpetrators of war crimes and atrocities can be held accountable, benign multicultural identities can be fostered, and international and civil wars will wane." The criticism to this, Snyder argues, is that anarchy gives rise to an "inescapable logic of insecurity and competition that culture cannot trump."

The study of political communication, at least twenty-five years old, is now asking questions that overlap concerns in international relations. Work on media influence, public diplomacy, propaganda, agenda-setting, democratic theory, and many other areas are all concerned with intra-state affairs or inter-state conduct. It also has the wonderful potential to begin vast amounts of comparative work in communication among distinct social groups that help explicate how they organize and produce their social worlds. Where then is space for mating these two fields and advancing the concerns if, as Snyder says, "anarchy trumps culture"?

One place to start is with the notion of communication itself. A communication approach to studying inter-state (or inter-communal) affairs will necessarily encourage attention toward the study of distinct premises of social interaction shared by some actors and not by others and hence to applied questions about communication as the source material for devising theories relevant to assisting in the conduct of statecraft. It will allow us to move beyond the aberrant and normal, the rational and irrational, to the comparative study of distinct social systems, normal or otherwise, rational or otherwise. In fact, we will be able to move beyond such terms entirely and ask two simple questions that are notably different from the questions about the immutable laws of state behavior. First *is social action here organized, produced, and interpreted according to some patterned system of premises internal to it that have significance to international affairs?*[14] If so, *what are they?* Wendt directed our attention to the notion of social interaction between units called states, and now it is time to move into the distinct social systems of the actors themselves. Once understood, their social interaction is no longer seen as merely "constructed" but is recognized as the intercultural communication of two social systems challenged by a similar concern (e.g., environmental degradation, nuclear proliferation, territorial disputes, etc.).

I wish to argue that these two questions (italicized in the previous paragraph) should *precede* debates on anarchy, realism, and rationalism. And what's more, a careful reading of Morganthau himself will demonstrate an appreciation for this sort of approach. I would argue that in his pre-Waltzian treatment of the balance-of-power system and anarchy, Morganthau *never* advocated for a universal treatment of war causation or system analysis. Rather, for Morganthau, the balance of power system *was unique to Europe itself*, and consequently, the critiques of Morganthau's work that followed—starting with Waltz in 1954 (and published in 1959)—are therefore arguments only against his analysis of a distinct social world as it existed (and presumably exists) in a culturally unified community called "The West" with its own communicative system and premises of social behavior. Morganthau's terminology may have been a bit different, but his meaning was extremely clear.

For Morganthau the very foundations of the balance-of-power system in Europe were contingent on *shared moral ideas and hence a community of practice* in international relations defined loosely as a European one or a Christian one. Though the tenets or rules of this system were not necessarily explicit, they were nevertheless shared and implicitly significant in governing inter-state relations. Morganthau built a very plausible case for the uniquely cultural foundations of the European balance-of-power system he described, and was blunt in saying it was Western civilization and its *own* laws of state behavior that commanded his attention in *Politics among Nations*.

Building on the ideas of Gibbon and Toynbee about the uniqueness of Europe as a cultural sphere and as "one great republic," he goes on to show how Fénelon, Rousseau, and Vattel were all in complete agreement on this point. "The great political writers of that age were aware of this intellectual and moral unity [of Europe], upon whose foundations the balance of power reposes and which makes its beneficial operations possible."[15]

For Morganthau, it would have been problematic to argue or even consider whether "anarchy trumps culture" (or the opposite) because the balance-of-power system he described and explained was in itself a cultural response—a *unique and distinct* cultural response—to the anarchy, or unruliness, he believed was inherent to the relations among states. Following a scholastically requisite list of quotations and anecdotes about this cultural substratum to the balance of power system, he starts the subheading called "Moral Consensus of the Modern State System" by writing, "[t]he confidence in the stability of the modern state system that emanates from all these declarations and actions [just reviewed] derives, it will be noted, not from the balance of power, but from a number of elements, intellectual and moral in nature, upon which both the balance of power and the stability of the modern state system repose."[16]

This could not be clearer. Anarchy was not chaos for Morganthau. It was a system defined by the absence of a leviathan, to be sure, but it was a social system with distinct and known rules of interaction. In this system, power emanates from "material, charismatic and ideological" realities (his terms) understood to function in certain ways by a community of European states who share common understandings about that anarchic world. From this reading, one cannot possibly compare and then rank a balance-of-power system to a cultural system, because for Morganthau *a balance-of-power system is a cultural system* that gained and maintained its rules and moral cohesion on the basis of common cultural orientations to international relations. "One might even say," he writes, "that society as a dynamic force is nothing but the sum total of its rules of conduct imposing patterns of action upon its members."[17]

One way to untangle ourselves from the false dichotomy between structure and socialization is to recognize that anarchy and chaos are not synonymous. Snyder would have us believe that the world is unruly and in chaos and this reality is the central fact of inter-state life. But it isn't, it never has been, and it never will be.

It is tempting for political scientists, mimicking the world of physicists, to ask how a distinct social system can emerge from chaos, like the birth of the universe from the void. But of course there never has been a world of chaos from which a social system is expected to emerge. History builds day by day and in the context of the given social world. There is always a social world from which change is derived and social interaction can only take place in the extant social order. What can emerge as new rules or structures (and indeed they do arise) are therefore *contingent* on the extant order. Strictly speaking, it is irrelevant, or even nonsensical, to ask whether a social order can take form out of complete chaos.

And it is just here that the new constructivists are a bit too "timely" and theoretically oriented. It is important for us to appreciate that society has been "under construction" for a remarkably long time. What exists and sustains societies through time is how they communicate, share meaning, and make social action productive.

It is here that comparative study in communication starts to align with the study of international relations in general and implies its own research agenda. What happens when differently socialized societies, with different rules of social behavior and different primary structuring ideas, encounter one another in a given form of interaction—such as the General Assembly of the United Nations, at a bilateral negotiation, as witnesses to each other's domestic political speech, or through physical confrontation on the battlefield? Assuming one society is not destroyed by the other (which of course happens with yawning regularity in international history) then some form of intercultural intercourse is taking place.

If the European balance-of-power system from 1648 to 1772 and then again from 1815 to 1933 was, as Morganthau described it, "an aristocratic pastime, a sport for princes, all recognizing the same rules of the game and playing for the same limited stakes" (p. 214)—and we appreciate that this system and set of rules was distinct with determinable modes of sociation (not to be confused with laws of state behavior)— then it only stands to reason that other such systems exist, or can exist.

This was precisely the conclusion of Adda B. Bozeman. Drawing heavily on her 1971 book *The Future of Law in a Multicultural World*, she wrote in 1992 that "the world society consists today as it did before the nineteenth century of a plurality of diverse political systems, and that each of these is in the final analysis the product of culturally specific ideas and modes of thinking rather than of particular political and economic arrangements. The challenge," she wrote, "of comparative studies is therefore to identify the structuring concepts and values that lend uniqueness or distinction to 'the other' society, region, or culture—namely those that provide moral and mental security because they stubbornly resist compromise under the impact of international and intercultural relations."

Bozeman's lifetime dedication of study to the Middle East, Africa, Indianized Asia, and China accorded fully with observations made by other legal scholars such as Harold Lasswell. In his 1959 piece called *The Identification and Appraisal of Diverse Systems of Public Order*, written with Myres McDougal for the *American Journal of International Law*, he wrote: "it is a commonplace observation that the world arena today exhibits a number of systems of public order, each demanding and embodying the values of human dignity in very different degree." McDougal and Lasswell were not concerned with the laws of state behavior and were not seduced by the contemporary physics-envy of political scientists keen on devising a unified theory of political history and warfare. Theirs was a concern for the law, and whether the Western orbit of ideas could indeed be universalized throughout other social systems that did not share the same primary structuring ideas. In law as in international relations theory, Lasswell and McDougal noted how scholars in their field displayed urgency with the "universal" and were uncomfortable with the idea of the culturally particular.

"Among traditional legal scholars," they wrote, "it has long been customary to give unquestioning verbal deference to the proposition that if there is any international law at all, it is a universal law, embracing the organized governments of the world community as a whole, or at least all those bodies politic admitted to the ever-enlarging European 'family of nations.' The existence of regional diversities in the interpretation of allegedly universal prescriptions and in the fundamental policies about the allocation of power and other values sought by such interpretation, has been cloaked in the shadow of 'decent mystery' by hopeful insistence that such divergent interpretations are but occasional aberrations which will disappear when the real universality of the relevant concepts is appropriately understood." They called this approach "make-believe universalism."

If international law sought to push off the differences in the ideas and values of alternatives social orders, then international relations theory sought to push them down. By looking ever upward toward more and more generalist—or even banal—observations about anarchy and rationalism, it was easy to forgive aberrant behavior by states on the basis of exogenous preferences, or failures to act rationally, or as local manifestations of inherently universal principles, or as thin rhetoric that made "real" motives more palatable to local populations or coalition partners. One way or another, the distinct, the local, the cultural, the non-universal, the evidently historical differences could be shunted off in favor of universal laws be they legal or natural.

In *Covert Action and Foreign Policy in World Politics*, Bozeman provided a list of dozens of questions she considered necessary for policymakers to answer, or have answered, to assist in the conduct of international relations. Accepting as given that a plurality of social systems exist and that understanding each, on its own terms, was central to advising state conduct, she divided her questions into Domestic and Foreign, and included, among others, the following:

- Which fundamental beliefs, ideas, and values seem to sustain the society in time?
- In which circumstances is violence condoned? What is the ceiling for tolerance of violence within society?
- What do men regard as "law"?
- Is law distinct from religion and from the political authority of the day?

- Is citizenship a developed concept?
- How is political authority rendered?
- Is war considered "bad" by definition?
- How do people think about peace? Is it a definable condition? What is its relation to war?
- What typifies the society's negotiating style?
- What is subsumed under the term "diplomacy"?

In her 1976 article, *War and the Clash of Ideas* (not to be mistaken with *War and the Clash of Civilizations* by Samuel Huntington published later and with no reference to Bozeman's piece), she lamented the distance political science had come from these essential questions.[18]

> The image of the world that is being rendered today by social and political scientists with a strong interest in war, peace, and conflict resolution is one of a global order of states that are structurally alike in essence or destined to become so under the impact of irresistible leveling forces. In the logic of this tight and finite scheme, all international relations—including belligerent confrontations—are seen as manifestations of national interests that converge on three main unifying themes: the survival of the state, the maintenance of the international system, and the avoidance of war . . . since there is no essential difference between State A and State B, there can be none between A's war and B's war . . .
>
> No allowance is made for the possibility that war-related phenomena are also, perhaps even predominantly, aspects of locally prevalent values, images, traditions, and mental constructions. Indeed, explorations of the ways of thought that make or do not make for war, or the meanings assigned to war and violence in culturally different parts of the world, would quite logically be out of place in the conceptually closed circuit of modern war and peace studies; for how can cultural diversity be perceived if "culture" (or "civilization") is not accepted as a relevant variable or factor?
>
> The Student embarking on war and peace studies today will look in vain for rigorous analyses of Occidental, Oriental, or African philosophies, ideologies, myths and religions . . .

There is always the fear that such observations are either dated or else the product of a lone, marginal scholar. In the first instance, this is certainly not the case, and in the second, I believe the problem is rather that the vast and varied academics who would agree with such an orientation to analysis are marginal only to international relations scholarship. What's needed is to bring them into the fold as welcome contributors.

In 1998, Kwesi Yankah, a scholar from Ghana, made the Plenary Address to the American Folklore society—not an event generally attended by international relations scholars. He asked questions that would have been very familiar to Bozeman: "How susceptible is traditional [African] society to Western norms and systems of communication, and how have African folk coped with attempts to graft modern communicative norms onto indigenous institutions?"

According to Yankah, "African folk have not hidden a lingering mistrust for advanced communication systems beyond the spoken word and face-to-face communication." He explains how the Akan of Ghana refer to the telephone as *ahomatrofo*, "meaning 'liar,' 'the tale-bearing wire,' 'string or wire that conveys lies, unverified information, not to be trusted, unreliable, dealing in falsehoods.'" This implies, he argues, that "fast-traveling news, whose veracity cannot be checked, is not trustworthy." He explains that the "general suspicion" of, or dispreference for, non-indigenous modes or channels of communication may also be seen in the general word for foreign language, *apotofoo kasa*, implying a language hurriedly improvised for ad hoc use, lacking permanence or authenticity. To speak a foreign language itself is *poto*, to "mix, craft, improvise."

An abductive and comparative approach to studying the plurality of forms that "international relations" really takes among culturally distinct communities will eventually arrive at a series of ethnographies (however so named). These series can then be compared, if so desired, to try and understand any global characteristics of international relations and hence reveal any extant "fundamental laws" if that is the researcher's interest. It may well be that there are such laws. It may also be that what laws exist are merely of scholastic interest because they are too banal to be interesting or informative for actual policy or decision making. In any case, this purposive approach to comparative social research in international relations would map and explain the distinct forms and meaning given to particular practices—like polluting the environment, engaging in espionage, attending "peace" discussions, or proliferating nuclear weapons—so that we might whisper from the voice of philosophers to the ears of kings, and in so doing, design and plan policies more conducive to constructive international engagement.

It is worth recalling, as a final thought, the words of Isaiah Berlin who wrote: "[i]t is only a very vulgar historical materialism that denies the power of ideas, and says that ideals are mere material interests in disguise."[19] Political communication will open new doors to the comparative study of ideas and ideals and how they impinge and communicate with one another across different social worlds. In doing so, it may bring some light to the darkest and dullest places of modern scholarship in international relations.

From Challenges to a
Research Agenda

Speaking of dull, a few final thoughts are needed. The measurement technique devised to test the Positioning Hypothesis is not without problems that are worthy of attention. By treating all questions posed by the media identically for the purpose of measurement; by making no effort to separate out more intensive or damaging scrutiny from more benign questions that still meet the minimal standard of pressure being used here; and by treating acts of repositioning the same as acts of redescription, the social dynamics of the questions have been flattened, thereby certainly negating highly useful pieces of information for social analysis. Instead of measuring the political significance of the questions asked, *we have only measured the density of media pressure* as experienced by the executive.

An analogy may be helpful: a line of soldiers are all firing at a selected target. Some are expert marksmen. Others are blindfolded. Sometimes, they all fire nearly at once. Other times, the shots are staggered. In treating the shots of the marksmen and the blindfolded men as equally effective, we deny ourselves the possibility of measuring the significance of the shots in terms of targets hit and damage done. What can be said with reasonable precision is how intensive the firing is at any given time. Damage assessments (i.e.. impact) cannot be measured. If we make the reasonable, though not indisputable, claim that the more shots that are fired at any given time the more damage is *likely* to be caused we can use the measure of the volley as a proxy measure for determining likely damage. This is what was achieved in chapter 6.

Some "pressure questions" are off the mark, and others are right on target. Some journalists are simply better than others and are more in tune to the crux of the issues being faced by the administration, and are equally willing to challenge those matters in the press conference. The measurement technique developed so far only tells us the intensity of the media barrage, not the damage caused. Further work will be needed to refine the process and—in all cases—the historical record must be consulted where possible to find alternative explanations for the policy changes.

The choice to use U.S. and British decision making allowed for useful comparative analysis. Their experience in the same event furthermore allowed for media coverage and pressure and influence to be compared in a highly refined manner. But another solution may have been to look at one historical case and one contemporary one within one country. This historical comparison would have shed less light on the media in democratic Liberal states, but more on the uniqueness of the present era—or conversely, its profound similarity to past ones. Chapter 2 attempted to contribute to this need, but could not provide comparative empirical data.

An interesting lesson learned from this study, which could not have been known *a priori*, but presents new opportunities for study and analysis, is the important difference between *policy pressure* and *accountability pressure*. In the period spanning 5 April, when the airdrops began, and 16 April, when the introduction of ground forces was announced, the White House was under extraordinary pressure from the press (though it was dropping) and Whitehall was under moderate to strong pressure (which was also dropping). But what was the nature of the pressure? Whereas the period leading up to 5 April was notable as being policy pressure—or pressure to take some action—the period after was mostly accountability pressure—or the pressure to account for *past* action (or inaction). The difference is enormous, but the two were not coded separately.

They need to be. Accountability pressure can indeed affect the reputation and authority of the executive and challenge policy coalitions, in conformity to the Positioning Hypothesis. What it cannot do, however, is change policy. And yet, do policymakers fear it? And if they do, is it considered during the policymaking process itself?

In the United States and United Kingdom, the president and prime minister are both politicians. This means they worked themselves up through some political machinery and suffered the slings and arrows of the voting process to achieve office. Consequently, they understand full well how to make decisions, and how to consider their consequences. One can assume that there is a self-selection process involved in reaching these offices whereby those who do, more often then not, are good at making these assessments. It might also be reasonably assumed that at some point in their prior political histories they suffered the backlash of an unpopular decision. This assumption can easily be confirmed by biography. And so, how might the accountability pressure influence the decision-making process? In any given society, what sorts of actions are most likely and least likely to be held to account? The method developed here allows for the measurement of pressure across societies, and therefore facilitates answers to these questions.

In chapter 2, two sources of valuable information came to light. The first was the rediscovery of lost voices and theories about media–government relations from the eighteenth and nineteenth centuries that will broaden and enrich the scope of present inquiries. At the center of this material is the legal record, and after the record itself is the legal exegesis on the rules and then the popular writings about those rulings.

The legal record and the controversy surrounding the law have been understudied in the field of political communication for Western cases. Due to the centrality of law as a source of stability and justice in society, the form it takes and the meaning given to its actions speaks volumes about the thought processes of a society. Each trial and sentence is a meaningful expression and reconstruction of a culture and its incumbent philosophy. In particular, the legal exegesis on seditious libel, libel, and slander contain within them a complete, serial record of the evolution of thinking about political communication and its consequences. *Media Pressure on Foreign Policy* has identified the value of the material and developed a modern theory consistent with it—though not actually built on it as the survey was too limited in scope. Consequently, what is now needed is a greater examination of this material in a thorough and systematic manner.

Such an undertaking will provide a wellspring of both data and explanation about how Western states conceived of media power. This can be confidently concluded because so many areas of social life were contingent on those understandings and found expression in daily life. What were the laws? What were the consequences of breaking those laws? What were the justifications for the sentences? What were the consequences to society understood to be? What philosophies of statecraft were being supported and challenged by these rulings and their enforcement? Under what political circumstances were laws strengthened and weakened? In what manner? The answers to all these questions will further develop or refine the Positioning Hypothesis as a theory of political communication. It will likewise form the basis for comparative studies.

The second was the need for comparative work. If reputation and authority are qualities constituted by clusters of concepts, forms of talk and practices within a given moral world, they serve as ways into cultural analysis. What constitutes a good reputation? A bad one? What makes someone authoritative? Or not?

Work in the field of ethnography of communication uses the assumption that all social action is organized, produced, and interpreted according to some patterned system of premises internal to it.[20] In this case, this means both the world of the decision makers themselves, and the media–government dialogue as cultural practice. That meaning is internally generated and constituted implies that meaning across cultural domains may well be different. The media–government dialogue may therefore be an enactment of cultural expression that varies from country to country whereby the purpose, meaning, and consequences of that dialogue are different from place to place, and in a single place through time. Whereas the act of positioning another person may be a universal phenomenon (e.g., all insults are hurtful by definition), the actual questions posed or descriptions made about the executive or its policies cannot be expected to have the same moral force in one locality and another. In short, what looks like pressure in one place may even be complimentary in another place. We can only know by (i) suspending our assumption that we know pressure when we see it, since that assumption is built on the researcher's own understandings of social frameworks in his or her own moral world, and (ii) by coding for the perlocutionary impact of media utterances on the executive itself.

Comparative studies that are culturally sensitive to the use of language and positioning will open vast areas for analysis. If bad press forces issues up the executive hierarchy, what constitutes bad press for a given executive? What does that in turn tell us about that executive's moral parameters for action? What does that, in turn, tell us about the range of choices for action considered good, or acceptable, or bad and unacceptable?

The major importance of identifying some of the limiting norms in a society are well explained by M.F. Burnyeat, who writes, "[t]here is a rhetoric in public life which surely does not determine the behaviour of our leaders, but does set limits, however loose, to the kinds of policy they can get away with and the kinds of things they can do without having to resign. It is a matter of enormous importance what values are acknowledged—sincerely or insincerely—in public discussion."[21] Recognizing that these limits are different in different localities allows us the opportunity to find out what they might be and how they work. By understanding the premises of "good" and "valuable" and "worthy," the logic of decisions in a community begins to take form. This is the essence of foreign policy decision making. And if actions in the international theater are accepted as coming from choices rather than mechanical reactions to structures, then it goes right to the heart of international relations itself.

Notes

Introduction

1. During this early period, I treat the terms "press" and "media" synonymously.
2. For some of the earliest twentieth-century discussions that followed Lippman's 1922 interest in public opinion and explored press–government relations through that general approach, see the following: Norman Angel, *The Public Mind* (London, 1926); Thomas Bailey, *The Man in the Street: The Impact of American Public Opinion on Foreign Policy* (MacMillan: New York, 1949); Jerome S. Bruner, *Mandate from the People* (New York, 1944); Walter Lippman, *The Phantom Public* (New York, 1925) and *Public Opinion* (New York, 1922); A.L. Lowell, *Public Opinion and Popular Government* (New York, 1926); and Charles W. Smith, *Public Opinion in a Democracy* (New York, 1942).
3. The term "press" in this period includes pamphleteering. This practice died out but Internet "blogs" today may bring the practice back in a new form.

Chapter 1   The Contemporary Debate

1. Livingston followed up this technological angle and explicitly questioned, with W. Lance Bennett, whether event-driven news stories in the international theater—which are technologically dependent—are "changing the reliance of journalists on [state] officials in selecting and cuing their political content [as determined by frame analysis]." This study concluded that technological advancement has increased event-driven coverage, but not necessarily its dependence on official sources. See Livingston and Bennett, "Gatekeeping, Indexing, and Live-Event News."
2. Kennan, "Somalia, through a Glass Darkly."
3. Natsios, "Illusions of Influence: The CNN Effect in Complex Emergencies."
4. Bennett and Paletz, *Taken by Storm*; Rotberg and Weiss, *From Massacres to Genocide*; Hoge, "Media Pervasiveness"; Gowing, "Real-Time Television Coverage"; Hindell, "The Influence of the Media on Foreign Policy," p. 77; and McNulty, "Television's Impact on Executive Decisionmaking and Diplomacy," pp. 67–83. This is by no

means an exhaustive list, as editorials appeared in newspapers all over the United States. These are a sampling of the more significant pieces.

5. Livingston and Eachus, "Human Crises."
6. Gans, *Deciding What's News.*
7. Hallin, *The Uncensored War.*
8. Bennett, "Towards a Theory of Press-State Relations in the United States," pp. 103–125.
9. Mermin, "Television News and American Intervention in Somalia." Document received through ProQuest, which changes the page numbers; hence page numbers unavailable.
10. Ibid.
11. Zaller and Chiu, "Government's Little Helper," p. 385.
12. Ibid., p. 387.
13. Ibid., pp. 386–387.
14. The 1956 Suez Crisis, the Cuban Missile Crisis of 1962, and the deployment of U.S. troops to the Gulf in 1991 were the three events when Congress was out of session.
15. Zaller and Chui, "Government's Little Helper," p. 392.
16. Television did not become affordable until the 1950s.
17. To the best of this author's knowledge, no study has properly looked at media pressure via radio news coverage. Radio was the first mass media where neither literacy nor education was required to understand the content. Beginning with Roosevelt (and Hitler in Germany) it was a powerful tool for the dissemination of news as well as official statements and propaganda by the government. It may be that the reason has to do with the practical difficulty of studying the subject for researchers. Recordings are not available in most libraries. The historic effects of radio on the public agenda are highly underappreciated; however, it gained global attention with the Rwandan genocide and the role that radio played. See Wood, *History of International Broadcasting.*
18. Robinson, "The CNN Effect."
19. Ibid., p. 302.
20. Ibid., pp. 301–302.
21. Ibid., p. 304.
22. Ibid., p. 305. Robinson attributes these descriptions to Minear et al., *The News Media,* pp. 51, 57, and 46 respectively.
23. Robinson, *The CNN Effect,* p. 3.
24. Ibid., p. 4
25. Ibid., p. 16
26. O'Heffernan, *Mass Media and American Foreign Policy,* p. xii.
27. Ibid., p. 82.
28. See Bernard C. Cohen's works in the Bibliography.
29. Ibid.
30. Ibid., p. 6.
31. O'Heffernan, *Mass Media and American Foreign Policy,* p. 88.

32. Gergen, "Diplomacy in a Television Age," p. 54.
33. Kalb, "Foreword," p. xv.
34. Bruner, *Acts of Meaning*, p. 2.
35. Ibid., p. 4.
36. Ibid., p. 6.
37. Kintsch, "The Representation of Knowledge in Minds and Machines," pp. 411–420.
38. Bruner, *Acts of Meaning*, p. 8.

CHAPTER 2   BEYOND THE CONTEMPORARY DEBATE

1. Defamation is an attack on the good reputation of a person. Slander is verbal defamation whereas libel is defamation in written form. Shakespeare's phrase comes from *Macbeth* ("foul whisperings are abroad").
2. Discourse analysis is one obvious tool for approaching this material because of the rich and plentiful vocabulary available from all the argumentation before the bench. Likewise, the researcher has the added benefit of seeing—over an extended period—what a legal community viewed as a threat to one's reputation, thereby providing a grounded analysis of a community's social values and changes to it over a period of time.
3. Jay M. Zitter (1986), "Excessiveness or Inadequacy of Compensatory Damages for Defamation," American Law Report 4th, 49 A.L.R. 4th, 1158, originally cited as 50 Am Jur 2d, Libel and Slander, §1.
4. Bozeman, *Strategic Intelligence and Statecraft*, p. 215.
5. Bozeman, *The Future of Law in a Multicultural World*, pp. 35–38.
6. Democracy in ancient Greece lasted in Athens for only two centuries, and less than that in a small number of other Greek states.
7. As cited. Original found at the Bodleian Library, Oxford University.
8. Squire, "A Faithful Report," pp. 2–3.
9. Ibid.; all italics from original.
10. Ibid., p. 15.
11. Ibid., p. 17. He uses a simple literary device of taking three men, two with extreme views and a third to moderate between them. Squire himself, supposedly the fourth and otherwise silent member of the party, takes no particular views but nods in agreement when agreement is met by all members. It cannot be known, of course, whether the conversation in fact took place.
12. Ibid., p. 22.
13. Ibid., p. 29.
14. It is possible that Squire arrived at this idea from the 1735 case in America against the New York publisher John Peter Zenger. Zenger wrote slanderous, but accurate, accounts of the notoriously corrupt

mayor of New York who was running for reelection. The case was handled by the lawyer Andrew Hamilton, who famously argued that truth in libel cases *should* be a proper defense. The common law of the period stated that any account of events that slandered or defamed an official was libel, and the truth of the slander was no defense. Hamilton argued the case, and against the instructions of the judge, the jury found in favor of Zenger. Though this case would not produce a strong nation-wide precedent, it was nevertheless a seminal case for the ensuing philosophical arguments and public discourse that would fuel resentment against Britain and the monarchy, leading to both the American Revolution and the establishment of freedom of expression as a fundamental right in the new republic.

15. National security, as is often noted, is a misnomer. State security is more accurate, as a nation tends to denote a people whereas a state is a legally defined entity comprising a government, a territory, and a population (by standards of modern international public law).

16. Harry Kalven (1964), "The *New York Times* Case: A Note on the Central Meaning of the First Amendment," 1964 Supreme Court Review 205. As quoted in American Bar Association, Central and East European Law Initiative (CEELI), "Concept Paper on Media Law," November 1996, available at http://www.abanet.org/ceeli/publications/conceptpapers/medialaw/media_law_concept_paper.pdf.

17. The term "non-Liberal" is deliberately used. Whereas "pre-Liberal" would be historically accurate when speaking of—say—the United States, Britain, and France, it is inappropriate to speak of states with no Liberal tradition as "pre-Liberal" as there is no *a priori* reason to assume that the complicated clusters of ideas and experience that led to Liberalism in the West will necessary be replicated and followed elsewhere. Evidence, indeed, suggests otherwise.

18. American Bar Association (1996).

19. It is argued that the Liberal state cannot legally sustain seditious libel laws. The 1798 *Seditious Libel Act* in America proves that in times of threat, freedom of speech can be viewed as a threat to national security, one of the main reasons being implicitly that communicative attacks on the government can weaken the state in its war against a foreign power by creating a "house divided," to employ Shakespeare's apt phrase.

20. Pigot, *Liberty of the Press*, p. 5; available at the Bodleian Library, Oxford University.

21. Chafee, *Free Speech in the United States*, p. 23.

22. Bentham, *The King against Edmonds, and Others*, p. 13.

23. Christopher Brewin (1996), book review of "Reputation and International Relations" by Jonathan Mercer, *International Affairs (Royal Institute of International Affairs, 1944)*, Vol. 72, No. 4, The Americas: European Security.

24. A mirror of this, of course, is the propaganda crafted to turn the enemy into an evil, and often feckless, adversary. The latter is more difficult to do, as the enemy might often win battles but demonizing

the enemy is rather easy and positions the domestic executive as not only moral, but comparatively *more* moral than the enemy. It is a testable hypothesis whether propaganda against the enemy increases the baser one's own actions become so that the comparative advantage is never lost. This would be an interesting study.

25. Gallup Tuesday Briefing, 18 September 2001, Special Edition, "Attack on America: Public Opinion," available at http://www.listserv.gallup.com.

26. Daniel Dobbs (2000), *The Law of Torts*, St. Paul, MN: West Group, pp. 1189–1195. Special thanks to John D. Rue for this source and explanation.

27. American Bar Association (1996), Section (G) Remedies: Relationship of Injury to Damages.

CHAPTER 3   TOWARD A THEORY OF MEDIA PRESSURE

1. The phrase "instrument of faction"—appropriated here—was first encountered in 1770 in *Thoughts on the Cause of the Present Discontents*, London: J. Dodsley, available at the Bodleian Library, Oxford University. It was used to discuss the power of the written word and its impact on the government. The pamphlet appears to have been authored anonymously. I thank that author for this useful idea.

2. Harré, "The Dynamics of Social Episodes," in Harré and Langenhove, *Positioning Theory*.

3. Ibid., pp. 2 and 3.

4. White House press conference, 25 March 1991.

5. Strobel, *Late-Breaking Foreign Policy*, pp. 1 and 2.

6. Britain does not have press conferences and the relationship of the prime minister and the press is quite different. Smith's comments—for the moment—are general enough to apply to both executives but distinctions will later be drawn in great detail. See Smith, "The Prime Minister and the Press: Britain," for a good introduction.

7. Aristotle, *On Rhetoric*.

8. Billig, *Arguing and Thinking*, p. 49.

9. Harré and Secord, *The Explanation of Social Behaviour*, p. 142.

10. Billig, *Arguing and Thinking*, p. 52.

11. Smith, *Presidential Press Conferences*, p. xvii.

12. It has not yet been determined that there is a consistent pattern of fewer press conferences during crises, though the Carter period, as well as this case study period, both defend the claim, and the Positioning Hypothesis provides an argument for why the phenomenon is likely.

13. Murray Edelman (1967), *The Symbolic Uses of Politics, With a New Afterward*, Urbana and Chicago: University of Illinois Press (reprint, 1985), p. 132.

14. This case will be explored in detail in chapter 4.

15. *BBC World*, 14 May 2003, has reported the discovery of 10,000–15,000 bodies in Shiite areas of Iraq, allegedly the result of mass killings and burials in 1991 (as reported in Geneva, Switzerland).

16. A *Washington Post* article of 9 April 1991 said that Voice of Free Iraq had been saying since January that, "we stand by you in whatever you carry out and in every step you take."

17. CNN (1994), "Reliable Sources," 16 October, as quoted in Moeller, *Compassion Fatigue*.

18. Powell et al., "The Relationship of the President and the Press," p. 26.

19. Gardner, *The Art of Fiction*, p. 53.

20. Ibid., p. 48.

21. Ibid., p. 55.

22. Again, this should be taken as a rule of thumb, because one can—in some circumstances—gain an upper hand through silence if the other is likely to fill that silence with some sort of prattle.

23. Harré, "Agentive Discourse," in Harré and Stearns, *Discursive Psychology in Practice*, pp. 124–126.

24. Ibid.

25. Issues of coalition governments and minority governments will not be dealt with specifically, but pose no challenges to the following discussion points.

26. Kaminsky, "On the Comparison of Presidential and Parliamentary Governments," p. 221.

27. Ibid.

28. Details from Gregory Treverton (1990), "Intelligence: Welcome to the American Government," in Thomas E. Mann (ed.) *A Question of Balance: The President, the Congress and Foreign Policy*, Washington, D.C.: The Brookings Institute, pp. 73–74.

29. Shaw, *Civil Society and Media in Global Crises*, p. 31.

30. A coalition government here means a parliamentary government whereby no single party has autonomous legislative power. This differs from my more casual use of the term coalition, which is any formal or informal arrangement necessary to implement or maintain a desired policy.

31. Müller and Strøm, *Coalition Governments in Western Europe*, p. 2.

32. Snyder, "Alliances, Balance, and Stability."

CHAPTER 4   THE IRAQI CIVIL WAR
AND THE AFTERMATH, 1991

1. The term "Gulf War" is used here only because of its common meaning in the United States and Britain.

2. Shaw, *Civil Society and Media in Global Crises*, p. 79.

3. Colin Powell, then chairman of the Joint Chiefs of Staff, provides the period with a three-page reflection; Brent Scowcroft, writing with

George H.W. Bush, offers four factually dubious pages in a 500-page book (*A World Transformed*); and then Middle East expert to the National Security Council, Richard N. Haass, offers four paragraphs about the largest, most expensive, and logistically complex humanitarian intervention in history (of which he was a major player) in a book called *Intervention: The Use of Military Force in the Post–Cold War World*.

4. Called "Operation Safe Haven" by Britain. The American code name is used because it is more widely known in military circles, and because Operation Safe Haven had a much shorter duration, and operated subordinately—but with distinction—to the American relief.

5. In 1998, the U.S. Congress passed the *Iraq Liberation Act* (HR 4655). Section 4, paragraphs 2A and 2B read, "(2) Military assistance: (A) The President is authorized to direct the drawdown of defense articles from the stocks of the Department of Defense, defense services of the Department of Defense, and military education and training for such organizations. (B) The aggregate value (as defined in section 644(m) of the *Foreign Assistance Act* of 1961) of assistance provided under this paragraph may not exceed $97,000,000."

6. Shaw, *Civil Society and Media in Global Crises*, p. 79.

7. The most in-depth study thus far was produced by Martin Shaw, who covered only the British media (though more extensively than examined here as it included tabloid papers as well as broadsheets and television) and only from 1 March to the end of April.

8. Among those examined.

9. See in the following sections the graphs of media influence as measured by minutes or paragraphs of coverage per week in all newspapers and television networks reviewed. Note that by the end of May, all media studied had effectively lost interest in the story.

10. Strobel, *Late-Breaking Foreign Policy*, p. 128. As will be discussed, Strobel's observations were astutely made, but his conclusions did not look beyond them. Media accounts did reach this very conclusion but were actually wrong. Aides also confirmed these statements, but it will be seen that this was in response to a change in the White House communication strategy that did not reflect the real reasons for the intervention.

11. Seib, *Headline Diplomacy*, p. 38.

12. Deborah Amos, "Foreign Policy by Popular Outrage," *Neiman Reports*, Summer, p. 74, as quoted in Seib, *Headline Diplomacy*, p. 39.

13. Shaw, *Civil Society and Media in Global Crises*, p. 156.

14. Carruthers, *The Media at War*, p. 211.

15. Lincoln P. Bloomfield (1994), "The Premature Burial of Global Law and Order: Looking Beyond the Three Cases from Hell," *The Washington Quarterly*, Vol. 17, No. 3, Summer, p. 142. Bloomfield is factually incorrect on two accounts here. First, it was not the coalition but rather the United States, Britain, France, and Turkey (primarily)

who moved in troops and aid. No Arab country participated. Second, the Shiite rebellion was over and "pacified" before Operation Provide Comfort was initiated, with the possible exception of isolated incidents. Whether the move was in response to public outrage will be examined in detail.

16. Schorr, "Ten Days that Shook the White House," pp. 21–23. Notable is that Schorr himself wrote during this period of alleged influence, a significant piece of obvious condemnation of the White House, 1975: "Background to Betrayal; How Kissinger, Nixon and the Shah Rallied—Then Shrugged Off—an Uprising," *Washington Post*, 7 April 1991.

17. All are local times for Iraq unless otherwise indicated.

18. Initial estimates of Iraqi casualties were not released by the Pentagon. In May 1991, in response to an inquiry filed under the *Freedom of Information Act*, the Defense Intelligence Agency produced an estimate with a error factor of "50 per cent or higher." The estimates were as follows: killed in action: 100,000; wounded in action: approximately 300,000; deserters: approximately 150,000. However, the Pentagon later retracted support for these figures although the number of 100,000 continues to live on.

19. Great controversy remains over whether this "chicken shoot" of Iraqi forces was a legitimate military necessity. As the question is one of morality, there is no simple answer. There are, however, two complicating factors. At the time, these soldiers were retreating with their weapons in an active war zone. Retreat is not surrender. From the position of International Humanitarian Law, it would need to be argued that these troops were "non-combatants" because they were unable to fight. The matter is further complicated, if only with hindsight, because we now know that many of those surviving these events would be later implicated in the murder of tens of thousands of civilians during the civil war.

20. The *Independent* reported on 1 March 1991 an AFP story stating that "Iraqi soldiers were banned from wearing white underwear so they could not use it to surrender, according to French intelligence officers who monitored Iraqi radio messages during the war." I have no idea whether this was true. If it was, it would have been a good indicator that Saddam Hussein was under few illusions about the caliber and morale of his front-line troops.

21. See Galbraith, *Civil War in Iraq*, p. vi. This report has numerous factual inaccuracies and this estimate should not be taken as definitive.

22. Nakash, *The Shi'is of Iraq*, p. 274.

23. Ibid., p. 275.

24. Khadduri and Ghareeb, *War in the Gulf 1990–91*.

25. Galbraith did not cite the original source of his information, and it is possible that he created his story from the very reports I am using here to confirm his own, which would create a circular problem (not unknown to scholarship). This possibility could not be verified.

26. No original citation was mentioned in their study.
27. Notable is that this paragraph does not say the uprising in fact began in Nasiriyah, only that it was the first city taken by rebel forces. It is therefore inconclusive.
28. What the press spokesmen were told to downplay or direct attention away from is unknown.
29. The Badr Brigade were originally Iraqi Shiite prisoners of war from the Iran–Iraq war and who converted to fundamentalism. See Randal, *After Such Knowledge, What Forgiveness*, p. 47.
30. Khadduri and Ghareeb, *War in the Gulf 1990–91*, p. 191.
31. According to Martin Woolacott of the *Guardian* (9 March), "All agree that the uprisings in both north and south Iraq were not launched in any planned way, and that there is little co-ordination between those fighting in different areas." Whether this was as true in the Kurdish north as in the Shiite south, however, is unlikely as will be discussed.
32. *Independent*, 24 March 1991.
33. ABC News, *Nightline*, 5 March 1991. All quotes from television programs are taken directly from the published transcripts rather than recorded by the researcher.
34. The question of Iranian material support is very uncertain. Suggestions of Iranian helicopters supplying aid have been discussed, but there is no confirmation. Furthermore, the United States dominated the Iraqi airspace, and no Iranian planes would have been able to make airdrops of aid or arms without immediate US intelligence knowledge (from AWACs and other systems). Second, all bridges across the Tigris, which separates Iraq and Iran near the southern border, were bombed making the river uncrossable. That said, the *Independent* in 26 March wrote, "[f]ew US officials now deny seriously that Tehran is supplying Shia rebels in the south with arms, if not troops." However, this was never confirmed at a White House press briefing.
35. One report in the *Independent* suggested that Massoud Barzani secretly visited Israel in mid-March to request material support. The Israelis supported the Kurds in the 1970s and early 1980s in order to weaken the Arab states. The article ambiguously implied that the Israelis may have been supplying the Kurds, but one is dubious about how that might have been accomplished and at what expense; see "Washington Dithers as Iraqi Rebels Claim More Victories," 24 March 1991.
36. Izzedine Barawi, a Kurdish spokesman in Damascus, as quoted in the *New York Times*, 11 April 1991.
37. Not to mention that the might of 500,000 U.S. troops in the region probably functioned as a rather convincing deterrent to Iranian adventurism.
38. *Guardian*, 4 March 1991.

39. Rabat Domestic Service, in Arabic, 23:00 GMT, 5 March 1991 (FBIS, 6 March, FBIS-NES-91-044), p. 12.
40. Remarks at a meeting of Veterans Service Organizations, 27 Weekly Comp. Pres. Doc. 246, Public Papers of the Presidents, 4 March 1991.
41. Public Papers of the President, 27 Weekly Comp. Pres. Doc. 257, 6 March 1991. *Address before a Joint Session of the Congress on the Cessation of the Persian Gulf Conflict.*
42. The tenacity with which American officials clung to the idea of a palace coup orchestrated by the Iraqi military was so strong there is great urge to conclude that they must have known something the public record has yet to reveal. Suspicions of a possible CIA-led operation inside Iraq or some such hidden policy, however, are not verifiable and remain only unsupported speculation. Evidence suggests instead a profound failure of U.S. strategic intelligence about Iraqi society and its dynamics.
43. Traditionally, Western states have issued declarations of war prior to initiating hostilities, followed by a peace treaty at their end. Since World War II, however, the United States, like other countries, has not issued a declaration of war, thereby making a peace treaty as such an untenable follow-up. The permanent ceasefire functioned in a manner similar to a peace treaty by setting terms and making agreements that were designed to act as law, in the form of a contract, between the parties.
44. Politically, Israel's complicity was considered vital to the war effort as no Arab state would have likely been willing to fight on the same side as Israel against another Arab country. Israel's joining the fighting was therefore considered a sure way to end the coalition against Iraq.
45. Baker's trip was not secret insofar as it was widely reported that he left for the region with these general instructions. What was confidential was the order in which he would speak to international actors, what he would say, and what promises might be made. The objective was to give him sufficient grounds to maneuver across the political terrain. Bush would often joke with reporters that he was not doing to tell them anything about the trip until it was over, and American journalists generally accepted of this position.
46. *Washington Post*, 1 March 1991.
47. Conversation with Alan Makovsky, Washington Institute of Near East Policy.
48. Whether the United States and the United Kingdom coordinated in the British contact is unknown, and it is therefore premature to conclude that the latter was necessarily acting against U.S. State Department policy. In all likelihood, the United Kingdom was passing on any relevant information to the United States. Britain had also been meeting with other Iraqi opposition leaders as early as January. According to the *Guardian* of 6 March, the Foreign Office met with Fahkri Karim, a politburo member of the Iraqi Communist Party and general secretary

of the Syrian-based Action Committee of Iraq on 5 March, making it the fourth Iraqi opposition leader visit since January.

49. *Washington Post*, 3 March 1991.
50. *Guardian*, 12 March 1991.
51. UN resolutions are not viewed, in international public law, as legal rulings that explicitly build the common law of international relations. However, the resolutions are viewed as binding due to the treaty obligations of the states who are members.
52. *Independent*, 8 March 1991.
53. 27 Weekly Comp. Pres. Doc. 301, Public Papers of the Presidents, 13 March 1991.
54. 27 Weekly Comp. Pres. Doc. 308, 13 March, 1991. *Statement by Press Secretary Fitzwater on Iraqi President Saddam Hussein's Use of Force against the Iraqi People.*
55. *Guardian*, 16 March 1991.
56. HANSARD, 12 March 1991.
57. HANSARD records were examined individually on a day-by-day basis and then downloaded electronically from the parliamentary website. All relevant sections were then copied out and pasted into a separate document so that all records could be grouped and examined without the distraction of the other House discussions. Word counts are considered estimates as Microsoft Word 98 also counted dates, the title, column indications, and other incidentals, and the author found it impractical—and frankly, much too boring—to remove them. Both figures should be considered accurate, well above 98 percent.
58. *Report on humanitarian needs in Iraq in the immediate post-crisis environment by a mission to the area led by the Under-Secretary-General for Administration and Management*, 10–17 March 1991 S/22366, 20 March 1991. As prepared by (then) Under-Secretary-General Martti Ahtisaari.
59. Press conference, 22 March 1991.
60. See chapter 3 for a discussion of storylines and how they end.
61. *Washington Post* editorial, 26 March 1991.
62. ABC News, *World News Tonight with Peter Jennings*, 27 March 1991.
63. Shaw, *Civil Society and Media in Global Crises*, p. 85.
64. White House press conference, 28 March 1991; available through Lexis/Nexis. Popadiuk also said: "we have a lot of reports to the effect that chemical weapons have been used, but we cannot confirm any of this at this time." There was no request to the White House by journalists to have this confirmed.
65. HANSARD, 28 March 1991, column 1106.
66. *Guardian*, 16 April 1991.
67. Ibid.
68. *Washington Post*, 1 April 1991.
69. See *U.S. News and World Report*, 15 April 1991, pp. 10 and 11 for a full-page spread of the photograph.

70. Danielle Mitterand would in fact be in occasional contact with the Kurdish leadership at least through the end of April, when she met Barzani and four journalists on 23 April in Iraq, three miles west of the Iranian border; see the *Guardian*, 24 April 1991.
71. As quoted on ABC *Evening News*, 3 April 1991.
72. *Guardian*, 4 April 1991.
73. Ibid.
74. As quoted in the *Guardian*, 26 March 1991.
75. Hella Pick and Michael White of the *Guardian* would write on 18 April 1991 that "[t]he fact that Margaret Thatcher went public first with a 'something must be done' statement wrongly created the impression that she had goaded Whitehall into action." As this runs counter to the findings here, it is noteworthy, but regrettably, the writers did not support the statement, which is otherwise worth greater investigation.
76. Quoted in the *New York Times*, 9 April 1991, in the editorial "A Leader for Some Seasons." It was stated that the Thatcher quote was made "last week."
77. *New York Times*, 7 April 1991, "The Week in Review," "Iraq is Left to the Mercy of Saddam Hussein."
78. Ibid., 10 April 1991.
79. See, for example, the regular use of this phrase in the 23 April Congressional hearings.
80. Rudd, "Operation Provide Comfort."
81. Public Papers of the Presidents, 27 Weekly Comp. Pres. Doc. 392, 5 April 1991.
82. Ibid., pp. 118–119. Rudd's source was a taped interview with General Colin Powell, chairman of the Joint Chiefs of Staff, General Collin Powell's office in the Pentagon, 30 September 1992; USAFE (United States Air Force Europe) history, pp. 17–19, 47.
83. Ibid., p. 121.
84. Ibid., p. 378.
85. *Guardian*, 10 April 1991.
86. *New York Times*, 9 April 1991.
87. Rudd, "Operation Provide Comfort." Taped interviews between Rudd and Galvin, and Rudd and Powell.
88. Ibid., p. 219.
89. Ibid., p. 220. Rudd added that General Galvin "stated that he perceived the need for intervention almost from the beginning of the operation. After several phone conversations with General Colin Powell, Chairman of the Joint Chiefs of staff, a consensus developed among senior American military leaders that intervention was necessary."
90. Ibid.
91. *New York Times*, 10 April 1991.
92. *Washington Post*, 6 April 1991.

93. *Newsweek*, 25 March 1991 (U.S. edition).
94. ABC *News with Peter Jennings*, 9 April 1991, quoting Iraqi officials.
95. *Guardian*, 9 April 1991.
96. Public Papers of the President, 16 April 1991. 27 Weekly Comp. Pres. Doc. 444
97. Ibid., 17 April 1991.
98. Ibid., 18 April 1991.
99. Ibid., 11 April 1991.
100. Ten years after the invasion of Kuwait, Thatcher would tell the *Daily Telegraph*, "I only wish that I had stayed on to finish the job properly. Perhaps then we wouldn't be where we are today with this cruel and terrible man still securely in power." See the *Daily Telegraph*, 26 February 2001, "Gulf War Ended too Soon, Says Thatcher."
101. *Washington Post*, 5 May 1991.
102. *Guardian*, 12 April 1991.
103. Rudd, "Operation Provide Comfort," p. 162.
104. *New York Times*, 27 May 1991.
105. Ibid., 22 April 1991.
106. Public Papers of the President, 11 April 1991. 27 Weekly Comp. Pres. Doc. 421
107. Iraq, which has no indigenous history of liberalism or democracy, often demonstrated its failure to understand what it meant. Iraq's prime minister, Saddoun Hammadi, explained to a journalist that, "[d]emocracy is a spirit and a concept, but the way one expresses it varies from one place to another" (*Guardian*, 26 April 1991).
108. Ibid.
109. ABC *Evening News*, 23 April 1991.
110. *Guardian*, 7 May 1991.
111. Rudd, "Operation Provide Comfort," p. 341.
112. Ibid., p. 343.
113. Ibid., p. 344.
114. Khadduri and Ghareeb, *War in the Gulf, 1990–91*, pp. 207–208.
115. *Washington Post*, 29 May 1991.

CHAPTER 5   MEASURING COVERAGE

1. ABC and NBC news transcripts were taken from Lexis-Nexis, but CBS news was only tracked by the information available from the website of Vanderbilt University's media center.
2. The list of material examined is available in the bibliography.
3. The British newspapers are on the liberal or "Labour" side of the British political spectrum. Because the hypothesis advanced in this study relies on the importance of oppositional voices to position executives and their policies, these papers were selected over their

comparable counterparts such as the *Times* and the *Daily Telegraph*. No implication should be drawn that the author favored one newspaper over another, although certain papers—such as the *Guardian*—demonstrated a comparative advantage in fielding such reporters as Martin Woolacott during sensitive periods.

4. Both sections were also aided by the daily news clippings gathered and generously made available by the Washington Institute for Near East Policy.

5. Or, as the Public Relations Society of America would have it instead, "the space around advertising in a publication for editorial content"; http://www.prsa.org/_News/leaders/byrum042103.asp.

6. See figure 5.2 and the discussion on units of measure to follow.

7. Again, other factors can be included to increase refinement of the measure, including font used for headlines, available word count as determined by typeface, and other such minutia.

8. The available data may be used for this purpose, however, by other researchers.

9. See chapter 4. There were a total of fifty-nine opinion articles between 2 March and 2 June 1991 in the *Independent*.

10. These cases were as follows. ABC: none; CBS: 12 March and 6, 7, 8 April; NBC: 18 March 1991.

11. E-mail correspondence with Martin Shaw.

12. Discussion with Steve Livingston, George Washington University, 2001.

13. Parliamentarians around the world have been known to leak material to the press specifically so that it becomes public information and can therefore be used against the executive.

14. The official Bush Library website was found insufficient. Lexis/Nexus was selected for downloading press briefings and was found to be, in this case, complete.

15. Scollon, *Mediated Discourse as Social Interaction*, p. viii.

16. BBC 1, late night news, 3 March 1991, as quoted by Shaw, *Civil Society and Media in Global Crises*, p. 81.

17. *Independent*, 4 March 1991.

18. BBC 1, late night news, 2 March 1991, as quoted by Shaw, *Civil Society and Media in Global Crises*, p. 81.

19. Toney Howitz and Craig Forman (1991), "Southern Iraq Is Ablaze with Protests, Challenging Saddam's Grip on the Region," *Wall Street Journal*, 5 March, p. A3.

20. *Washington Post*, 5 March 1991.

21. Horwitz and Forman, "Southern Iraq Is Ablaze with Protests."

22. *Guardian*, 6 March 1991.

23. Military personnel in the Gulf were at all times deeply concerned about possible reinitiation of hostilities and remained constant consumers of intelligence information of a tactical nature. The possible motivations for the uprisings were nevertheless beyond these military concerns.

24. Haass, *Intervention*, p. 35.
25. ABC News, *Nightline*, 6 March 1991; from transcripts. It is no small irony that Bush would soon be defeated by Bill Clinton for the presidency.
26. *Washington Post*, 23 March 1991.
27. *Washington Post*, 8 April 1991.
28. CBS News, 14 March 1991
29. On 18 March, ABC News anchorman Ted Koppel would begin his segment saying, "As usual, there are conflicting reports tonight about the fighting by insurgent forces inside Iraq." In the broader context, this reads more as an admission of journalistic frustration than an apology.
30. *Washington Post*, 23 March 1991. Zelnick had a continued interest in this matter and presented a lecture at Duke in 1998. See Zelnick, "Media and National Security Issues."
31. Why this was reported on 26 March but appeared in the *Washington Post* on 24 March is unclear.
32. *Independent*, 29 March 1991.
33. *Guardian*, 29 March 1991. Based on a conversion rate for 15 March 1991, there were 136.4 dinars to the U.S. dollar (from www.oanda.com), making the value of a child or woman $1.83, and $36.64 for each man.
34. ABC News, *World News Tonight with Peter Jennings*, 26 March 1991.
35. This material is graphically represented in figure 5.18.
36. *Guardian*, 6 April 1991; lead article.
37. *Guardian*, 10 April 1991.
38. *New York Times*, "6 U.S. Planes Begin Airlifting Relief to Kurds in Iraq," 8 April 1991, p. 1.
39. *Guardian*, 17 April 1991.
40. Hoagland would also argue that it was the media that catalyzed the Bush team into action. In a 2 May editorial for the *Washington Post* he wrote, "[f]or a large group in the Bush administration, Iraq was a one-night stand. Or it would have been, had it not been for the power of the televised images of dying Kurdish children. Those pictures undid George Bush's determination to pursue a hands-off approach to post-war Iraq. Kurdish misery and the insistent prodding of Britain, France and Turkey brought American troops into northern Iraq to feed and protect the victims of Saddam's latest outrages."
41. *Washington Post*, 16 April 1991.
42. *Guardian*, 22 April 1991.
43. *Guardian*, 13 April 1991.
44. Notable was that on 9 May, a new CBS News/*New York Times* poll found that most Americans thought President Bush had ended the war against Iraq too soon. Sixty-three percent of those polled said the United States should have kept fighting until Saddam was removed from power.

45. See the *New York Times*, 13 May 1991, for the inappropriately titled article, "Latest Rock-Star Relief Effort Benefits the Kurds."

CHAPTER 6 MEASURING PRESSURE, TESTING FOR INFLUENCE

1. There is evidence to suspect that in this particular case the White House deliberately headed off suspected media pressure. Fitzwater explained at a press conference on 9 May 1991 that "there is a long-range planning group that considers these events [i.e., presidential speeches] and talks about the appropriate theme and strategy, all under the direction of the Chief of Staff, and decisions are made [about scheduling and audience] by that group." This is considered "by essentially the senior staff to the president."

2. This rather overwrought term was used to identify the following countries directly aiding the refugees (maximum troops deployed in parentheses): Australia (75), Belgium (150), Canada (120), France (2,141), Germany (221), Italy (1,183), Luxembourg (43), Netherlands (1,020), Portugal (19), Spain (602), Turkey (1,160), United Kingdom (4,192), United States (12,136). Notably absent were Muslim states who had participated in the war effort.

3. *Report on Humanitarian Needs in Iraq in the Immediate Post-Crisis Environment by a Mission to the Area Led by the Under-Secretary–General for Administration and Management*, 10–17 March 1991, S/22366, 20 March 1991, as prepared by (then) Under-Secretary-General Martti Ahtisaari. In this study, see chapter 3, Phase 2: Explicit Banning of Helicopters and Chemical Weapons.

4. *Washington Post*, 25 April 1991.

5. *Guardian*, 27 March 1991.

6. This is not to imply official endorsement of Gelb's views by the *Times*, but the parallel in their arguments is noteworthy.

7. *Washington Post*, 29 March 1991; editorial.

8. *CBS Evening News*, 6 April 1991.

9. It would raise again briefly, but only during the Zakho crisis.

10. Rudd, "Operation Provide Comfort," p. 118

11. Danielle Mitterand would, in fact, be in occasional contact with the Kurdish leadership at least through the end of April, when she met Barzani and four journalists on 23 April in Iraq, three miles west of the Iranian border; see the *Guardian*, 24 April 1991.

12. "Statement on Aid to Iraqi Refugees," 27 Weekly Comp. Pres. Doc. 392, Public Papers of the President, 5 April 1991.

13. Rudd, "Operation Provide Comfort," pp. 118–119. Taped interview with General Colin Powell, Chairman of the Joint Chiefs of Staff, General Powell's office in the Pentagon, 30 September 1992. USAFE History, pp. 17–19, 47.

14. *Guardian*, 4 April 1991.
15. Ibid.
16. As quoted in the *Guardian*, 26 March 1991.
17. Hella Pick and Michael White of the *Guardian* would write on 18 April 1991: "[t]he fact that Margaret Thatcher went public first with a 'something must be done' statement wrongly created the impression that that had goaded Whitehall into action." As this argument that Whitehall's policies were actually ahead of Thatcher's comments runs counter to the findings here, it is noteworthy. Regrettably, the writers did not substantiate the claim that is otherwise worth greater investigation.
18. Quoted in the *New York Times*, 9 April 1991, in editorial "A Leader for Some Seasons." Thatcher quote made "last week."
19. *Guardian*, 18 April 1991.

CHAPTER 7   SUMMING UP
AND PRESSING ON

1. Available at http://www.pbs.org/newshour/media/west_wing/fitzwater.html. It should also be mentioned that Fitzwater along with Dee Dee Meyers and Peggy Noonan were all consultants to the show (see end credits to second-season episodes if, like me, you have the series on DVD).
2. Richard Cohen, "Pictures and the President," *Washington Post*, 23 April 1991, editorial.
3. Victoria Brittain, "Environment (the Forgotten Famine): Pain and Priorities—Agenda," *Guardian*, 26 April 1991.
4. Worth noting is that Strobel does not provide any explanation for why executive decisions on peacekeeping are somehow different from decisions on "going to war," and therefore provides no foundation for the importance of his study. My own research has no provided any clues on why such cases should be treated any differently from others that involve U.S. troops.
5. Linsky, *Impact*, p. 128.
6. Ibid., p. 224.
7. Gergen, "Diplomacy in a Television Age," p. 54.
8. McNulty, "Television's Impact," pp. 67–83.
9. Zaller and Chiu, "Government's Little Helper."
10. Morganthau, *Politics among Nations*, p.1
11. Legro and Moravcsik, "Is Anybody Still a Realist," p. 5.
12. Walt, "Rigor or Rigor Mortis?" p. 5.
13. Bruner, *Acts of Meaning*, pp. 28–29.
14. This is inspired by the work of Gerry Philipsen (1990) "Speaking 'Like a Man' in Teamsterville: Culture Patterns of Role Enactment in an Urban Neighborhood." See also the work of Donal Carbaugh as

mentioned in the bibliography. I believe that a powerful new research agenda can be forged between political communication and IR theory if we seek to build an "ethnography of political communication" that applies their insights and tools to Bozeman's set of questions.
15. Morganthau, *Politics among Nations*, p. 209.
16. Ibid., p. 211.
17. Ibid., p. 222.
18. Reprinted in Bozeman, *Strategic Intelligence and Statecraft*, pp. 56–57.
19. Berlin, "Two Concepts of Liberty." The article was first an Inaugural Lecture delivered before the University of Oxford on 31 October, 1958, and published by Clarendon press in the same year.
20. Carbaugh, "The Ethnographic Communication Theory."
21. Burnyeat, "The Past in the Present," p. 364.

BIBLIOGRAPHY

THEORY AND METHODOLOGY

Alexseev, Mikhail A. and W.L. Bennett (1995) "For Whom the Gates Open: News Reporting and Government Source Patterns in the United States, Great Britain, and Russia." *Political Communication*, Vol. 12, pp. 395–412.

American Bar Association, Central and East European Law Initiative (CEELI) (1996) "Concept Paper on Media Law," 20 November, http://www.abanet.org/ceeli/publications/conceptpapers/home.html

Anonymous (1755) *Detraction: An Essay in Two Parts.* London: J. Bouquet, 1755.

Anonymous (1796) *A Letter to His Majesty's Attorney General, Soliciting Advice How to Act with Safety under the Two New Bills, called the Treason and Sedition Bills. By One of Many Astonished Royalists.* London: Southern, Parsons and Smeeton.

Aristotle (1991) *On Rhetoric: A Theory of Civic Discourse*, trans. George A. Kennedy. New York: Oxford University Press.

Arlen, Michael J. (1996) *Living Room War.* New York: Viking.

Austin, J.L. (1962) *How to Do Things with Words.* Oxford: Clarendon Press.

Bailey, Thomas A. (1949) *The Man in the Street: The Impact of American Public Opinion on Foreign Policy.* New York: Macmillan.

Bennett, W.L. (1989) "Marginalizing the Majority: Conditioning Public Opinion to Accept Managerial Democracy," in Micael Margolisad and Gary Mauser (eds.), *Manipulating Public Opinion.* Pacific Grove: Brooks/Cole.

Bennett, W.L. (1990) "Towards a Theory of Press–State Relations in the United States." *Journal of Communication*, Vol. 40, pp. 103–125.

Bennett, W.L. and D.L. Paletz (eds.) (1994) *Taken by Storm: The Media, Public Opinion, and U.S. Foreign Policy in the Gulf War.* Chicago and London: University of Chicago Press.

Bentham, Jeremy (1820) *The King against Edmonds, and Others: Set Down for Trial, at Warwick, On the 28th of March, 1820: Brief Remarks, Tending to Show the Untenability of this Indictment.* London: John McCreery.

Bentham, Jeremy (1821) *On the Liberty of the Press, and Public Discussion.* London: William Hone.

Billig, Michael (ed.) (1991) *Ideology and Opinions: Studies in Rhetorical Psychology.* London: Sage.

Billig, Michael (1996) *Arguing and Thinking: A Rhetorical Approach to Social Psychology*. Cambridge: Cambridge University Press.

Bozeman, Adda B. (1971) *The Future of Law in a Multicultural World*. Princeton: Princeton University Press.

Bozeman, Adda B. (1992) *Strategic Intelligence and Statecraft*. New York: Brassey.

Bruner, Jerome S. (1990) *Acts of Meaning*. Boston: Harvard University Press.

Bruner, Jerome S. (1944) *Mandate from the People*. New York: Duell, Sloan & Pearce.

Burnyeat, Myles F. (1996) "Enthymeme: Aristotle on the Rationality of Rhetoric," in Amélie Oksenberg Rorty (ed.), *Essays on Aristotle's Rhetoric*. London: University of California Press.

Burnyeat, Myles F. (1998) "The Past in the Present: Plato as Educator of Nineteenth-Century Britain," in Amélie Oksenberg Rorty (ed.), *Philosophers on Education*. London and New York: Routledge.

Campbell, Karlyn Kohrs and Kathleen Hall Jamieson (1990) *Deeds Done in Words: Presidential Rhetoric and the Genres of Governance*. Chicago: University of Chicago Press.

Carbaugh, Donal (ed.) (1990) *Intercultural Communication and Intercultural Contact*. Hillsdale, NJ: Lawrence Erlbaum Associates.

Carbaugh, Donal (1995) "The Ethnographic Communication Theory of Gerry Philipsen and Associates," in B. Kovacic (ed.), *Watershed Research Traditions in Human Communication Theory*. Albany: State University of New York Press.

Carruthers, Susan L. (2000) *The Media at War*. New York: St. Martin's Press.

Chafee, Zechariah (1954) *Free Speech in the United States*. Cambridge, Mass.: Harvard University Press.

Cohen, Bernard C. (1957) *The Political Process and Foreign Policy*. Princeton: Princeton University Press.

Cohen, Bernard C. (1963) *The Press and Foreign Policy*. Princeton: Princeton University Press.

Cohen, Bernard C. (1973) *The Public's Impact on Foreign Policy*. Boston: Little, Brown.

Cook, Fay Lomax, Tom R. Tyler, Edward G. Goetz, Margaret T. Gordon, David Protess, Donna R. Leff, and Harvey L. Molotch (1983) "Media and Agenda-Setting: Effects on the Public, Interest Group Leaders, Policy Makers, and Policy." *Public Opinion Quarterly*, Vol. 46, Spring.

Cook, Timothy (1989) *Making Laws and Making News*. Washington, D.C.: The Brookings Institute.

Cook, Timothy (1997) *Governing with the News: The News Media as a Political Institution*. University of Chicago Press: Chicago.

Cowan, Ruth Schwartz (1987) "The Consumption Junction: A Proposal for Research Strategies in the Sociology of Technologies," in W.E. Bijker, T.P. Hughes, and T.J. Pinch (eds.), *The Social Construction of Technological Systems: New Directions in the Sociology and History of Technology*. Cambridge, Mass.: MIT Press, pp. 261–280.

Crigler, Ann N. (1986) "Setting the Congressional Agenda: Public Opinion in a Media Age." Unpublished Ph.D. dissertation, MIT.

Davies, B. and Rom Harré (1999) "Positioning and Personhood," in Rom Harré and Luk van Langenhove (eds.), *Positioning Theory*. Oxford: Blackwell.

Dearing, James W. and Everett M. Rogers (1996), *Communication Concepts 6: Agenda-Setting*. Thousand Oaks, Calif.: Sage.

Dobbs, Daniel (2000) *The Law of Torts*. St. Paul, MN: West Group.

Edleman, Murray (1967), *The Symbolic Uses of Politics, With a New Afterward*, Urbana and Chicago: University of Illinois Press (reprint, 1985), p. 132.

Feaver, Peter (1998) "The CNN Effect and Information Warfare." Lecture at the DeWitt Wallce Center of Communications and Journalism, Sanford Institute of Public Policy, Duke University, April.

Foyle, Douglas C. (1997) "Public Opinion and Foreign Policy: Elite Beliefs as a Mediating Variable." *International Studies Quarterly*, Vol. 41, No. 1, pp. 141–169.

Foyle, Douglas C. (1999) *Counting the Public In: Presidents, Public Opinon and Foreign Policy*. New York: Columbia University Press.

Gamson, William A. and A. Modigliani (1966) "Knowledge and Foreign Policy Opinions: Some Models for Consideration." *Public Opinion Quarterly*, Vol. 30, pp. 187–199.

Gans, Herbert (1979) *Deciding What's News*. New York: Vintage Books.

Gardner, John (1991) *The Art of Fiction: Notes on Craft for Young Writers*. New York: Vintage.

Gergen, David (1991) "Diplomacy in a Television Age," in Simon Serfaty (ed.), *The Media and Foreign Policy*. New York: St. Martin's Press.

Goffman, Erving (1974) *Frame Analysis: An Essay on the Organization of Experience*. New York: Harper & Row. Reprinted, 1986.

Gow, James, Richard Paterson, and Alison Preston (eds.) (1996) *Bosnia by Television*. London: British Film Institute.

Gowing, Nik (1994) "Real-Time Television Coverage of Armed Conflicts and Diplomatic Crises: Does It Pressure or Distort Foreign Policy Decisions?" Working Paper 94–1, Joan Shorenstein Barone Center on the Press, Politics and Public Policy, John F. Kennedy School of Government, Harvard University, June.

Haass, Richard N. (1994) *Intervention: The Use of American Military Force in the Post–Cold War World*. Washington, D.C.: Carnegie Endowment for International Peace.

Hallam, Henry (1846) *The Constitutional History of England from the Accession of Henry VII to the Death of George II*, Vols. I and II. London: John Murray.

Hallin, Daniel (1996) *The Uncensored War: The Media and Vietnam*. NewYork: Oxford University Press.

Harré, Rom (1995) "Agentive Discourse," in Rom Harré and Peter Stearns (eds.), *Discursive Psychology in Practice*. London: Sage.

Harré, Rom and Grant Gillett (1994) *The Discursive Mind*. London: Sage.

Harré, Rom and Luk van Langenhove (eds.) (1999a) *Positioning Theory*. Oxford: Blackwell.

Harré, Rom and Luk van Langenhove (1999b) "The Dynamics of Social Episodes," in Rom Harré and Luk van Langenhove (eds.), *Positioning Theory*. Oxford: Blackwell.

Harré, Rom and P.F. Secord (1972) *The Explanation of Social Behaviour*. Oxford: Blackwell.

Harré, Rom and Peter Stearns (eds.) (1995) *Discursive Psychology in Practice*. London: Sage.

Herman, Edward S. and Noam Chomsky (1988) *Manufacturing Consent: The Political Economy of the Mass Media*. New York: Pantheon Books.

Hinckley, Barbara (1994) "Key decisions by Eisenhower and Johnson on Vietnam, by Reagan in Lebanon and Libya, by Bush in the Persian Gulf—All Were Weeks or Months in the Making," in *Less than Meets the Eye: Foreign Policy Making and the Myth of the Assertive Congress*, Chicago: University of Chicago Press.

Hindell, Keith (1995) "The Influence of the Media on Foreign Policy." *International Relations*, Vol. 12, No. 4.

Hoge, James F. (1994) "Media Pervasiveness." *Foreign Affairs*, Vol. 73, No. 4, p.136.

Holsti, Ole (1976) "Foreign Policy Decision-Makers Viewed Cognitively," in Robert Axelrod (ed.), *Structure of Decision*. Princeton: Princeton University Press, pp. 18–54.

Holsti, Ole R. (1996) *Public Opinion and American Foreign Policy*. Ann Arbor: University of Michigan Press.

Hunt, Frederick Knight (1998) *The Fourth Estate: Contributions towards a History of Newspapers, and the Liberty of the Press*. London: Routledge/Thoemmes Press.

Isaacs, Maxine (1998a) "Foreign Policy, Media, and Public Opinion." Lecture at the DeWitt Wallace Center of Communications and Journalism, Sanford Institute of Public Policy, Duke University, April.

Isaacs, Maxine (1998b) "Two Different Worlds: The Relationship between Elite and Mass Opinion on Foreign Policy." *Political Communication*, Vol. 15, pp. 323–345.

Iyengar, Shanto and R. Reeves (eds.) *Do the Media Govern? Politicians, Voters, and Reporters in America*. Thousand Oaks: Sage.

Jervis, Robert (2002) "Politics, Political Science, and Specialization," in *PS. Political Science and Politics*, Vol. 35, No. 2, pp. 187–189.

Kalb, Marvin (1991) "Foreword," in Simon Serfaty (ed.) *The Media and Foreign Policy*, New York: St. Martin's Press, p. xv.

Kalb, Marvin (1994) "A View from the Press," in W.L. Bennett and D.L. Paletz (eds.), *Taken by Storm: The Media, Public Opinion, and U.S. Foreign Policy in the Gulf War*. Chicago and London: University of Chicago Press.

Kaminsky, Elijah Ben-Zion "On the Comparison of Presidential and Parliamentary Governments." *Presidential Studies Quarterly*, Vol. 27, No. 2, Spring, pp. 221–228.

Kennan, George (1993), "Somalia, through a Glass Darkly" Op-Ed, *The New York Times*, 30 September 1993.

Key, V.O. (1961) *Public Opinion and American Democracy*. New York: Knopf.

Knightley, Phillip (1976) *The First Casualty: From the Crimea to Vietnam: The War Correspondent As Hero, Propagandist, and Myth Maker*. New York and London: Harcourt Brace

Langenhove, Luk van and Rom Harré (1999a) "Introducing Positioning Theory," in Rom Harré and Luk van Langenhove (eds.), *Positioning Theory*. Oxford: Blackwell, pp. 13–31.

Langenhove, Luk van and Rom Harré (1999b) "Positioning as the Production and Use of Stereotypes," in Rom Harré and Luk van Langenhove (eds.), *Positioning Theory*. Oxford: Blackwell.

Legro, Jeffrey W. and Andrew Moravcsik (1999) "Is Anybody Still a Realist," in *International Security*, Vol. 24, No. 2, p. 5.

Lindsay, James (1994) *Congress and the Politics of U.S. Foreign Policy*. Baltimore: Johns Hopkins Press.

Linsky, Martin (1986) *Impact: How the Press Affects Federal Policy Making*. New York: Norton.

Lipinksi, Daniel (1999) "Communicating the Party Record: How Congressional Leaders Transmit Their Messages to the Public." Paper presented at the Annual Meeting of the American Political Science Association, Atlanta.

Lippmann, Walter (1922) *Public Opinion*. New York: Simon and Schuster.

Livingston, Steven (1997) "Clarifying the CNN Effect: An Examination of Media Effects According to Type of Military Intervention." Research Paper R-18, Joan Shorenstein Center for Press, Politics and Public Policy, Harvard University, John F. Kennedy School of Government, June.

Livingston, Steven (1998) "Beyond the CNN Effect." Lecture at the DeWitt Wallace Center of Communications and Journalism, Sanford Institute of Public Policy, Duke University, April.

Livingston, Steven and Todd Eachus (1995) "Human Crises and U.S. Foreign Policy: Somalia and the CNN Effect Reconsidered." *Political Communication*, Vol. 12, pp. 413–429.

Livingston, Steven and W. Lance Bennett (2003) "Gatekeeping, Indexing, and Live-Event News: Is Technology Altering the Construction of News?" *Political Communication*, Vol. 20, pp. 363–380.

McCombs, M., E. Maxwell, and Donald L. Shaw (1972) "The Agenda-Setting Function of Mass Media," in *Public Opinion Quarterly* Vol. 36, No. 2, pp. 176–187.

McCombs, M., Donald L. Shaw, and Donald Weaver (eds.) (1997) *Communication and Democracy: Exploring the Intellectual Frontiers in Agenda-Setting Theory*. Mahwah: Erlbaum.

McNulty, Timothy J. (1993) "Television's Impact on Executive Decisionmaking and Diplomacy." *The Fletcher Forum of World Affairs*, Vol. 17, Winter, pp. 67–83.

Mermin, Jonathan (1997) "Television News and American Intervention in Somalia: The Myth of a Media-Driven Foreign Policy." *Political Science Quarterly*, Vol. 12, No. 3, Fall.

Michelson, Melissa R. (1998) "Explorations in Public Opinion—Presidential Power Linkages: Congressional Action on Unpopular Foreign Agreements." *Political Communication*, Vol. 15, pp. 63–82.

Mindich, David T.Z. (1998) *Just the Facts: How "Objectivity" Came to Define American Journalism.* New York: New York University Press

Minear, L., C. Scott, and T.G. Weiss (1996) *The News Media, Civil War and Humanitarian Action.* Boulder: Rienne.

Moeller, Susan D. (1999) *Compassion Fatigue: How the Media Sell Disease, Famine, War and Death.* New York and London: Routledge.

Mueller, J. (1973) *War, Presidents and Public Opinion.* New York: John Wiley.

Mueller, J. (1994) *Policy and Opinion in the Gulf War.* Chicago: University of Chicago Press.

Müller, Wolfgang C. and Kaare Strøm (eds.) (2000) *Coalition Governments in Western Europe.* New York: Oxford University Press.

Natsios, Andrew (1996) "Illusions of Influence: The CNN Effect in Complex Emergencies," in Robert I. Rotberg and Thomas G. Weiss (eds.), *From Massacres to Genocide: The Media, Public Policy, and Humanitarian Crises.* Washington, D.C.: The Brookings Institute.

Neuman, Joanna (1996a) *Lights, Camera, War: Is Media Technology Driving International Politics?* New York: St. Martin's Press.

Neuman, W. Russell, Marion R. Just, and Ann N. Crigler (eds.) (1992) *Common Knowledge: News and the Construction of Political Meaning.* Chicago: University of Chicago Press.

Neustadt, Richard (1990) *Presidential Power: The Politics of Leadership from FDR to Carter.* New York: John Wiley.

O'Heffernan, Patrick (1991) *Mass Media and American Foreign Policy.* Norwich, N.J.: Ablex.

Orren, Gary (1986) "Foreword," in M. Linsky, *Impact: How the Press Affects Federal Policy Making.* New York: Norton.

Philipsen, Gerry (1990) "Speaking 'Like a Man' in Teamsterville: Culture Patterns of Role Enactment in an Urban Neighborhood," in Donal Carbaugh (ed.) (1990) *Intercultural Communication and Intercultural Contact.* Hillsdale, NJ: Lawrence Erlbaum Associates.

Pigot, Robert (1790) *Liberty of the Press: A Letter addressed to the National Assembly of France.* Paris: publisher.

Powell, Jody, George Reedy, and Jerry terHorst (1986) "The Relationship of the President and the Press," in Kenneth W. Thompson (ed.), *Presidents, Prime Ministers and the Press.* Lanham: University Press of America.

Reston, James Barrett (1966) *The Artillery of the Press: Its Influence on American Foreign Policy.* New York: Harper and Row.

Risse-Kappen, Thomas (1991) "Public Opinion, Domestic Structure and Foreign Policy in Liberal Democracies." *World Politics*, Vol. 43, No. 4, pp. 479–512.

Robinson, Piers (1999) "The CNN Effect: Can the News Media Drive Foreign Policy?" *Review of International Studies*, Vol. 25, April, p. 2.

Robinson, Piers (2002) *The CNN Effect: The Myth of News, Foreign Policy and Intervention*. London: Routledge Press.

Rogers, Everett M., William B. Hart, and James W. Dearing (1997) "A Paradigmatic History of Agenda-Setting Research," in Shanto Iyengar and R. Reeves (eds.), *Do the Media Govern? Politicians, Voters, and Reporters in America*. Thousand Oaks: Sage.

Rorty, Amelie Oksenberg (ed.) (1998) *Philosophers on Education*, London and New York: Routledge.

Rotberg, Robert I. and Thomas G. Weiss (eds.) (1996) *From Massacres to Genocide: The Media, Public Policy, and Humanitarian Crises*. Washington, D.C.: The Brookings Institute.

Schorr, Daniel (1991) "Ten Days that Shook the White House." *Columbia Journalism Review*, July/August, pp. 21–23.

Scollon, Ron (1998) *Mediated Discourse as Social Interaction: A Study of News Discourse*. Longman: New York.

Scowcroft, Brent and George H.W. Bush (1998) *A World Transformed*. New York: Knopf.

Seib, Philip (1997) *Headline Diplomacy: How News Coverage Affects Foreign Policy*. Westport: Praeger.

Serfaty, Simon (ed.) (1991a) *The Media and Foreign Policy*. New York: St. Martin's Press.

Serfaty, Simon (1991b) "The Media and Foreign Policy," in Simon Serfaty (ed.), *The Media and Foreign Policy*. New York: St. Martin's Press.

Shaw, Martin (1996) *Civil Society and Media in Global Crises: Representing Distant Violence*. London: Pinter.

Skinner, Quentin, (1989) "Meaning and Understanding in the History of Ideas," in James Tully (ed.), *Quentin Skinner and His Critics*. Princeton, N.J.: Princeton University Press.

Smith, Carolyn (1990) *Presidential Press Conferences: A Critical Approach*. New York: Praeger.

Smith, Geoffrey (1986) "The Prime Minister and the Press: Britain," in Kenneth Thompson (ed.), *Presidents, Prime Ministers and the Press*. Lanham: University Press of America.

Snyder, Glenn H. (1991) "Alliances, Balance, and Stability." *International Organization*, Vol. 45, No. 1, Winter.

Squire, Francis (1740) *A Faithful Report of a Genuine Debate Concerning the Liberty of the Press Addressed to a Candidate at the Ensuing Election*. London.

Strobel, Warren, P. (1996) "The CNN Effect." *American Journalism Review*, Vol. 18, No. 4.

Strobel, Warren P. (1997) *Late-Breaking Foreign Policy: The News Media's Influence on Peace Operations.* Washington, D.C.: United States Institute of Peace Press.

Thompson, Kenneth W. (1986) *Presidents, Prime Ministers and the Press.* Lanham: University Press of America.

Walt, Stephen M. (1999) "Rigor or Rigor Mortis? Rational Choice and Security Studies." *International Security*, Vol. 23, No. 4, pp. 5–48.

Wanta, Wayne and Yu-Wei Hu (1993) "The Agenda-Setting Effects of International News Coverage: An Examination of Differing News Frames." *International Journal of Public Opinion Research*, Vol. 5, No. 3, Fall, pp. 250–264.

Wanta, Wayne and J. Foote (1994) "The President–News Media Relationship: A Time Series Analysis of Agenda-Setting." *Journal of Broadcasting and Electronic Media*, Vol. 38, pp. 437–448.

Willnat, Lars (1997) "Agenda-Setting and Priming: Conceptual Links and Differences," in M. McCombs, Donald L. Shaw, and Donald Weaver (eds.), *Communication and Democracy: Exploring the Intellectual Frontiers in Agenda-Setting Theory.* Mahwah: Erlbaum.

Wood, B. Dan and Jeffrey S. Peake (1998) "The Dynamics of Foreign Policy Agenda Setting." *American Political Science Review*, Vol. 92, March.

Wood, James (1992) *History of International Broadcasting.* London: Peter Peregrinus in association with the Science Museum.

Zaller, John (1992) *Political Competition and Public Opinion.* New York: Cambridge University Press.

Zaller, John (1994) "Strategic Politicians, Public Opinion and the Gulf Crisis," in W.L. Bennett and D.L. Paletz (eds.), *Taken by Storm: The Media, Public Opinion, and U.S. Foreign Policy in the Gulf War.* Chicago and London: University of Chicago Press, pp. 250–274.

Zaller, John and Dennis Chiu (1996) "Government's Little Helper: U.S. Press Coverage of Foreign Policy Crises, 1945–1991." *Political Communication*, Vol. 13, October–December.

Zelnick, C. Robert (1998) "Media and National Security Issues." Lecture at the DeWitt Wallce Center of Communications and Journalism, Sanford Institute of Public Policy, Duke University, April.

Zitter, Jay M. (1986) "Excessiveness or Inadequacy of Compensitory Damages for Defamation." *American Law Report 4th*, 49 A.L.R. 4th, 1158, originally cited as 50 Am Jur 2d, Libel and Slander, §1. Supplement, August 2004.

CASE STUDY REFERENCES

1. Bush, George and Brent Scowcroft (1998) *A World Transformed.* New York: Knopf.
2. Foreign Broadcast Information Service, Daily Report, Near East and South Asia, every day from 2 March to 1 June.

3. Galbraith, Peter W. (1991) *Civil War in Iraq: A Staff Report to the Committee on Foreign Relations, United States Senate.* Washington, D.C.: United States Government Printing Office.
4. Haass, Richard N. (1994) *Intervention: The Use of American Military Force in the Post–Cold War World.* Washington, D.C.: Carnegie Endowment for International Peace.
5. Khadduri, Majid and Edmund Ghareeb (1997) *War in the Gulf 1990–91: The Iraq–Kuwait Conflict and Its Implications.* Oxford: Oxford University Press.
6. Nakash, Yitzhak (1994) *The Shi'is of Iraq.* Princeton: Princeton University Press.
7. Randal, Jonathan (1999) *After Such Knowledge, What Forgiveness?* New York: Westview Press.
8. Rudd, Gordon W. (1993) "Operation Provide Comfort: Humanitarian Intervention in Northern Iraq, 1991." Unpublished Ph.D. dissertation, Duke University.
9. Sheri, Laizer (1996) *Martyrs, Traitors and Patriots: Kurdistan after the Gulf War.* London: Zed Books.

INDEX

Printed in the United States
121887LV00001B/96/P

·